VOLUME XXII • NUMBER 1 • WINTER 1992

PRESIDENTIAL STUDIES QUARTERLY

CENTER FOR THE STUDY OF THE PRESIDENCY

Editor   R. GORDON HOXIE

Associate Editors   ROBERT E. DENTON, JR., PHILIP R. RULON
AND WILLIAM C. SPRAGENS

**SELECTING THE PRESIDENT,
THE CONGRESS, AND THE C⌐**

The *Presidential Studies Quarterly* is published by the Center for the Study of the Presidency, 208 East 75th Street, New York, NY 10021. R. Gordon Hoxie, President, and Maria Rossi, Business Manager. Subscription is included with Center membership. Additional copies may be secured at $6.00 each.

Notice of nonreceipt of an issue must be sent to the Membership Secretary of the Center within three months of the date of publication of the issue. Change of address should be sent to the Membership Secretary. The Center is not responsible for copies lost because of failure to report a change of address in time for mailing. The Center cannot accommodate changes of address that are effective only for the summer months.

Correspondence: Manuscripts and editorial correspondence should be addressed to the Editor, *Presidential Studies Quarterly*, 208 East 75th Street, New York, NY 10021. Article manuscripts should be submitted in duplicate. A brief biographic paragraph and an abstract not to exceed 200 words should be included. The main text should be double spaced. In general, it should not exceed 6,000 words in length. Footnotes should be numbered consecutively throughout, and should appear in a separate section at the end of the text including the date and place of publication and publisher for books. The editors are the final arbiters of length, grammar, and usage. They may refer manuscripts to referees for counsel on acceptance and revisions. Manuscripts will not be returned.

Book reviews on historical works should be addressed to Dr. Philip R. Rulon, Professor of History, Northern Arizona University, Box 5725, Flagstaff, AZ 86001. Book reviews in the field of political science should be addressed to Dr. William C. Spragens, P.O. Box 682, Herndon, VA 22070. Book reviews in the field of communications and rhetoric should be addressed to Dr. Robert E. Denton, Jr., Head, Department of Communications Studies, Agnew Hall, Virginia Polytechnic Institute & State University, Blacksburg, VA 24061.

Correspondence regarding advertising, back issues, and reprint permission should be addressed to Paul Fitzpatrick, Editorial Associate, *Presidential Studies Quarterly*, 208 East 75th Street, New York, NY 10021.

The *Presidential Studies Quarterly* is available on University Microfilms. They may be ordered by calling toll free: 800-521-0600, or by writing University Microfilms at 300 North Zeeb Road, Ann Arbor, MI 48106-1346. It is abstracted and indexed in *ABC POL. SCI. Historical Abstracts*, and *America: History and Life* and in *United States Political Science Documents*, University of Pittsburgh Press. It is also abstracted in *Sage Public Administration Abstracts*, *Human Resources Abstracts*, *Sage Urban Studies Abstracts*, *Sage Family Studies Abstracts*, *Communication Abstracts*, Temple University, *Political Science Abstracts*, and *International Political Science Abstracts*. It is also indexed in the *Public Affairs Information Service Bulletin* and the *ABC POL. SCI. Advance Bibliography of Contents*. An index of articles and book reviews for each volume of the *Quarterly* is included in the Fall issue.

COVER ILLUSTRATION: Clay Model of Artist's Rendering of Center's Distinguished Service and Distinguished Public Service Medals (by Tiffany).

Contents

I. ABOUT THE AUTHORS   6

II. ABOUT THIS ISSUE, by the Editor, *Presidential Studies Quarterly*   8

III. ARTICLES

Communication in the First Primaries: The Voice of the People in 1912, by Paul E. Corcoran and Kathleen E. Kendall   15

General MacArthur and the Presidential Election of 1944, by Philip J. Briggs   31

Shattering the Myth About President Eisenhower's Supreme Court Appointments, by Michael A. Kahn   47

Eisenhower's Congressional Defeat of 1956, by Craig Allen   57

A Step in the "Right" Direction: Conservative Republicans and the Election of 1960, by Mary C. Brennan   73

Religious Periodicals and Presidential Elections, 1960–1988, by James D. Fairbanks and John Francis Burke   89

Scenario for a Centrist Revolt: Third Party Prospects in a Time of Ideological Polarization, by Edward N. Kearny and Robert A. Heineman   107

Peak Presidential Approval from Franklin Roosevelt to Ronald Reagan, by David C. Nice   119

Selected Fiscal and Economic Effects on Presidential Elections, by Alfred G. Cuzán and Charles M. Bundrick   127

The Democrats' "Southern Problem" in Presidential Politics, by Nicol C. Rae   135

IV. BOOK REVIEWS

Ronald Reagan, *An American Life: The Autobiography*, by Raymond J. Saulnier   153

Helene von Damm, *At Reagan's Side: Twenty Years in the Political Mainstream*, by Jeffry M. Burnam   157

Dilys M. Hill, Raymond A. Moore, and Phil Williams, eds., *The Reagan Presidency: An Incomplete Revolution?*, by William C. Spragens   159

Tom Whicker, *One of Us, Richard Nixon and the American Dream*, by George Shore   161

Louis Filler, ed., *The President in the 20th Century.* Vol. 2, *The Presidency in Crisis: From Lyndon B. Johnson to Ronald Reagan,* by D. Bruce Hicks 164

Michael Barone, *Our Country: The Shaping of America from Roosevelt to Reagan,* by Robert B. Thigpen 166

James P. Pfiffner, ed., *The Managerial Presidency,* by Barbara Kellerman 167

Richard E. Neustadt, *Presidential Power and the Modern Presidents: The Politics of Leadership from Roosevelt to Reagan,* by Barbara Kellerman 167

Peter G. Boyle, ed., *The Churchill-Eisenhower Correspondence: 1953–1955,* by Arlene Lazarowitz 168

Waldo Heinrichs, *Threshold of War: Franklin D. Roosevelt and American Entry into World War II,* by Susan Estabrook Kennedy 170

John Milton Cooper, Jr., and Charles E. Neu, eds., *The Wilson Era: Essays in Honor of Arthur S. Link,* by Richard H. Collin 172

Richard H. Collin, *Theodore Roosevelt's Caribbean: The Panama Canal, The Monroe Doctrine, and the Latin American Context,* by John D. Buenker 174

Mark E. Neely, Jr., *The Fate of Liberty: Abraham Lincoln and Civil Liberties,* by Eugene H. Berwanger 177

James M. McPherson, *Abraham Lincoln and the Second American Revolution,* by Judith A. Best 178

Robert V. Remini, *The Jacksonian Era,* by Warren M. Billings 180

George C. Edwards, III, *At the Margins: Presidential Leadership of Congress,* by Marcia Lynn Whicker 181

John R. Bond and Richard Fleisher, *The President in the Legislative Arena,* by Steven Puro 183

Stuart Bruchey, *Enterprise: The Dynamic Economy of a Free People,* by Raymond J. Saulnier 185

David Schmidtz, *The Limits of Government: An Essay on the Public Goods Argument,* by Robert B. Thigpen 187

L. Sandy Maisel, ed., *The Parties Respond: Changes in the American Party System,* by Ralph M. Goldman 188

James A. Smith, *The Idea Brokers: Think Tanks and the Rise of the New Policy Elite*, by William C. Spragens   191

Brian R. Fry, *Mastering Public Administration: From Max Weber to Dwight Waldo*, by James D. Ward   193

Richard Whelan, *Drawing the Line: The Korean War, 1950–1953*, by Edward Goedeken   194

Martin J. Medhurst, Robert L. Ivie, Philip Wander, and Robert L. Scott, *Cold War Rhetoric: Strategy, Metaphor, and Ideology*, by J. Justin Gustainis   196

John Le Boutiller, *Vietnam Now: A Case for Normalizing Relations with Hanoi*, by Thomas M. Egan   198

John Taft, *American Power: The Rise and Decline of U.S. Globalism*, by Bruce Nesmith   200

V.   BOOK NOTE

Carnegie Council on Ethics and International Affairs, *Ethical Traditions and World Change*, by William C. Spragens   203

VI.   GUEST EDITORIAL

Robert W. Selle, Trustee, James Monroe Memorial Foundation   205

VII.   LETTERS TO THE EDITOR   207

VIII.   NEWS NOTES   215

About the Authors

Craig Allen, Ph.D., Ohio University, is Assistant Professor of Journalism and Telecommunication at Arizona State University. He has contributed articles to professional journals on Presidential use of the media, concentrating on the Eisenhower and Nixon Administrations. He is completing a volume which examines this relationship in regards to the Eisenhower Administration.

Mary C. Brennan, Ph.D., Miami University, is Assistant Professor of History at Southwest Texas State University. She has presented several papers on various aspects of modern conservatism and is currently working on a manuscript on the development of conservativism in the 1960s.

Philip J. Briggs, Ph.D., Syracuse University, is Chair, Department of Political Science, East Stroudsburg University, also Executive Director, Research Committee on Armed Forces and Society, International Political Science Association. He is the author of *Making American Foreign Policy, President-Congress Relations from the Second World War to Vietnam*, and contributor to other volumes and professional journals.

Charles M. Bundrick, Ph.D., Florida State University, is Professor and Chairman of the Department of Mathematics and Statistics at the University of West Florida. He is the co-author of *Essentials of Abstract Algebra*. His present work has centered around experimental design and data analysis problems in government, industry, and scholarly research.

John Francis Burke, Ph.D., University of Notre Dame, is Assistant Professor of Political Science, University of Houston-Downtown. He is particularly concerned with Christian political and social thought and at present is engaged in articulating an American political theory which constitutes pluralism upon a communitarian as opposed to an individualist basis.

Paul E. Corcoran, Ph.D., Duke University, is Senior Lecturer in Politics at the University of Adelaide, Australia. He is the author of *Political Language and Rhetoric* (1979) and *Before Marx: Socialism and Communism in France 1830–1848* (1983), and has published numerous articles on political language, political theory and philosophy in scholarly journals.

Alfred G. Cuzán, Ph.D., Indiana University, is Professor of Political Science at The University of West Florida. The author of two dozen scholarly articles published in such journals as *Public Choice, Behavioral Science*, and *The American Journal of Economics and Sociology*, Dr. Cuzán is interested in the impact of fiscal policy on elections and, more generally, political stability.

James D. Fairbanks, Ph.D., Ohio State University, is Professor of Political Science and Executive Director of Planning and Institutional Research at the University of Houston-Downtown. His work on religion and politics has appeared in a variety of professional journals, including *Presidential Studies Quarterly*.

Robert A. Heineman, Ph.D., American University, is Professor of Political Science at Alfred University. He is author or co-author of a number of volumes including *Authority and the Liberal Tradition* (1984).

Michael A. Kahn, M.A. and J.D., Stanford University, is a partner in the law firm of Folger and Lavin in San Fransisco. He is a contributor to many professional journals. He is also a member of the State Senate Commission on Property, Tax, Equity and Revenue and of the National Advisory Council of the Center for the Study of the Presidency. He has participated in many of the Center's programs.

Edward N. Kearny, Ph.D., American University, is Professor of Government at Western Kentucky University. He is author, co-author or editor of a number of volumes including *Mavericks in American Politics* (1976) and has contributed to professional journals, including *Presidential Studies Quarterly*.

Kathleen E. Kendall, Ph.D., Indiana University, is Associate Professor of Communication at the State University of New York at Albany. She is the author of articles on political discourse and sources of political information, and is currently writing a book on communication in the presidential primaries, 1912–1992.

David C. Nice, Ph.D., University of Michigan, is Associate Professor of Political Science at Washington State University. His research interests include the presidency, Congress, and public policy making. He is the author of *Federalism: The Politics of Intergovernmental Relations* (1987) and has written extensively for professional journals.

Nicol C. Rae, D.Phil., Oxford University (England), is Assistant Professor of Political Science at Florida International University. He is the author of *The Decline and Fall of the Liberal Republicans: from 1952 to the Present* and has written in professional journals on party politics in America and Britain.

About this Issue

This issue of *Presidential Studies Quarterly* has as its theme SELECTING THE PRESIDENT, THE CONGRESS, AND THE COURT. As we begin the 1992 Presidential election year, it is helpful to perceive the climate of public opinion and the instruments related thereto over the past 80 years. Accordingly in this issue we examine such factors influencing this quadrennial event as the roles of political parties, presidential primaries, economic conditions, the media and pollsters.

We begin with the brilliant essay, "Communications in the First Primaries: The Voice of the People in 1912," by Paul E. Corcoran and Kathleen E. Kendall. The former is from the University of Adelaide, Australia and the latter from State University of New York at Albany. They bring together the perspectives from "down under" and from "the Empire State" in this manuscript to which, as they stated, "the authors contributed equally." They assert, "Primaries, once a 'solution' to remote and unresponsive government, have become a problem. Scholar reformers look to the future to propose changes that might be brought into play to rationalize the presidential selection process, all the while preserving an implicit nostalgia for a 'real' two-party system." They assert, "The underlying assumption is that a compromise may be struck between popular participation and the intractable force of the electronic media in modern government." They begin with the conceptions, the hopes, of the framers of political primaries which had begun with candidates for local primaries in California and New York in 1866, and with "presidential preference primaries" in Florida in 1904 and Wisconsin in 1908. The first big year of presidential primaries was 1912, pitting Senator Robert La Follette, Theodore Roosevelt and Taft in the Republican primaries and Woodrow Wilson and House Speaker "Champ" Clark in the Democratic. As the authors observe, "In many respects, the primary campaign in 1912 bears an uncanny resemblance to the primaries of today." Primaries did *not* in 1912 supplant national political conventions as the selector of the party candidates, nor did they supplant personality with policy; quite the contrary the media fed on personalities in 1912 and the media does so today. It was made clear in 1912, as it doubtless will be in 1992, "that the techniques of communication employed to create and mediate a candidate's image may be used with equal effectiveness to attack and recreate the image of one's opponent."

Beginning with our first President, George Washington, military service has been an avenue to the Presidency. Andrew Jackson, William Henry Harrison, and Zachary Taylor were all pre-Civil War military heroes. Beginning with Grant in 1868 through McKinley in 1900, every successful Republican candidate for President had served in the Civil War. McKinley's successor, Theodore Roosevelt achieved much of his prominence as Colonel Roosevelt, veteran of the Spanish American War. Of our modern presidents, only Dwight D. Eisenhower's career had been in the armed forces, though President Franklin Roosevelt's career had been enhanced 1913–1920 as Assistant Secretary of the Navy.

The Vietnam War had placed a pall on the political attraction of military leaders. However, now comes Operations Desert Shield and Desert Storm with the emergence of the first black Chairman of the Joint Chiefs of Staff, General Colin L. Powell, as an attractive candidate for future political office, perhaps in 1996 as the Vice Presidential running mate of his friend Dick Cheney, the present Secretary of Defense.

The political interests of one of the Nation's most extraordinary military leaders, Douglas MacArthur, have drawn little attention. Professor Philip J. Briggs corrects that oversight with his essay "General MacArthur and the Presidential Election of 1944." In doing so, he relates it to leading political persons of that war-time era, including President Roosevelt, Wendell Willkie, Governor Thomas Dewey, Secretary of War Henry L. Stimson, Democratic Senate Majority Leader Alben W. Barkley, Clare Boothe Luce, and, most significantly, Senator Arthur H. Vandenberg. As early as February 1942, Vandenberg had privately named MacArthur as his candidate for President. He was opposed both to Willkie, the 1940 Republican candidate, and the leading Republican aspirant, Governor Dewey, whom he was convinced could not defeat Roosevelt. In the Spring of 1943, Vandenberg and Representative Clare Boothe Luce, wife of the Editor-in-Chief, *Time, Life, Fortune*, met with MacArthur's Chief of Staff in Representative Luce's Washington apartment. In response to their overture, MacArthur cabled his receptivity. *Fortune* commissioned a Roper Poll which showed MacArthur had a popularity rating about equal to Willkie and Dewey combined. Vandenberg's strategy was to keep the heroic MacArthur in reserve until a draft movement could be mounted in the Republican convention. Contrary to Vandenberg's strategy, MacArthur declined to have his name withdrawn from the Illinois primary, where MacArthur polled 76% of the vote. However, while MacArthur was winning victories in the Pacific he was corresponding with Republican Representative A.L. Miller of Nebraska. The appearance of that correspondence in the public press caused MacArthur to issue a statement requesting that "no action be taken to link my name in any way with the nomination." Vandenberg, who went on in the post World War II era to become the Senate Majority Leader, and mentor of Gerald Ford, said of MacArthur, "he would have been our most eligible President, especially in his spokesmanship for America at the peace table." Ironically, it was the release of MacArthur's correspondence with another Republican, Minority Leader Joseph Martin, in 1951, which led to President Truman's dismissal of MacArthur in the Korean War.

As we approach the quadrennial election assessment of the President, one often neglected measure is the President's appointments, particularly the Cabinet, Senior White House Staff, and most especially the Supreme Court. It is through the Court that the President's appointments may have a continuing influence for a quarter century or more. Such was the case of John Adams' appointment of John Marshall as Chief Justice during his own last weeks in office in 1801. Marshall was to dominate much of national policy for the next 34 years, in that instance fortunately so, as he strengthened the Union, and is regarded as our greatest Chief Justice. In the same manner President Jackson appointed Roger B. Taney as Chief Justice in 1836, during his own last year in office. Twenty-one years later Taney was to lead in the Dred

Scott case, the court decision instrumental in the dissolution of the Union. As we approach the 1992 Presidential election the recent appointment of Justices Souter and Thomas may well weigh in the balance.

Only recently have scholars begun to appreciate President Eisenhower's political skills. Not yet have they come to grasp his moderate or "Modern Republicanism" and his liberalism in both domestic and foreign policy. In particular they have misunderstood his stand on Civil Rights and his Court appointments. In a highly perceptive essay, Michael Kahn, a practicing attorney and a member of this Center's National Advisory Council, portrays how Eisenhower laid the "foundation for the Court's broad expansion of civil rights in the 1950's and 1960's."

Eisenhower did so despite the concerns of the conservative wing of the Republican Party and the threats that he would lose the necessary support for his re-election in 1956 by his liberal stance on civil rights and the Court. As with his 1956 denunciation of British-French-Israeli aggression against Egypt, when he was threatened with the loss of the Jewish vote, he emphasized that in *no* way were his decisions predicated on enhancing his prospect for re-election. In the event the American people did not respect his Court appointments and his civil rights leadership, then, he said, let them cast their votes against him. In truth, they did respect him, and he won re-election in a landslide.

Michael Kahn examines Eisenhower's five appointments to the Supreme Court and finds him demonstrating "a strength of character" not so clearly made manifest by some more recent presidents in their Court appointments. Far more than *Roe* v. *Wade* on abortion, *Brown* v. *Board of Education* on segregation created a "supercharged political environment." Make no mistake, Eisenhower "did not select neutral appointees who refused to express their views on the central judicial and political issues of the time." In these appointments he had the counsel of that most remarkable Attorney General, Herbert Brownell. Kahn concludes, "the appointments of Warren, Harlan, Brennan, Whitaker and Stewart demonstrate clearly that Eisenhower intentionally appointed persons to the Supreme Court who would uphold liberal civil rights philosophies and implement them throughout the country. Eisenhower did *not* accidentally select persons whose civil rights philosophies of the day were liberal; he intended to do so, and he defied Southerners and conservatives who passionately urged him to take another course." It is especially interesting that Kahn, who did graduate work at Stanford on the American Presidency, before taking his law degree, and is active in Democratic Party leadership, concludes that Eisenhower is "one of the most masterful and productive Presidents in American history. . . ."

Eisenhower's 1956 landslide victory had no coattails with Republican candidates in the Congress. Dr. Craig Allen seeks to analyze why not, particularly with reference to this being "the first election in which a political party [the Republican] coordinated a truly national television campaign." It was also, Dr. Allen observes, "a beginning of a long Republican winter on Capitol Hill, with Eisenhower the first victorious president in 108 years [since Zachary Taylor, another general and war hero in 1848] to lose both houses of Congress." Dr. Allen attributes the loss on too great reliance on television. As the Republican Chairman, Leonard Hall, an old friend of this editor, observed, "We still have much to learn about how best to use [television] in a national campaign. Important as television and new transportation methods are, they don't replace the local organization. "There is," Hall concluded, "no substitute for this vital element, and there is no substitute for door bell ringing and shoe leather."

Where Dr. Allen focuses on the 1956 elections, in the ensuing essay, Dr. Mary C. Brennan examines the 1960 elections. She does so particularly in terms of the rise of the conservative wing of the Republican party. Liberal Republicans had led in the selection of Republican presidential candidates in 1940 with Willkie, in 1944 and 1948 Dewey, and in 1952 and 1956 with Eisenhower. Now comes 1960 with "the emergence of a more organized, astute and determined Right." The conservatives had become disenchanted with Senator Robert Taft, when, after his loss of the Republican nomination to Eisenhower in 1952, Taft gave his wholehearted support to Eisenhower. Indeed, Eisenhower relied on Taft as the new Senate Majority Leader and mourned his serious illness in the late Spring of 1953 and his death that summer.

The conservatives were no more comfortable with Vice President Nixon, despite his conservative credentials. By 1960, they perceived his having been tainted with liberalism in eight years as Eisenhower's Vice President. They found their man in Barry Goldwater, who had come to the Senate on Eisenhower's coattails in the 1952 election and had been re-elected in 1958, a lean Republican year. By 1960, Goldwater was referring contemptuously to the Eisenhower Administration's "dime-store New Dealism." Goldwater shared Senator John Bricker's view that the Nation was "in worse shape than at the depths of the New Deal." Even former president Hoover found the Eisenhower Administration in 1960 infected with the "Karl Marx virus."

Nixon in 1960 was less concerned with Goldwater's challenge from the right than with Nelson Rockefeller's from the left. Conservatives viewed the meeting between Nixon and Rockefeller as an agreement made in hell, rather than in Rockefeller's house. Goldwater termed the meeting the "Munich of the Republican Party." Nixon lost the election to Kennedy literally by a few thousand contested votes, which may be attributed to intellectual right wingers sitting on their hands. The conservatives gained control of the Republican Party with Goldwater as their candidate in 1964, running against Johnson and suffering a devastating defeat. Nonetheless, from 1960 on they have been a formidable force in the Republican Party.

Although the separation of church and state is a basic constitutional tenant, so also is freedom of the press. Moreover, the Nation's social fabric and its political system have a moral and religious foundation. This foundation, our first President, Washington; our Civil War President, Lincoln; and among modern Presidents, Eisenhower, especially emphasized. Indeed, Eisenhower had the words "under God" added to the pledge of allegiance.

Dr. David Fairbanks and Dr. John Francis Burke examine the roles of four of the Nation's leading religious periodicals, two Catholic and two Protestant, in terms of their addressing candidates and the issues in the presidential elections from 1960–1988. The two Catholic periodicals are *America* and *Commonweal* and the two Protestant are *Christianity Today* and *Christian Century*. Their circulations range from 20,000 to 185,000. While the numbers are not large, their readers are "opinion leaders" in their respective religious communities.

Over time, the Catholic publications have given more editorial space to campaign issues than have their Protestant counterparts. However, from 1976 on, with the rise of the evangelical movement, the Protestant publications have led in editorial coverage. The authors conclude, quite respectfully, "Both *America* and *Commonweal* are unequivocally committed to evaluating the stance of the candidates on public policy issues from the standpoint of Catholic social thought." The Protestant journals do not have a comparable "explicit policy agenda rooted in religious principles." Editorially, all four have a bond of unity in concern for lack of issues, lack of leadership and questionable campaign tactics.

Professors Edward N. Kearney and Robert A. Heineman make a strong case for the proposition that the time may be approaching for what they term "a centrist revolt" resulting in the creation of a major third party. They base this on a number of phenomena. Today the two major parties are at a stand-off, the Democrats in control of the Congress and the Republicans in control of the White House. There are tendencies for both parties to desert this centrist position where most of the votes are. The Democrats, with such leaders as Jesse Jackson, are being pulled to the left with racist overtones. The left moving position, the authors predict, will be enhanced in the Democratic Party in 1992 by rule changes increasing the power of special interests. The Republicans, with Pat Robertson in 1988 and now with Pat Buchanan and Ex-Klansman David Duke, are being pulled to the right.

The authors perceive that out of a crisis a new party may be born, such as the Republican Party was born in the 1850s. This may not be as far-fetched as it may seem. Even President Eisenhower contemplated it in 1956 when he was re-elected in a landslide while the Republicans were defeated in both houses of Congress. The authors conclude, "Ideology and flexibility and political moderation have been the foundations of the American political process. When the two party system can no longer assure their strength, other democratic options deserve consideration."

We are now in the season where we are examining presidential approval ratings as an augury of prospects for re-election. Dr. David C. Nice traces Gallup approval ratings of Presidents from Franklin Roosevelt through Reagan. He observed (before the war to liberate Kuwait), "Peak presidential approval may . . . be shaped by the presence of military conflict. . . ." This is certainly true in the case of President Bush, whose approval rating peaked with the successful conclusion of Operation Desert Storm. Dr. Nice finds "the most highly rated presidents tend to be war presidents." Nice also finds "that a faltering economy leads to a loss of public support." That is precisely what has happened to President Bush as this issue of the *Quarterly* goes to press. Over time, the weakening of the role of political parties and the increasing "public cynicism regarding government" has seen a lowering of presidential approval ratings. These are not happy auguries for the present incumbent or his near term successors.

Dr. Alfred G. Cuzán and Dr. Charles M. Bundrick examine the relationships between economic conditions and policies and presidential elections. The clear keys to re-election success are prosperity and reduction in expenditures. Surprisingly whether the incumbent president is running again or whether it is the successor selected by the president's party seems to have little effect on retaining occupancy of the White House. Nor is economic growth as significant as fiscal policies and deflationary factors such as we are now seeing. In brief "the best predictor is the role of inflation/deflation in the year of the election." The authors conclude, "There is a certain rationality in this fiscal policy, and inflation/deflation seem to be more directly, or ar least more immediately affected, by governmental decisions on spending and the money supply, respectively, than economic growth, which is driven largely by the choices of producers, consumers, and investors, including many from abroad. This is not to say that economic growth does not matter—only that its importance as a predictor seems to have been overrated." President Bush may well take comfort from these conclusions.

Finally, most appropriately as we near the 1992 presidential election, we have the essay by Dr. Nicol C. Rae, "The Democrats' 'Southern Problem' in Presidential Politics." Dr. Rae writes this essay with the detached perspective of an observer from abroad. A native of Scotland, born in 1960, with a master's degree from Edinburgh (1982) and his doctorate from Oxford (1986), he had prior to coming to the United States already written extensively on American elections.

Dr. Rae explains how the Republicans have come to secure southern support for their presidential candidates, while the Democrats have retained control of other elective offices including the Congress, the state legislatures and governors. By 1936, the beginnings of this problem were apparent. First, the Republicans, the party of Lincoln, had lost the black vote, north and south, with the attractions of the New Deal economic safety net. In the debacle of 1936, the Republicans presidential candidate, Alf Landon, carried only Maine and Vermont. That same year, Franklin Roosevelt had secured the removal of the two-thirds rule for selecting the Democratic party's candidate in the nominating convention, replacing it with a majority vote. This meant the Solid South could no longer veto selection of a presidential candidate. The Eisenhower civil rights measures had secured black enfranchisement. With the right to vote, blacks began to demand seats in the Democratic National Convention. Then came the increase in party presidential primaries and state party caucuses. The Southern whites could not secure candidates of their choice in the key early states, Iowa and New Hampshire. The exception was in 1976 with Carter, where the trauma of Vietnam and Watergate, made him appealing. However, he soon alienated southern whites. Nor did the Southern creation of "Super Tuesday" primaries prove an antidote for Iowa and New Hampshire, especially in 1988 when Jesse Jackson emerged the Super Tuesday winner! Compounding the dilemma is the fact that the kind of conservative candidate southern whites would like to mount for their Super Tuesday primaries would be viewed unfavorably by the northern liberal Democrats. The Democrats best hope for regaining the White House seems to be not a mild recession but rather a severe depression. Without the depression, Dr. Rae concludes, "the recreation of a presidentially Democratic South will likely prove to be a hopeless task for the Democrats."

This issue of *Presidential Studies Quarterly* is rounded out by book reviews, a guest editorial, letters to the editor, and news notes. The Center mourns the death of one of the early members of the Center's advisory board, Dr. Jacob I. Hartstein. Beginning in 1969, Dr. Hartstein came on the Center's Board of Educators, which was transformed into the Board of Editors in 1976. In 1978, he transferred to the National Advisory Council. Always faithful in his attendance, and creative in his recommendations, he participated in the September 1991 meeting, and, again, renewed his Center membership in October 1991. Dr. Hartstein passed away on November 19, 1991.

A respected dean at Long Island University, Dr. Hartstein had been persuasive in overtures sent to me at Columbia University in 1954 inviting me to come to LIU. We were colleagues in the University until 1964 when he departed to become the Founding President of Kingsborough Community College. One of his life-long concerns was the teaching of democratic values. He perceived and developed this as a goal of the Center for the Study of the Presidency. He will be much missed as a colleague and a friend.

R. GORDON HOXIE
Editor, *Presidential Studies Quarterly*
December 19, 1991

Communication in the First Primaries: The "Voice of the People" in 1912*

PAUL E. CORCORAN
Senior Lecturer in Politics
University of Adelaide
Australia

KATHLEEN E. KENDALL
Associate Professor of Communication
State University of New York at Albany

Abstract

Presidential primaries were instituted early in this century as a passionately democratic reform in American politics. Eighty years later, there is a consensus that primaries tax the patience of the electorate, exhaust the candidates, trivialize public discourse, and fail to produce nominees whose qualities are commensurate with the expense and effort. Successful primary candidates, by then the inevitable party nominees, are survivors, but somehow not winners. Primaries, once a "solution" to remote and unresponsive party government, are now viewed as a problem demanding repair and revision.

This study focuses on the structures and procedures of the party nominating process and the critical role of the newspapers in the "first primaries" in 1912, the inaugural year for presidential primaries on a national scale. It was a spectacular debut for a process that fascinated and disappointed then as it does today. In particular we examine how campaign strategies evolved in 1912, the process by which the primary emerged from the outset as a campaign issue itself, and the role of the media in presenting the campaign. The analysis of the 1912 primary campaigns is based upon campaign rhetoric and news reporting in leading East and West coast newspapers.

Similarities in style and in perceived defects between 1912 and contemporary presidential primaries cast "old" light on what are conventionally deemed to be peculiar features of campaign strategies and media practices of the 1990s.

Introduction

Instituted as a sweeping reform in American politics, the presidential primaries were conceived in passionate democratic debate. Eighty years later, there is a growing consensus that primaries need repair. They tax the patience of the electorate, exhaust the candidates, trivialize public discourse, and fail to produce

15

nominees whose qualities are commensurate with the expense and effort of all concerned. Four long months of state primary elections, combined with an ever-lengthening "pre-primary" campaign, now dominate the quadrennial political calendar. Successful candidates, by then the inevitable party nominees, are survivors, but somehow not winners. Primaries, once a "solution" to remote and unresponsive government, have become a problem.[1] Scholar-reformers look to the future to propose changes that might be brought into play to rationalize the presidential selection process,[2] all the while preserving an implicit nostalgia for a "real" two-party system. The underlying assumption is that a compromise may be struck between popular participation and the intractable force of the electronic media in modern government.

A different perspective would be to look to the past. What did the originators of the primaries have in mind? How did the experience of the early presidential primaries conform to their hopes and dreams? Powerful ideals lay behind "direct" democracy. If those aspirations have now been frustrated, it could be instructive to review one of its elements, if only to ascertain when, if ever, there was a golden age of party democracy — the "voice of the people" being heard in the selection of its one national elected official.

Even a preliminary examination of these questions reveals a surprising dearth of scholarship on the origins and early history of presidential primaries. The first primaries seem to have arisen over too long a period of time, in too many states, with too great a variety, to gain close attention. Scholars have tended, not surprisingly, to focus on the vivid personalities of the party nominees and (especially) the winners, the color and bombast of the party conventions, and the fascinating patterns of party organizations. Hence the primaries are mentioned only in passing, and viewed in retrospect as the prelude to entertaining *faits accomplis* in the convention halls. Studies in depth of the presidential primaries are rare,[3] focus on recent decades,[4] or are devoted to projects of future reform.[5] Scholars of communication, the mass media, opinion dynamics, and political behavior study the primaries in ever-increasing intensity because they offer an ideal opportunity for quantitative research.[6] Often these studies try to locate underlying processes in primaries which are functional to a liberal democratic system.[7] An alternate theme is that something is amiss in the law (too many primaries, bad timing) or the role of the mass media.[8] These approaches take for granted that primaries are supposed to exemplify democratic principles in the achievement of substantive political outcomes, but routinely conclude that these principles are honored only in the breach. This paradox suggests shaky assumptions or unsound principles. Consequently, it may be useful to go back to the beginning. As an initial step, this study focuses on 1912, the first major trial for presidential primaries.[9] It was a spectacular debut for a process that fascinated and disappointed then as it does today.

In particular we examine primary campaign strategies in 1912, the process by which the primary itself emerged from the outset as a campaign issue, and the role of the media in presenting the campaign. This analysis is largely based upon reporting that year in leading East and West coast newspapers: the *New-York Daily Tribune* (later known as the *Herald Tribune*), *The New York Times*, the *San Francisco Chronicle*, the *San Francisco Examiner*, and the *Los Angeles Times*.

Bosses and Machines: The Conventional Problem

In 1910, the People's Power League proposed a bill to establish a direct presidential primary in Oregon. Its aim was "to increase the people's power" in four ways. It would enable voters to express a choice for their party's presidential candidate; allow all party members to elect party delegates to national conventions; give party voters (rather than party bosses) the power to nominate presidential electors; and "extend the publicity rights of candidates" in primary campaigns. The League argued that "the power to nominate is more important than the power to elect." The Oregon bill was a sharp alternative to "the convention system of appointing delegates to the national conventions," thereby making it impossible "for our President to control officeholders and build a huge political machine, with which he may dictate the nomination of his successor."[10]

Identical sentiments on behalf of direct democracy had been expressed in Wisconsin by the Wisconsin Senator Robert M. La Follette, Sr., a Progressive Republican and long-standing leader of the direct democracy movement. In 1905, the Wisconsin legislature enacted a presidential primary law. La Follete too aimed to overturn the bosses: "No longer . . . will there stand between the voter and the official a political machine with a complicated system of caucuses and conventions, by the manipulation of which it thwarts the will of the voter and rules of official conduct."[11] What is perhaps most striking about this vision is that these same aspirations remain today the orthodoxy of political reform in American party politics. Yet in a curious paradox, anyone advancing them now, in the face of the 1992 election, would be regarded as hopelessly naïve.

The Origins of Primary Elections

Party primaries are a peculiarly American institution,[12] first used for nominating candidates for local office in California and New York in 1866 and increasingly in other states in the late nineteenth century.[13] The first "presidential preference primaries" were held in Florida in 1904 and Wisconsin in 1908, and quickly spread to twenty states in 1916. The number of primaries thererafter declined sharply, and fluctuated between twelve and fifteen into the 1970s.[14] Between 1917 and 1949, only one state, Alabama, enacted a presidential primary law. Presidential candidates could often afford to ignore them. After 1948, primaries were important or decisive in a handful of cases.

In 1972, the Democratic Party's McGovern-Fraser Commission prepared guidelines to ensure that state parties would select convention delegates in a fair, open, and timely fashion. These reforms echoed the aspirations of the earlier reformers. They were intended to correct perceived abuses of the past, particularly the control over the selection of national convention delegates by party "bosses." The Democratic state parties complied with these guidelines, and the Republicans followed suit, with the result that many states adopted new or revised presidential primary laws. The number of state presidential primaries has grown from fifteen in 1968 to thirty-seven in 1988.

Ranney[15] defines the direct primary system in this way:

(1) the parties' nominees to public office are chosen directly by rank-and-file party members rather than indirectly by their representatives in caucuses and conventions; and (2) they are chosen by primary elections—that is, elections administered by *public* authorities (not party authorities) using virtually the same *statutory* rules (not party rules) for printing, distributing, casting, and counting ballots that are used in general elections.

In 1912, there was no such clarity. It was a year of intense debate as state legislatures considered adopting a primary, and some passed enabling legislation just one month prior to the actual primary. Since only Wisconsin and Florida had any prior experience with primaries, there were differing interpretations of how they should be run.

Davis reports that thirteen states held primaries in 1912.[16] Contemporary newspaper accounts, however, mention eight others.[17] The confusion arises over the term itself. The Missouri primary described in the *New-York Daily Tribune*[18] took place in one congressional district only, for delegates to the Republican convention. Other states had primaries in only one or two counties, or in one party only.

The 1912 Primaries
The Candidates. In 1912, the main candidates in the Republican primaries were former president Theodore Roosevelt (1901–1909), incumbent President William Howard Taft, and Wisconsin Senator Robert La Follette. The Democratic race developed as a fight between New Jersey Governor Woodrow Wilson and Champ Clark, Speaker of the House of Representatives from Missouri. Ultimately, Taft's control over state Republican organizations gained him the nomination at the June convention in Chicago. Tactical maneuvers reversed Roosevelt's overwhelming primary victories, replacing or nullifying the Roosevelt delegates with "at-large" or substitute delegations pledged to Taft.[19] Though Clark was the decisive winner in the Democratic primaries, taking nearly double Wilson's delegate strength to the convention in Baltimore, successive ballots eventually led to Wilson's nomination with the required two-thirds majority.

Roosevelt and Taft had obvious advantages in exemplifying the *gravitas* of political leadership. Roosevelt had twice selected Taft for the highest offices,[20] and no one could seriously doubt Taft's abilities. Roosevelt's image was already legendary. A military hero as Colonel of his "Rough Riders," he dramatically succeeded to the White House upon the assassination of McKinley in 1901, rose to national popularity as President and international fame as a naturalist and recipient of the Nobel Peace Prize. "Professor" Wilson was little known outside of the East, and despite extensive national tours fared poorly in the primaries, losing even his "home" states of Georgia and Virginia. Most of his delegate strength come from state conventions.

The Media. Newspapers were the dominant medium in 1912, although the telegraph played a critical role in national news reporting, and was also used by candidates to monitor their rivals' speeches and respond with counterattacks throughout the day's speaking itinerary. Candidates and their staff courted the journalists, and the newspapers actively supported a favored candidate. The newspapers in this study conveyed the impression that only one contest mattered in the primary elections: the race between "Colonel" Roosevelt and his handpicked successor in the White House, Taft. The Taft campaign received massive coverage, Roosevelt was relentlessly vilified, and La Follette received only token coverage. There was never any attempt to hide the favorable treatment and open support Taft was given by the majority of newspapers in this study. The same newspapers gave the impression that no Democratic primary campaign existed. The exception was Clark's endorsement by the *S. F. Examiner*, part of the Hearst chain's active support for his candidacy. The newspapers were remarkably pliant to President Taft and his campaign spokesmen, often publishing unedited news releases. Roosevelt, though less favorably covered, was still a dominant figure in the news. He was available to reporters on a daily basis, and his warm relations with the press were apparent in his regularly addressing them as "Boys," while they called him "Colonel."

The newspapers presented the primaries as important events, but little emphasis was given to the novelty of the 1912 presidential preference primaries. Primaries at the state and local level were not uncommon. The primaries were reported simply as an extension of the top-priority, page-one coverage traditionally given to presidential elections. Primaries in the populous states received the largest coverage. The news reporting was reinforced by newspaper advertisements paid for by campaign organizations. The ones appearing in *The N. Y. Times* and the *Tribune* on the day before the New York primary were all for Roosevelt.

The Primary as a Contested Symbol

The primary system itself became one of the most hotly contested issues of the campaign in 1912. Early enthusiasm for the hastily implemented presidential preference primaries quickly led to controversy. Progressive democratic ideals were one thing, but actually allowing popular participation in selecting party candidates was something else. It threatened to subvert state and local party systems and provided an opening for candidates whose popularity and resources transcended state or even national party discipline. The introduction of this "progressive" reform involved major changes for party machinery and presidential campaigns. On the other hand, opponents had to tread a very careful line in criticizing what they saw as "unchecked" democracy.

Far easier to trumpet in public were the "immediate benefits" put forward by the proponents of presidential primaries: closer democratic ties between voters and elected officials, the elimination of party bosses and machines, and an overthrow of party nominations by back room deals. Against the sinister forces of party favoritism and the influence of wealth, the primaries would, as Nebraska's Governor Aldrich put it, "sound the death knell of corrupt political machines."[21] The "Roosevelt boomers" had strongly advocated primaries even before they succeeded in persuading him to enter the race, and early in 1912 Roosevelt himself had urged states to adopt primaries. He personally favored a national presidential primary. Addressing the Massachusetts legislature, he argued that the primary and other progressive reforms would "make representative government genuinely representative."[22]

Taft claimed to favor presidential primaries, but he saw their purpose differently from Roosevelt, describing them as a way to safeguard the "privilege" of party members to have a voice in the choice of their party candidates.[23] Roosevelt welcomed Taft's statement, and called upon him to act upon those beliefs by supporting primary bills pending in several states.[24] In Maine a few days later, Roosevelt attacked Taft for altering Abraham Lincoln's belief in "government of the people, for the people, and by the people" to a government "of the people, for the people, and by a representative part (or class) of the people." Roosevelt called this an endorsement of "minority government," of "government of the people, for the people, by the bosses."[25] Taft forces supported the idea of primaries, emphasizing that each state should decide for itself, but this lukewarm endorsement was chilled by their legal and political maneuvers to undermine primary bills in Michigan and other state legislatures.[26] The most deeply symbolic terms of the American Revolution and Constitution could hardly be questioned in a frontal attack.

Establishing a Model of Primary Campaigning

Enacting presidential primaries on a nationwide basis soon became a moot issue. By the end of March, most of the states had made their decisions for or against. All candidates were actively campaigning around the nation, whether they wished to or not. Their honorific titles — President Taft, ex-President Roosevelt, Senator La Follette, Governor Wilson and Speaker Clark — suggest, despite the optimism of "direct" democracy progressivists, that the primaries brought forth few fresh voices with intimate ties to the common people. That presidential primaries served as vehicles for established national leaders in a struggle for power seems a stronger hypothesis than the hope that new candidates would emerge from a process of democratic selection to represent interests previously suppressed by party organizations.

The first candidates to take part in presidential preference primaries established precedents for future elections. While this may seem obvious, quite different, but no less plausible, precedents might have been set. The entry of Roosevelt, with his extraordinary personality and popularity, was an unusual case. Having rejected another term in 1908, he might well have refused again. It is equally plausible that, quite apart from Roosevelt, Taft and his rivals could have reached an agreement not to engage actively in this novel process, thus establishing a very different precedent.[27]

The 1912 primary campaigns were pursued in much the same way as full-scale presidential general elections. Special attention was given to the more populous states; whistle-stop tours carried the candidates through the hinterlands to rallies in major cities. Local party organizations were mobilized, and "spontaneous" support groups sprang up independently of the local party machines. Candidates toured extensively, and where the distances were too great, well-known Washington officials, prominent national figures, and prestigious locals served as "surrogate" orators at mass rallies.

Gangs of newspaper reporters followed the candidates on speaking tours, wiring dispatches to editors each evening. In many respects, the primary campaign in 1912 bears an uncanny resemblance to the primaries of today.

The need for candidates to publicize their cause was not new in 1912. The traditional state convention system for selecting delegates to the national convention had also required candidates, albeit more quietly and on a much smaller scale, to mobilize financial and personnel resources, legitimate their candidacies through endorsements, publicize their achievements, and take positions on issues. Thus the presidential primary campaign did not suddenly appear as a novel form of electoral behavior. Yet the momentum of the primaries in 1912 was special, and fed on itself. It was a campaign in large part about whether or not to have a campaign. This forced the candidates as well as the parties to improvise as the primaries unfolded. The novel strategies, at least for the Republicans, led to catastrophic decisions.

The Campaign Process

The primaries commenced March 19th in North Dakota and ended June 4th in South Dakota. Taft, Wilson, and La Follette campaigned early. Roosevelt, despite agitation on his behalf, was slow to enter. La Follette's victory in North Dakota raised the ante for other candidates. He had campaigned actively there, whereas Roosevelt had not, and Taft, who received only 3% of the vote, had barely a token presence. The primary had introduced a dramatically new contest of aspirants. Even the President of the United States was a mere "candidate" for the people's votes. The signal from North Dakota was that the candidate who campaigned in person had a clear advantage.

The campaign trail took its toll. On February 2, La Follette was on the verge of physical collapse during his two and a half hour speech to a dumbfounded audience at the Periodical Publishers' Association dinner in Philadelphia. It was Wilson's good fortune to precede La Follette at the podium. His nationally reported speech received a standing ovation, and was a turning point for Wilson being considered a serious candidate. La Follette took a two-week break, pleading exhaustion from the campaign and his senatorial duties.[28]

The candidates travelled extensively in the populous states of the East and Midwest, often giving ten to fifteen whistle-stop speeches each day. Taft made a three-day speaking tour to Ohio and Pennsylvania. After Wilson's speech in Philadelphia, he set off on a speaking tour of Kentucky and Illinois. In April, Roosevelt travelled through Kentucky, West Virginia, Ohio, and Pennsylvania by train, and then went on to Nebraska and Iowa. La Follette resumed his strenuous campaigning, including visits to Oregon in April and California in May. Wilson went to Illinois to give speeches in ten cities in April, and made a point of praising the presidential primaries, though his 56% to 44% loss to Clark was the prelude to further primary defeats in Nebraska, Colorado, Massachusetts, Maryland, Wyoming, and California.

Managers and Handlers

Simons'[29] analysis of persuasive campaigns in terms of five basic stages — planning, mobilization, legitimation, promotion, and activation — seems clearly appropriate to the 1912 presidential primaries. Each of these stages was explicitly discussed by campaign managers in the newspapers we studied. The reader is regularly confronted with interviews, press releases, and telegrams, printed verbatim, from persons identified as "managers" or "handlers."[30] Their access to the press was remarkable. After Taft's poor showing in the Oregon and Nebraska primaries, a front-page headline in the *S. F. Chronicle*, "Taft Managers Score Roosevelt's Tactics," introduces the verbatim text of a press release with this candid preface.

> The Taft national headquarters at Washington has sent to the headquarters of the Taft Republicans in this city a statement indicating its belief that President Taft will be nominated at Chicago on the first ballot, with votes to spare.[31]

In the East, Roosevelt's manager seemed to wield the same influence. The *Tribune* published his letter of March 7 complaining that the New York newspapers were "moving heaven and earth to avoid the nomination of Roosevelt." Managers also knew how to put a favorable "spin" on bad news in 1912. When La Follette won the North Dakota primary, "the Taft people called it a victory, because every vote taken from Roosevelt means a gain for them, and the Roosevelt followers called it a victory because Taft ran third, and a bad third at that."[32] Assurances that a candidate's nomination was certain, or that sufficient delegates were in hand, repeatedly appeared in published press releases for both Taft and Roosevelt. In mid-May, Roosevelt's managers claimed that he had over 500 delegates; the next day the Taft leaders claimed 543 for their candidate.[33]

Looking back to 1912, one is struck by a paradox. Presidential preference primaries immediately *focussed and intensified* pre-convention candidacy to a four-month period. At the same time they *opened up and diffused* the campaign in its scale of appeal, its demand for resources, and the enlarged scope of competition beyond party organizations. The timing of Roosevelt's entry into the primary campaign, its impact on the Republican Party, and the energetic campaigning by all the candidates illustrate the dramatic effect of the primaries on presidential politics in 1912.

The last month of the primaries received the most attention from both candidates and the press. In Massachusetts, the headlines read, "Taft and Roosevelt Rock Old Bay State. President and Ex-President Dash Through Massachusetts Town in Final Appeals for Votes at Primary Today. Cheering Crowds Greet Them."[34] The candidates participated in what *The N. Y. Times* called "the most remarkable political joust that the United States has ever seen," following each other around from city to city. Roosevelt received regular telegraphic reports of Taft's speeches and began "a long distance debate by retorting to Mr. Taft's statements."[35] The "sleaze factor" became a major issue. Roosevelt charged that Taft was backed by corrupt bosses and "the sinister special interests which stand behind the bosses." Taft replied that Roosevelt was fostering class hatred.[36] After Roosevelt won in a close vote in Massachusetts, both spent more time in Maryland, which Roosevelt won (May 6) by a larger margin.

Taft campaigned nine full days in his home state of Ohio, speaking in every Congressional district. He was closely followed again by Roosevelt, who won by a 16% margin. In the New Jersey primary (May 26), Roosevelt and Taft, still in tandem, kept in touch by telegraph with his rival's speeches and prepared an immediate response to the latest challenges.[37]

The voter turnout was generally reported as "light." In the Pennsylvania primary, for example, the *Tribune*[38] reported that in some districts the vote was not much over 50% of the total vote cast in the last general election. Indeed, most of the primaries had turnouts of less than 50% by the same comparison. In New York, reporters speculated about the reasons for the low turnout, which today would be considered a heavy primary vote. They concluded that people were simply not educated about primaries. Only the "excitable few" took part, except in Wisconsin, where "the people have grown accustomed to them."[39]

Imagery and Strategy in the 1912 Primaries

Savage[40] has noted that presidential aspirants strive to develop a "statesman" image during the critical early months (and now years) of "surfacing." To survive the "pre-campaign" and primary tour a candidate must project a "presidential" image, a rhetorical vision, and a rhetorical agenda.

Compared to the "cool medium" blandness of recent presidential candidates, the "images" and "rhetorical visions" of the candidates in 1912 stand out in bold relief. A self-styled hero of mythic proportions, Roosevelt bristled with energy and revelled in his exploits as a charismatic military officer, big-game hunter, naturalist, diplomat, and political reformer. Even enemies considered him a figure larger than life, whose ego was a diabolical force. Roosevelt's persona was powerfully projected even in a hostile press.

Roosevelt formulated his candidacy in terms of vision. There were, he said, two types of men. One stands for "the spirit of uplift and betterment of mankind," possessed of a "fervor and broad sympathy and imagination, with faith in the people to rule themselves. The other type has "narrow vision and small sympathy," is "not stirred by the wrongs of others," distrusts people and wishes to "exploit them for their own benefit." No one doubted that he saw himself as the first type, and Taft the second.[41]

Roosevelt's agenda, if it can be split from his activist image, was Progressivism. He advocated the adoption of a nationwide presidential primary, the initiative, referendum, direct election of senators, recall of judges, and "a competent administrative body" in addition to anti-trust law to control big business.[42]

Taft's image and rhetorical vision were not nearly so sharply defined, even though he had the advantage of incumbency. The press continued to report his official duties: showing empathy for those left homeless in a flood, recommending legislation to Congress, and initiating the Titanic disaster inquiry.[43] But his surrogate speakers at election rallies and his campaign manager's regular press statements did little to dramatize his image. These testimonials took the form of dubiously long, unfocussed lists of programs and policy positions, having the paradoxical effect of being effusive while striving to be objective.[44] The proclaimed certainty of his nomination at the Chicago convention unintentionally reinforced Roosevelt's repeated warnings that the Taft forces would spurn the popular vote in the primaries with a "fixed" convention. Thus Taft: "The Chicago convention will be organized by the friends of the constitutional government and the success of that great cause now seems assured."[45] Roosevelt could hardly have said it better.

Wilson and Clark were barely noticed in the newspapers examined in this study.[46] Reports of Wilson's speeches, described as serious and intelligent, were consigned to the back pages. The theft of Wilson's suitcase from a Chicago hotel provided a rare opportunity to develop Wilson's image into front page material. Deprived of his belongings by those "believed to have been employed by political enemies,"[47] he arrived in Syracuse with only the clothes on his back to deliver a speech to the Chamber of Commerce. For "two hours the suit question gave Gov. Wilson more anxiety than the political situation." A borrowed suit saw him through the evening, but the readers were assured that he had a "shopping tour" in Syracuse to purchase socks, shirts, ties, and underwear.[48]

Wilson's agenda for progressive reform stressed the theme of change. The trusts and the tariff were especially attacked. His speech in Topeka, Kansas, "The Relationship of Business to Government," declared that he did not want to "hamper the great processes of our economic life." But those who "are making use of our corporation laws for their own advantage" must not be allowed to "establish monopoly."[49]

La Follette continued to receive coverage as a champion of progressive causes. Candidates such as Governor Judson Harmon and Representative Oscar Underwood received only token coverage of their official policy positions. Their lack of "image" is aptly measured by their absence[50] from political cartoons, where the stolid, respectable bulk of Taft[51] is less popular than caricatures of Roosevelt as a Neanderthal, complete with "big stick," a buffoon on a treadmill,[52] or a demagogic hell-raiser.[53]

Offensive Campaigning

Perhaps because of the undoubted qualifications of both candidates, their primary campaigns became embittered and "negative." Roosevelt regularly proclaimed that "A vote for Mr. Taft is a vote for the bosses."[54] Taft retorted by naming political bosses who supported Roosevelt.[55] The attacks on Taft began when Roosevelt lost the New York primary. In his "most stinging speech thus far," Roosevelt charged Taft's managers with fraud and trickery, resorting to practices "worse than Tweed's."[56] Then he accused Taft of "political chicanery" in "cooking" the southern primaries.[57] He released a letter accusing Taft of using Federal officeholders in acts of vote fraud in Kentucky.[58] In Massachusetts, his attacks were described as a "torrent of hot denunciation."[59]

As Taft met successive defeats, he attacked Roosevelt more aggressively, charging him with demagoguery and "Caesarism" for violating the unwritten law against a third presidential term and for breaking the spirit of his own promise in 1908 that "under no circumstances" would he accept another nomination.[60] But he refrained from direct personal attacks on Roosevelt until the Massachusetts primary. Now, his supporters said, he had "decided to abandon his attitude of silence" because of the "severe criticism which Colonel Roosevelt has made of him." Henceforth he would not only reply, but even mention him by name.[61] Repeatedly Taft spoke of his disdain for personal attacks—while making them.

It is not pleasant and it is not a dignified position for the President of the United States. But I did not seek it. I am forced against the wall, with my back to it, and if I have any manhood I am forced to fight.[62]

The crowds loved it. They "broke into tremendous cheering." "'Go for him! Soak it to him! Go at him!'" Taft complied, warning that Roosevelt might become a dictator in the White House.[63]

These increasingly abusive attacks on so popular a rival contradicted the Taft campaign's aim of projecting an image of competence, stability and assured victory.[64] Under a wild headline on the day of the California primary—"Roosevelt Would Wipe Out Civil War Victory"—Taft was quoted as saying it would be "dangerous" to elect a man with Roosevelt's views of the Constitution.[65] Days later, Taft returned to this theme "The arrogance of his statement that he is the Republican Party . . . finds no parallel in history save for the famous words of Louis XIV: 'The State, I am it.'"[66]

The most vicious attack, alleging that Roosevelt had a drinking problem, appeared in a Salina, Kansas, newspaper and spread through the Midwest. In a letter to the *Tribune* in May, Roosevelt denounced the charge, protesting that he was "exceedingly temperate," never touched whiskey, and doubted if he drank "a dozen teaspoonsful of brandy a year." A sign of the Taft campaign's desperation was the "Washington scandal" uncovered during the Ohio campaign alleging that, in 1907, Roosevelt intervened in a U.S. Attorney's investigation of International Harvester.[67] The falling out of Roosevelt and Taft, two old friends, was exceptionally bitter.

Conclusion: *Plus ça Change*

Advocates of a more democratic electoral process had reason to believe that the Progressive cause of presidential primaries was advanced in 1912. Roosevelt and La Follette supporters could be pleased that Taft's machine-engineered renomination was a Pyrrhic victory. Under the old system, Taft almost certainly would have been smoothly renominated and re-elected. Yet the 1912 campaign was hardly a victory for direct popular control of the nominating process. The primary "winners," Roosevelt and Clark, were both denied nomination at their party conventions. Wilson's "progressive" candidacy was also a victory for old-style state machine politics and vote-trading at the national convention. Although a party would never again reject the clear mandate of the primaries after 1912, the first primaries revealed tendencies that reformers had not anticipated.

Presidential primaries in this first national trial were regarded by some as a problem rather than a solution. The 1912 presidential primaries enabled popular, charismatic, and well-established national figures such as Roosevelt and La Follette to mobilize national campaigns. Both to the electorate at large as well as to powerful backers, primaries enhanced the appeal of personality as a rival force to the established national parties. Nevertheless, the overwhelming popular mandate of both parties' primaries was negated by the combined forces of state machines and national conventions, and neither candidate was able to translate the "voice of the people" into an endorsement by the national party organization. For the Republicans especially, the first primaries imposed a heavy toll. Their resistance to the force generated by Roosevelt's four-month primary campaign led to a fractious convention in Chicago, the splitting of the party, and electoral defeat for the incumbent president of what had been the nation's majority party. The Democrats won by a minority vote with a candidate who had lost most of his party's primaries. Finally, Roosevelt's "Bull Moose" campaign led to humiliating defeat and self-caricature for a man then widely regarded as the greatest president since Lincoln, and the most popular Republican president ever. This was quite a début for presidential primaries.

The 1912 primaries changed the character of pre-convention presidential campaigning by involving the parties, the candidates, the press, and the electorate in a new range and intensity of political communication. The primaries gave a scope to candidates to build upon an already established national reputation. The primaries also seemed tailor-made — La Follette was one of the tailors — for political personalities to intervene and significantly influence the presidential selection process, not only within the party organization, but outside and against it. The national scale of primary campaigning also enabled Wilson, a newcomer even to state politics, to develop internal party alliances and an electoral image sufficient to gain the nomination of a major party.

The early and arduous campaigning by all candidates in the 1912 primaries set up a momentum for a surge in the number of state primaries in 1916. This force was spent by 1920, not to be revived for a half-century. Nevertheless, the 1912 primaries offer a revealing perspective on a now familiar concern that the campaign requires an ever sharper popular focus on the personalities of presidential aspirants. The 1912 experience illustrates how the primaries engendered an *inherent* conflict between the power of personality and the power of party organizations. Such campaigns shifted the emphasis to *mass mediated perceptions* of candidates: "experience," image, and symbolic context. The emphasis on image so frequently lamented in recent campaigns appears to be an *inherent* factor in primary contests dating back to these first primaries. In spite of the fact that Taft received more favorable coverage in the newspapers, Roosevelt's persona, rhetorical vision, and unique personality still emerged, built upon the already vivid communal memory of Roosevelt the former president.

Thus the primary process is both a struggle to generate popular "recognition" and a test of its vividness: in the mass media, the primary elections, and the parties *in descending order of importance*. Inevitably, this process competes with ideology, policy, and issues — candidates and managers rightly see these as remote — and gives priority to "personal" factors: physical appeal, charm, and skills of communication. Even in the clash of issues among Roosevelt, Taft, and La Follette in 1912, candidate personalities and communicative skills played a dominant role in the media coverage. The very first primary campaign illustrated that the techniques of communication employed to create and mediate a candidate's image may be used with equal effectiveness to attack and recreate the image of one's opponent.

* At the request of both authors the following statement is included: "The authors contributed equally in the preparation of this manuscript."

Notes

1. See William J. Crotty and John S. Jackson III, *Presidential Primaries and Nominations* (Washington, D. C.: Congressional Quarterly Press, 1985), pp. 62–79; Thomas R. Marshall, *Presidential Nominations in a Reform Age* (New York: Praeger, 1981), pp. 157–171.
2. Austin Ranney, *Curing the Mischiefs of Faction: Party Reform in America* (Berkeley, California: University of California Press, 1975); *The Federalization of Presidential Primaries* (Washington, D.C.: American Enterprise Institute Studies, #195, 1978).
3. James W. Davis, *Presidential Primaries: Road to the White House* (Westport, Connecticut: Greenwood Press, 1980).
4. Austin Ranney, *Participation in American Presidential Nominations, 1976* (Washington, D.C.: American Enterprise Institute Studies, #149, 1977).
5. Ranney, *Curing the Mischiefs of Faction*, 1975; *The Federalization of Presidential Primaries*, 1978.
6. Two recent examples of this genre are Gary R. Orren and Nelson W. Polsby, *Media and Momentum: The New Hampshire Primary and Nomination Politics* (Chatham, New Jersey: Chatham House, 1987), and Kathleen E. Kendall and Judith S. Trent, "Presidential Surfacing in the New Hampshire Primary," *Political Communication Review* 14 (Fall 1989), pp. 1–29. *Political Communication Review* 11 (1986) is a special issue devoted to the "early campaign" and provides extensive references to recent research literature. Surveys and primary voting data provide grist for regular milling in *Public Opinion Quarterly* and the *American Political Science Review*.
7. Bruce Gronbeck, "Functional and Dramaturgical Theories of Presidential Campaigning," *Presidential Studies Quarterly* 14 (1984), pp. 487–498.
8. Scott Keeter and Cliff Zukin, *Uninformed Choice: The Failure of the New Presidential Nominating System* (New York: Praeger, 1983); George Grassmuck, *Before Nomination: Our Primary Problems* (Washington, D. C.: American Enterprise Institute, 1985).
9. For a general account of the campaign, see Frank K. Kelly, *The Fight for the White House. The Story of 1912* (New York: Thomas Y. Crowell Co., 1961). Biographies provide good candidate perspectives but typically do not differentiate primaries from the presidential campaign. Ray Stannard Baker, *Woodrow Wilson, Life and Letters*, 8 vols. (London: William Heinemann Ltd., 1932), Vol. 3, 1910–1913; Arthur S. Link, *Wilson*, 5 vols. (Princeton: Princeton University Press, 1947), Vol. 1, *The Road to the White House*; Henry Fowles Pringle, *Theodore Roosevelt* (New York: Harcourt, Brace, 1931); George E. Mowry, *Theodore Roosevelt and the Progressive Movement* (New York: Hill and Wang, 1960); H. F. Pringle, *The Life and Times of William Howard Taft*, 2 vols. (New York: Farrar and Rinehart, 1939), Vol. 2.
10. Allen Hendershott Eaton, *The Oregon System. The Story of Direct Legislation in Oregon* (Chicago: A. C. McClurg & Company, 1912), pp. 109–112.
11. Ranney, *Curing the Mischiefs of Faction*, p. 124.
12. See Leon D. Epstein, *Political Parties in Western Democracies* (New York: Praeger, 1967), Chapters 7–8, for a comparative study of machinery and procedures for electoral nominations in other countries.
13. Arthur Coffman Wolfe, *The Direct Primary in American Politics*, Ph.D. dissertation, University of Wisconsin, 1966.
14. Crotty and Jackson, p. 16.
15. Ranney, *Participation in American Presidential Nominations*, 1976, p. 4.
16. California, Illinois, Maryland, Massachusetts, Nebraska, New Jersey, North Dakota, Ohio, Oregon, Pennsylvania, South Dakota, and Washington. New York law provided for an optional primary in 1912, but only the Republican Party elected pledged delegates (Davis, pp. 279–281). Depending on the definition, the number cited in the literature ranges from 12 to 15.
17. Kansas, Michigan, Minnesota, Missouri, Nevada, New Hampshire, Rhode Island, and Texas.
18. *New-York Daily Tribune*, March 7, 1912. Hereafter referred to as *Tribune*.
19. Having been denied the Republican nomination, Roosevelt forces returned to Chicago six weeks later to nominate his "Bull Moose" candidature for the Progressive Party. The three-way split of votes in the general election produced a Democratic victory for Wilson, with Taft running third.

20. Roosevelt both times prevailed over Taft's genuine opposition, naming him Secretary of War and then his successor as the Republican nominee in 1908. A professor of law at Yale, Taft had wanted to stay on as Governor in the Philippines in what was conceded to be an impossibly difficult job. He was later appointed Chief Justice of the Supreme Court.
21. *Tribune*, February 26, 1912.
22. *Tribune*, February 27, 1912.
23. *Tribune*, March 19, 1912.
24. *The New York Times*, March 20, 1912.
25. *Tribune*, March 24, 1912.
26. Davis, p. 44.
27. In fact, as a result of intensive campaigning by La Follette and Roosevelt, the Republican primaries produced polling figures several times greater than the more sedate Democratic primary. Davis, pp. 279–281.
28. *Tribune*, February 4, 1912. La Follette's rambling performance "eliminated him as a serious contender for national leadership of the progressive movement." R. S. Baker, *Woodrow Wilson*, Vol. 3, pp. 275–278.
29. Herbert W. Simons, *Persuasion: Understanding, Practice, and Analysis* (2nd ed.; New York: Random House, 1986), Chapter 12.
30. This term was used by George A. Knight, an "old war horse of the G.O.P.," and seconder of Taft's nomination at the 1908 convention, in describing his disillusionment with Taft and conversion to Roosevelt's candidacy: "It is because of the 'evil hands into which the President has fallen,' Knight declared, that Taft cannot win . . . and that his handlers are preparing to knife him and throw an unknown candidate into the field. . . ." *San Francisco Examiner*, May 7, 1912. Hereafter referred to as *Examiner*.
31. *San Francisco Chronicle*, April 23, 1912. Hereafter referred to as *Chronicle*.
32. *The New York Times*, March 21, 1912.
33. *Tribune*, May 16–17, 1912.
34. *Tribune*, April 30, 1012.
35. *The New York Times*, April 30, 1912.
36. *Ibid*.
37. *Tribune*, March 30, 1912.
38. *Tribune*, April 15, 1912.
39. *Tribune*, June 1, 1912.
40. Robert L. Savage, "Statesmanship, Surfacing, and Sometimes Stumbling: Constructing Candidate Images During the Early Campaign," *Political Communication Review* 11 (1986), pp. 43–57.
41. *Tribune*, April 4, 1912.
42. *Tribune*, February 22 and March 15, 1912.
43. *Tribune*, April 4, 17, 19, and 29; May 6 and 11, 1912.
44. *Tribune*, May 5 and 13, 1912.
45. *Los Angeles Times*, May 17, 1912.
46. Wilson did receive widespread press support, including the *New York Evening Post, Philadelphia Record, Cleveland Plain Dealer, Baltimore Sun* and the Scripps chain of thirty-four newspapers. On Wilson's press support, see A. S. Link, *Wilson*, Vol. 1, pp. 371–374 and 391–92. Clark received strong backing from the Hearst newspapers. After his victory in Illinois, Clark cabled the editor of Hearst's *New York American* (April 10, 1912) that he was "profoundly grateful" for "the powerful influence of the Hearst newspapers, which have stood by me loyally, manfully and unselfishly from the beginning from Massachusetts to California." Quoted from A. S. Link, p. 412, n. 77.
47. *Tribune*, April 8, 1912.
48. *The New York Times*, April 9, 1912.
49. *Tribune*, February 23, 1912.
50. *The Examiner*'s cartoon celebrating Clark's victory in the Democratic primary, May 15, 1912, is

an exception that proves the rule. The bemused and featureless drawing of Clark is paired on the front page with a cartoon of Roosevelt as a crowing rooster, complete with bow tie and beribboned spectacles.

51. *Los Angeles Times*, May 14, 1912.
52. *Chronicle*, April 21 and May 14, 1912.
53. *Tribune*, April 16, 1912.
54. Letter dated May 10, to I. A. Caswell, chairman of the Roosevelt committee in Minneapolis. *Examiner*, May 11, 1912.
55. *Tribune*, May 7, 1912. The same charges flew back and forth among the Democrats in the Clark-Wilson race. A. S. Link, *Wilson*, Chap. XI.
56. *Tribune*, March 28, 1912.
57. *Tribune*, April 9, 1912.
58. *The New York Times*, April 9, 1912.
59. *Tribune*, April 27, 1912.
60. *The New York Times*, March 20, 1912.
61. *Tribune*, April 20, 1912.
62. *Tribune*, April 27, 1912.
63. *Tribune*, April 26, 1912.
64. *Los Angeles Times*, May 21, 1912.
65. *Chronicle*, May 14, 1912.
66. *Tribune*, May 20, 1912.
67. *Los Angeles Times*, May 8, 1912.

General MacArthur and the Presidential Election of 1944

PHILIP J. BRIGGS
Professor and Chairperson
Department of Political Science
East Stroudsburg University

Abstract

Beginning with the first President of the United States a recurring pattern has emerged in which successful generals have become presidents. However, just as the successful general-become-president scenario is clear in the broad sense, it is less clear how such commanders become available for political office, especially while serving on active duty during wartime. This study examines the role of General Douglas A. MacArthur in the presidential election of 1944. Related events, policies and leading personalities, including Senator Arthur H. Vandenberg and President Franklin D. Roosevelt are also examined. The study's conclusions are then briefly evaluated against conclusions drawn by major scholars on civil-military relations including Huntington, Janowitz and Mills.

The success of American military commanders achieving high political office is well known. Beginning with the foundation of the Republic itself a recurring pattern has emerged in which successful generals have become presidents. George Washington's election was, for instance, all but certain from the moment he declared his willingness to serve. In fact, Dwight D. Eisenhower, a World War II general who became president in 1953, was the tenth former general elected to the nation's highest office.[1]

However, just as the successful general-become president scenario is clear in the broad sense, it remains much less clear how such commanders become available for political office, especially while serving on active duty during wartime. Using the case study method, the role of General Douglas A. MacArthur in the presidential election of 1944 is examined. The events, policies and leading personalities, especially those of Senator Arthur H. Vandenberg and President Franklin D. Roosevelt, are also evaluated. A concluding section refers to pertinent literature in the study of civil-military relations, against which this episode in the relationship of the military and electoral politics may be evaluated.

Nomination Politics

Senate Republican foreign policy spokesman Arthur H. Vandenberg of Michigan noted in a letter to a family member during February, 1942: "This is Roosevelt's private war! He sends troops where he pleases—all over the map—and

31

meanwhile MacArthur fights alone! *Ugh*! If he gets out alive, I think he will be my candidate for President in 1944."[2]

Arthur H. Vandenberg was the former isolationist leader of his party and a powerful member of the Senate Foreign Relations Committee — especially after the congressional elections of 1942 in which the Democrats lost heavily, but maintained reduced voting majorities in both chambers. His choice of MacArthur for the nomination was critical because of his influential position within the Republican Party. His support for the General was mainly attributable to the following three lines of reasoning: First, MacArthur had long been the darling of conservative Americans, probably beginning with his rout of the Bonus Marchers during the Hoover Administration and his subsequent conflict with Roosevelt over Army appropriations while serving as Chief of Staff prior to World War II. Secondly, Vandenberg opposed Wendell Willkie, the front running candidate for the Republican nomination who was defeated by FDR in 1940. Finally, he was unconvinced that Governor Thomas E. Dewey of New York, who also eventually sought the nomination, could win against Roosevelt. Therefore, basically for pragmatic reasons he backed the charismatic General.

On February 25, 1943, the War Department issued an order stating, "No member of the military forces on active duty will hereafter become a candidate for or seek or accept election to any public office not held by him when he entered upon active duty." The order precipitated a sharp exchange in the Senate regarding its motives and meaning between Vandenberg and Democratic Majority Leader Alben W. Barkley from Kentucky.[3]

Barkley referred to the Republican Secretary of War Henry L. Stimson who, he reminded his audience, "is not a Democrat, as everyone knows," and his defense of the order as an update with "did not alter or modify anything in the foregoing. It merely consolidated the various outstanding directives which were scattered in different places and put them into one place. . . ." Vandenberg responded by emphasizing the recent inclusion (February, 1943), of "the word 'acceptance' — of public office by men in the armed service of the country. That is the sinister word to which I apply my total indictment."[4]

Vandenberg drew a sharp distinction between disallowing "any sort of political activity within military units," and the "acceptance of high public office independent of any personal pursuit of it." Barkley responded by noting that a soldier nominated by a convention could comply with the order by simply resigning from military service, but Vandenberg stated that the right of resignation is not automatic and in fact is a "very narrowly guarded right."[5]

President Roosevelt's announcement the following year that he would accept a fourth presidential term "as a good soldier," made Vandenberg's final remarks on the order prophetic. The Senator noted that "if there is any person under the flag who is in fact a member of our military forces on active duty it is the Commander in Chief, and he would be the first one in this country to insist that he was." He therefore added that "the spirit of this order certainly should apply to the President in his role of Commander in Chief if it is to apply to anybody in the military service."[6]

Secretary of War Stimson subsequently claimed the order would not affect MacArthur, but Vandenberg still regarded it as "an attempt to keep the General out of the 1944 campaign."[7]

General MacArthur was not the only member of the military forces on active duty who was under consideration for the 1944 Republican nomination. Harold E. Stassen, the young former Governor of Minnesota who, along with Wendell Willkie represented the internationalist wing of the Republican Party, was a naval officer serving on the Staff of Admiral William "Bull" Halsey in the Pacific. His chances of receiving the number one spot on the ticket were very slim, but according to Richard H. Rovere writing for *The Nation* on the eve of the Republican Convention, Stassen had "a very good chance of being named for Vice President."[8]

Dwight D. Eisenhower, who was not a candidate for either party's Presidential nomination during the war, nevertheless recalled receiving during 1943, "the earliest serious suggestion that I might become a presidential candidate." Newspaper correspondent Virgil Pinkley remarked to Eisenhower that he would "as the wartime commander of large and successful military groups, inevitably be considered as a strong presidential possibility." In addition, Republican Senator Arthur Capper of Kansas favored his nomination in 1944.[9]

During the spring of 1943 Vandenberg and Republican Representative Clare Boothe Luce, a strong admirer of MacArthur, met with the General's Chief of Staff Richard Sutherland and his Air Chief George Kenney in Representative Luce's Washington apartment. Vandenberg made what he described in his diary as a "vigorous statement" at the meeting and on April 13th he received his only communication from the Southwest Pacific Commander. It came in cable form addressed personal and confidential and hand delivered by a Colonel McArdle who had just arrived by plane from Australia. It stated:

> I AM MOST GRATEFUL TO YOU FOR YOUR COMPLETE ATTITUDE OF FRIENDSHIP. I ONLY HOPE THAT I CAN SOME DAY RECIPROCATE. THERE IS MUCH THAT I WOULD LIKE TO SAY TO YOU WHICH CIRCUMSTANCES PREVENT. IN THE MEANWHILE I WANT YOU TO KNOW THE ABSOLUTE CONFIDENCE I WOULD FEEL IN YOUR EXPERIENCED AND WISE MENTORSHIP. MACARTHUR.[10]

The General was willing and what Senator Vandenberg would later describe as the MacArthur "adventure" was underway. After a subsequent meeting with Brigadier General Charles Willoughby, another MacArthur staff officer in Washington along with other prominent Republicans including General Robert E. Wood, of Chicago, Vandenberg began a "quiet boom for the General." Again, his reasoning in the final analysis was pragmatic: "that MacArthur could defeat Roosevelt and that he was probably the only man who could do it."[11]

There were public opinion reasons for Vandenberg to believe in a successful MacArthur candidacy. A Roper pool conducted for *Fortune* in 1942 reported that his popularity rating of 57.3 percent was almost equal to Willkie's 35.8 percent and Dewey's 24.7 percent taken together. He was a hero in Australia where a MacArthur Day had been proclaimed a national holiday and at Southwest Pacific Headquarters in Brisbane people dialed his number just to hear the switchboard operator say "Hello, this is Bataan." *The New York Times* stated there was "glamour even to his name —

Douglas MacArthur, compound of the Hollywood ideal of a soldier with pure Richard Harding Davis." Senator Robert M. La Follette, Jr. introduced a resolution for the establishment of a "Douglas MacArthur Day" and numerous localities were using his name to designate new public projects: "a bridge in Detroit; . . . a dam in Tennessee; . . . a baseball park in Syracuse."[12]

MacArthur's speeches heightened his potential as a political candidate. They were frequently statements that went beyond military affairs to include political and especially moral considerations. For instance, in 1943 he said of Corregidor, the doomed Philippine fortress from which he had escaped by PT boat the year before: "Until we lift our flag from its dust, we stand unredeemed before mankind. Until we claim again the ghastly remnants of its last gaunt garrison, we can but stand humble supplicants before Almighty God. There lies our Holy Grail."[13]

He also managed news from his theater. Exclusive interviews were given to reporters who pictured his efforts in extravagant terms as well as information on what to expect next. In addition, through his "somewhere in Australia" dispatches came MacArthur's view that supplies and men sent to the Central Pacific Command under Admiral Chester W. Nimitz could hasten the defeat of Japan if they were instead sent to his command in the Southwest Pacific.[14]

However, the single most important political asset the General possessed besides his own legendary military reputation amongst the American public was Senator Vandenberg's support. Vandenberg had been a dark horse contender for the Republican nomination in 1940 as a leading isolationist and he knew intimately the problems and pitfalls of nomination politics.

The initial leading contender for the Republican nomination in 1940 had been Dewey followed by Robert A. Taft of Ohio. Through an emissary at the convention Dewey offered Vandenberg the vice presidency with him, but he declined, saying "my place on the Senate floor is more important than on the Senate rostrum." In return Vandenberg made the same offer in reverse: Dewey to be Vandenberg's Vice President with the added provision that he would be a "pre-pledged one-termer," thus giving Dewey a "direct line for the White House in 1944." Finally, Vandenberg added "if this is too much for him to swallow all at once, I'll make him a sporting proposition. I'll meet him at eleven o'clock and flip a coin to see which end of the ticket we each take."[15]

Vandenberg did not hear from Dewey again until late in the convention. "But [according to the Senator] it was too late. He missed the boat when he clung to his own first place ambitions." Instead a rising tide of popular support and cleverly packed convention galleries shouting "We Want Willkie" gave a former Democrat, Wendell L. Willkie, the nomination on the sixth ballot.[16]

Commenting later on the convention's outcome Vandenberg noted that "The Willkie blitzkrieg hit me just as it hit everybody else," but the lesson was not lost. Vandenberg knew "outside" candidates could win and this fact undoubtedly influenced his nomination strategy for MacArthur. In 1943 he wrote in his diary as follows: "I believe that his nomination must essentially be a spontaneous draft — certainly without the appearance of any connivance on his part (of which he would never allow himself to be consciously guilty)."[17]

It was also Vandenberg's view that discussions of MacArthur's candidacy should be devoid of political issues. The General, however, held controversial political-military views. To begin with he did not agree with the basic strategy upon which the war was being fought as reaffirmed at the ARCADIA Conference in 1941. The conference decision to defeat Germany before Japan was therefore at odds with MacArthur's Asia First position.[18]

MacArthur also regarded the Philippines as "the key that unlocks the door to the Pacific," which was in danger of being overlooked or disregarded by the Navy and the Commander in Chief. His growing frustration and anger over this issue was augmented by his personal distrust of Roosevelt and exclusion from any of the big wartime conferences.[19]

However, although MacArthur was a political conservative he was not an isolationist. This latter fact was undoubtedly another reason why Vandenberg wished to "de-politicize" the General's draft movement for too many of his backers were or had been isolationists. The Southwest Pacific Commander was in fact an early supporter of aid to the allies. In the fall of 1940, a period during which Vandenberg was considered the leading isolationist candidate for the Republican presidential nomination, MacArthur wrote to William Allen White, Chairman of the Committee to Defend America by Aiding the Allies, regarding aid to Great Britain. He supported "coordinated help as may be regarded as proper by our leaders . . . synchronized with the British effort so that the English-speaking peoples of the world will not be broken in detail."[20]

After the Japanese attack upon Pearl Harbor few if any differences existed over the isolationist issue between the General and his mentor in the Senate. Vandenberg knew the credibility of an isolationist foreign policy was ended by the December 7th attack and he began to act politically in ways that would eventually establish him as a leader of the internationalist cause. Yet, during 1941 and early 1942 he shared with MacArthur a deep frustration over a lack of consultation with the Administration regarding the prosecution of the war and postwar planning.[21]

Eventually Vandenberg won for the Republicans the right to be consulted, thus complying with a necessary precondition for effective bipartisanship: Executive consultation with party foreign policy leaders in the Congress prior to the implementation of policy. A direct result was passage of the Fulbright and Connally Resolutions in 1943, which placed the Congress on record as favoring a foreign policy of collective security through an international organization.[22]

Wendell Willkie was the initial leading contender for the 1944 Republican Nomination. He had won a sizeable vote as the GOP presidential candidate in 1940 and his widely read book, One World, espoused strong support for a postwar international peacekeeping organization. In addition to being an internationalist he also attacked economic privilege as Roosevelt had done, but he claimed publicly: "I never read any New Deal textbooks to get my views. I learned them the hard way of business experience."[23]

However, his liberalism offended conservative midwestern Republicans and he did not receive party organization support. Willkie nevertheless entered the Wisconsin primary during the spring of 1944 and was completely defeated. He received not one delegate of the twenty-four total with MacArthur and Stassen in absentia winning three and four respectively. Dewey won fifteen plus two more uninstructed delegates accredited to him. Willkie withdrew stating: "It has been my conviction that no Republican could be nominated for President unless he received at the convention the votes of some of the major midwestern states. For it is in this section of the country that the Republican Party has had its greatest resurgence."[24]

Ironically, conservative Republicans' successful efforts to "stop Willkie" may well have insured that the opposition Democrats would renominate Roosevelt, easily their most formidable opponent. Although Roosevelt and Willkie had waged a bitter campaign in 1940, a degree of mutual admiration and respect, based presumably upon their important shared beliefs, had developed between the two men in the interim period. Robert E. Sherwood had written that although he had no specific evidence, "it was my belief in 1943 and early in 1944 that if Willkie were to win the Republican nomination Roosevelt would not run for a fourth term."[25]

With Willkie out of the race the front runner was clearly Governor Dewey of New York. Dewey was already well known to the public as the special prosecutor of Lucky Luciano and Legs Diamond during the 1930's and his strong gubernatorial victory in 1942 meant he could command his state's large bloc of delegate votes at the convention. Also, by remaining only vaguely supportive of a postwar international peacekeeping organization he had not alienated the party's remaining isolationists. However, Dewey lacked the charisma of his only remaining rival for the nomination — General MacArthur. Perhaps Alice Roosevelt Longworth summed up most clearly his lack of popular appeal based upon his personal appearance when she stated: "After all, how can you vote for a man who looks like the bridegroom on a wedding cake?"[26]

Yet, the primaries had established Dewey as the party's choice, but not necessarily a candidate who could defeat Roosevelt. In addition to his Wisconsin victory he won in Nebraska and Pennsylvania. In the keystone state MacArthur came in second, but nowhere close to Dewey who received almost 150,000 votes to the General's 8,000. Also, Harold Stassen was particularly disliked by former Willkie supporters for having entered the Wisconsin primary, thus splitting (they believed) the liberal Republican vote.[27]

Republican governors John Bricker of Ohio and Earl Warren of California had also been possible nominees. Warren's strength came from the fact that California's electoral vote was second only to that of New York State in 1944, plus his own impressive gubernatorial election victory two years before. However, party professionals had typecast him as a vice presidential candidate — a possibility he was to decline at the convention.[28]

Governor Bricker was the personal choice for the nomination of Ohio's leading isolationist Senator, Robert A. Taft. Bricker's more commanding figure contrasted with Dewey's appearance and style. He had entered public service immediately following law school attendance at Ohio State University, holding various positions including city solicitor and attorney general of Ohio before becoming Governor, thus earning the academic label "Professional Politician" during his later tenure in the U.S. Senate. However, he was also referred to as an "honest Harding" by the always glib Alice Roosevelt Longworth and in fact was recognized as occupying the conservative wing of the party with Taft, while Willkie and Stassen were identified as liberal on foreign policy issues with the middle ground left to Dewey.[29]

On March 10, 1944, President Roosevelt announced a joint Army and Navy agreement regarding the participation of armed forces personnel in political campaigns. The agreement bore the signatures of Secretary of War Stimson and Secretary of the Navy Frank Knox. The key phrase in the agreement read: "A member of the regular components of the land or naval forces, while on active duty, may accept a nomination for public office, provided such nomination is tendered without direct or indirect activity or solicitation on his part." This small but significant change eliminated the prohibition against accepting election which Vandenberg had referred to as "sinister" the year before.[30]

The agreement differentiated between the requirements of regular and reserve officers because of the latter's primary civilian status. Reserve officers could seek public office by filing as candidates prior to a political party's convention. The most obvious results of the agreement were that General MacArthur could now "accept" a nomination if selected by a convention and Lieutenant Commander Stassen, who was a reserve officer, could "seek" election by filing as a candidate prior to the Republican Convention. All other restrictions on both categories of officers remained the same. They could not perform duties to which they may be elected while on active duty, or take time from military duties to devote to politics. Speechmaking or the conducting of political campaigns were also prohibited. Finally, if elected any such officers would be retired or honorably discharged as appropriate.[31]

At the same time the Administration was eliminating the controversial aspects of its regulations concerning members of the armed services participating in political campaigns, a related election conflict with Vandenberg was brought to an end by Stimson.

During January, 1944, an article titled "General MacArthur: Fact and Legend" by John McCarten, a former associate editor of *Fortune* and *Time*, was published in the *American Mercury*. McCarten purported to separate "fact from fancy" in his highly critical analysis of the General and his backers, including Vandenberg. According to the author, "Hero worship of MacArthur was deep and non-partisan; but the specialized noises, with political overtones, were from the outset peculiarly Old Guard Republican, 'nationalist' in the latest and worst meaning of the word, and isolationist." McCarten also made reference to a "disgruntled general" whose friends "like Vandenberg are immensely helpful. They serve as home-front aides-de-camp, insuring that his every wish will have staunch support in high political quarters."[32]

Incredibly enough this broadside against the General and the Senator was included in the Army Library Bulletin for February as one of the ten outstanding magazine articles available to the Army. Vandenberg's reaction was swift and predictable. During a March 9th debate in the Senate he referred to the article as a "smear" and in a letter to Stimson noted that his own recent article titled "Why I Am For MacArthur" in *Collier's Weekly* was written largely in reaction—his opening remarks in *Collier's* do in fact refer to ". . . a number of MacArthur critics now significantly busy trying to head him off. . . ." However, with reference to any similar use of his own analysis by the Army he stated to Stimson, "I should vigorously protest against its circulation even as an offset to the Mercury smear. But the obvious impropriety in the use of War Department facilities to circulate the Army with my statement about General MacArthur simply confirms the equal impropriety in the circulation of Mr. McCarten's article or any other article appraising any Presidential timber, as such."[33]

Once again the Senator had seized upon an incidence of ill-timed and mistaken judgment in the Administration's conduct of civil-military relations during the critical period prior to the presidential election. In this case, however, Stimson moved quickly to rectify the War Department's error. In a reply letter to Vandenberg he stated that the list would be eliminated from the Bulletin and he assured the Senator of his "complete agreement with your statement that 'the War Department must be scrupulously careful to avoid the official distribution of partisan or prejudicial material to the Army,' either at this time or at any other."[34]

Senator Vandenberg's strategy for MacArthur remained firm: he must be held in reserve until the convention at which time an opportunity for a dramatic draft movement among the delegates might suddenly take place. However, Vandenberg was unable to control the General's campaign. With respect to the pivotal Wisconsin primary — the state MacArthur had referred to previously as "home" — his entrance was strongly against the Senator's wishes. On March 18, 1944, Vandenberg expressed his frustration on the matter by writing "I have simply had to wash may hands of the Wisconsin situation."[35]

MacArthur's poor showing in Wisconsin coupled with Dewey's strong victory followed by Willkie's withdrawal, eliminated any chance of a convention deadlock between Dewey and Willkie and a dark horse candidacy for the General. The Southwest Pacific Commander's chances were fading and on April 10th Vandenberg assessed the situation as follows:

> If people in Wisconsin were flocking to Dewey on Dewey's own account then it is all over but the shouting. . . . But if they were flocking to Dewey because he looked like their best chance to "stop Willkie" then there may be a complete reassessment of values during the next sixty days. . . . I think we should wait until at least the first of May before we take any active step toward joining the Dewey parade. . . . I have written Australia and frankly presented the picture.[36]

The Boom Bursts

The high-water mark of the MacArthur quest for the nomination was reached shortly before it ended. His name was entered in the Illinois Republican presidential preference primary, against the wishes of Vandenberg. When General Wood sent him the necessary papers to sign dropping him from the primary the General chose not to withdraw, thus making it clear he was a candidate.[37]

Illinois gave MacArthur his only primary victory. Running in effect unopposed he received 76% of the vote with about a half-million votes cast for the General. Yet, Dewey had polled 86% of the Republican vote in the same primary four years before. Theoretically MacArthur should have received more votes than Dewey in the conservative midwest, but the Governor still appeared stronger.[38]

The Southwest Pacific Commander had all along corresponded with various civic groups and office holders on the "homefront." One such correspondent was Representative A. L. Miller, a Nebraska Republican. Miller was a first term isolationist with the exception that he voted for the Fulbright Resolution in 1943. He was also an intense anti-New Dealer who, in a letter to MacArthur, expressed the assumption "that unless this New Deal can be stopped this time, our American way of life is forever doomed." MacArthur responded by describing Miller's letter as "complete wisdom and statesmanship" with which "I do unreservedly agree."[39]

In a second letter to Miller, MacArthur's expression that "I will be glad when more substantial forces are placed at my disposition," appeared to suggest that he wanted the Congress to exert pressure on his superiors to obtain what he wanted. In a second letter from Miller which MacArthur described as "scholarly," he referred to a "monarchy" being established in the United States by "left-wingers and New Dealism." I. F. Stone's highly critical comments on the Miller-MacArthur correspondence in *The Nation* included the view that a general in agreement with Representative Miller "is too unreliable politically to be entrusted with command, for Miller obviously believes that the great menace to America is at home and not abroad."[40]

Roosevelt's supporters were not the only political observers to see the folly in MacArthur's comments. Although the General answered his critics by stating that the letters "were never intended for publication," (Miller had turned them over to the press on April 14th), and that they were not "politically inspired," the damage was done for all to see.[41]

As the possibility of a MacArthur candidacy was disintegrating, the luster of his military prowess was increasing. With careful planning and deception his forces landed on the northern coast of Dutch New Guinea on April 22nd at Aitape and Hollandia almost unopposed. A *Yank* article covering the invasion was titled "Push-Over at Hollandia" and it described the invasion force as the "largest armada ever assembled in the Southwest Pacific." MacArthur received much praise for the operation which brought him within striking distance of the Philippines. Congratulatory messages were received from Chief of Staff General George C. Marshall, Admiral Nimitz, the British commander in Southeast Asia, Lord Louis Mountbatten, and Australian Prime Minister John Curtin who described him as a "great genius."[42]

In spite of these successes, Vandenberg recommended through a "mutual friend" (Brigadier General Willoughby), that the furor over the Miller-MacArthur correspondence had to be answered in a dignified fashion. A formal withdrawal from the race was required and during late April MacArthur issued the requisite statement from his headquarters in New Guinea. He requested that "no action be taken that would link my name in any way with the nomination. I do not covet it nor would I accept it."[43]

Within twenty-four hours Vandenberg analyzed MacArthur's statement and failure to gain the nomination in his diary. According to the General, the reason he withdrew was the "widespread public opinion that it is detrimental to our war effort to have an officer in high position on active service at the front considered for President." However, Vandenberg wrote: "That is not the *real* reason. If it were, he would have said it long ago." Instead the Senator listed the publication of the Miller-MacArthur correspondence which made the General's position "untenable" and the powerful momentum of the Dewey movement making it unlikely "that any other candidate can overtake him."[44]

Vandenberg deeply regretted that MacArthur could not be nominated because "he would have been our most eligible President, especially in his spokesmanship for America at the peace table." He also believed that his backing of the General had cost him the temporary chairmanship of the Republican National Convention, yet he was still "proud of *everything* I have done in this connection." The Senator was also convinced that MacArthur would have accepted a draft, but later noted: "I was shocked that he should have ever written the letters which Miller made public. If he hadn't written them Miller couldn't have used them."[45]

According to Roosevelt's Chief of Staff, Admiral William D. Leahy, who was with him at the time, the President did not show any particular interest in MacArthur's withdrawal statement when it was published. Nevertheless, Leahy remarked to him "that if General MacArthur should get the nomination he would be a very dangerous antagonist for anybody, including Roosevelt."[46]

Perhaps the President felt he had sufficient leverage over MacArthur to insure his own victory in November even if the Republicans nominated the Southwest Pacific Commander. In addition to his own view that MacArthur had acted most inappropriately by raising false hopes amongst the Philippine defenders during early 1942, the President had taken the extra precaution of having his secretary locate a stenographic report of a discussion between Admiral Thomas Hart of the Far East squadron and MacArthur a week before the Pearl Harbor attack. In that discussion MacArthur stated unequivocally that he could defend the Philippines without reinforcements and that: "My greatest security lie in the inability of our enemy to launch his air attack on our islands."[47]

Given the fact that ten hours after the December 7th Japanese attack in Hawaii, MacArthur's B-17 Flying Fortresses parked at Clark Field on Luzon were destroyed by Japanese aircraft, his recorded miscalculation had provided FDR with a brickbat if the General had been nominated and decided to make an issue of Pearl Harbor in the campaign. As it was, Pearl Harbor did not become an election issue because General Marshall cautioned Dewey during September, 1944, against making it part of the public debate for fear that the Japanese would learn that their codes had been broken. However, Dewey believed FDR "knew what was happening before Pearl Harbor and instead of being reelected he ought to be impeached." Yet, the New York Governor accepted Marshall's admonition given the wartime circumstances of the election and the issue was "kept from the public" during the campaign according to one prominent World War II historian.[48]

As the Republican Convention was reaching its final ballot on June 28th to nominate Dewey unanimously, Vandenberg's MacArthur "adventure" played its last act. A MacArthur delegate from Wisconsin was determined to make a thirty minute nominating speech for the general even though he had formally withdrawn from the race over eight weeks before. Tipped off, Vandenberg pushed his way through the crowd to head off the delegate who he believed would humiliate the General by being yelled down or wind up receiving only one or two votes. The Senator did intercept the delegate—Dr. Koehler of Milwaukee—and stalled him long enough for the roll call to begin without his speech. However, one vote was cast for MacArthur by the delegate scheduled to make the seconding speech for the General, thus denying Dewey a unanimous nomination. It was, according to the Senator, "a narrow escape. . . ."[49]

MacArthur's nomination drive had ended, but the influence of the Senator and the General on the 1944 presidential election was not over. Vandenberg had served as the chairman of his party's Mackinac Foreign Policy Committee during September, 1943. With his guidance, the Committee's resolution favoring "responsible participation by the United States in post-war cooperative organization among sovereign nations to prevent military aggression and to attain permanent peace with organized justice in a free world," was incorporated into the Republican platform. At the same time the General was vigorously pressing his case for the liberation of the Philippines and careful attention to his arguments by the Commander in Chief would be necessary to avoid an explosive breakdown in civil-military relations during the presidential election campaign.[50]

In late July General MacArthur was summoned to Pearl Harbor for a conference. He was not told with whom he would meet, but the Southwest Pacific Commander felt "something closely affecting me must be involved." He was correct. Roosevelt had decided to intervene personally between the Navy and MacArthur as to the next line of attack against Japan.[51]

Despite his failing health the President, who had just been nominated for the fourth time by his party, effectively presided over the meetings with Admiral Nimitz presenting the Navy's position. Nimitz argued basically for the central Pacific approach, emphasizing that "Formosa should be the next objective, instead of Luzon, which MacArthur wanted." While the Navy's argument was purely strategic, the thrust of MacArthur's counter argument was moral.[52]

The General's view was that to bypass the Philippines again—referring to the plight of Bataan and Corregidor in 1942—would not be "condoned or forgiven." Later, talking with Roosevelt privately, his argument became more personally focused: "If your decision be to bypass the Philippines and leave its millions of wards of the United States and thousands of American internees and prisoners of war to continue to languish in their agony and despair—I dare to say that the American people would be so aroused that they would register most complete resentment against you at the polls this fall." The President shot back—"We will not bypass the Philippines, . . . Carry out your existing plans. And may God protect you."[53]

MacArthur had in part replicated the same approach he used successfully during FDR's first administration while serving as Army Chief of Staff. During their disagreement at that time over cuts in the Army budget, the General quickly broadened the context of the argument from purely military concerns and at the same time personalized the issue's consequences to the President. At Pearl Harbor his approach was basically the same, but devoid of the acrimony which marked the previous budget disagreement. To the President's credit at Hawaii, he accepted the moral superiority of MacArthur's position and he certainly understood its potential political consequences at the polls. By so doing the Commander in Chief avoided a possibly disruptive civil-military conflict during wartime.

In Conclusion

Consultation in civil-military and legislative-executive relations therefore emerges as an important point in this study. MacArthur's always heightened sensitivities were especially aroused by a series of issues or events as seen from his perspective beginning with the non-reinforcement of Bataan and Corregidor during early 1942 and including, among other matters, the relative amount of supplies sent to his command. Yet, resentment and suspicion were largely swept aside in a two day conference and a clear degree of cordiality became evident in the Roosevelt-MacArthur relationship following their meeting in Hawaii. Senator Vandenberg was an "outsider" until he succeeded in gaining for himself and other members of his party the right to be consulted on the prosecution of the war and postwar planning, resulting in a period of bipartisanship in the formulation of foreign policy.

D. Clayton James in his 1975 volume, *The Years of MacArthur*, has offered a different interpretation of the Pearl Harbor meeting. He suggests that an "informal deal was made at Pearl Harbor, probably without explicit verbalization," whereby FDR agreed to support MacArthur's Philippine plan in return for battlefield releases extolling increased Washington support. According to James, both Roosevelt and MacArthur were "clever schemers of the first order," thus making his informal deal theory plausible, "even if unprovable."[54]

However, James' supposition must be viewed with strong skepticism given its unprovability. A more plausible analysis suggests that the weight of MacArthur's known moral and political arguments were sufficient to sway the President, especially during an election year.

The Roosevelt-MacArthur consultation at Pearl Harbor must also stand as an exception to a conclusion reached by Samuel P. Huntington in his 1964 volume, *The Soldier And The State*. Huntington concludes that: "The prime deficiency in the conduct of World War II was, therefore, the insufficient representation of the military viewpoint in the formulation of national strategy." MacArthur was heard by the President in the summer of 1944, and eventually the General's strategy was implemented.[55]

Vandenberg's decision to back MacArthur for his party's nomination was made alone while the General was on Corregidor facing possible death from the enemy in 1942. In addition, it was the General who accepted the Senator as his wise political mentor in his 1943 cable to Vandenberg. Finally, it was Vandenberg who recommended to the General that a formal withdrawal from the race was required following the furor over the Miller-MacArthur correspondence during the spring of 1944. The General was clearly subservient to the Senator during the quest for the nomination. However, MacArthur could not or would not accept the full meaning and wisdom of their mentor-pupil arrangement. Thus, the relationship between the Senator and the General contradicts a conclusion drawn by C. Wright Mills in his 1959 volume, *The Power Elite*. Mills concluded: "Since the early forties the traditional Congressional hostility toward the military has been transformed into something of a 'friendly and trusting' subservience." Senator Vandenberg was clearly not subservient to General MacArthur.[56]

Even if MacArthur had completely accepted Vandenberg's "experienced and wise mentorship" as noted in the General's cable to the Senator, the outcome of the 1944 presidential election would almost certainly have been the same given the consummate political skill of the Commander in Chief under wartime conditions. Vandenberg's backing of MacArthur was in part based upon their shared conservative beliefs even though the General was not an isolationist and the Senator had been strongly identified with that policy. More importantly, his support for the General was pragmatic — that he would be a far more viable candidate to run against Roosevelt than Willkie or Dewey.

MacArthur's use of the term "reciprocate" in his lone cable to Vandenberg suggests he might have offered the Senator the number two position on the ticket (had he been nominated), or a cabinet position, i.e. Secretary of State, in a MacArthur Administration. Whether or not Vandenberg would have left the Senate floor for any such offer, given his reply to Dewey in 1940 regarding a possible vice presidential nomination, remains open to question.

The War Department order forbidding active duty personnel from becoming a candidate or seeking or accepting election to any office not held upon entering active duty, did in fact represent a significant obstacle to the General's nomination. At a minimum, it reinforced the public's view as outlined by MacArthur in his withdrawal statement: ". . . that it is detrimental to our war effort to have an officer in high position on active service at the front considered for President." However, Roosevelt's announcement of a joint Army and Navy agreement on March 10, 1944, which allowed personnel to accept a nomination while on active duty eliminated any possibility that the orders would become a political issue.

The fact that MacArthur continued to hold command while a "boom" was in process for his nomination therefore stands in contrast to the case of General George McClellan who was relieved as Commander of the Army of the Potomac by Abraham Lincoln during the Civil War and then became the Democratic candidate for President in 1864. McClellan was easily defeated by Lincoln in the election — although the results surprised the Great Emancipator.[57]

The principal reasons for the Southwest Pacific Commander's withdrawal were the disastrous Miller-MacArthur correspondence, as noted by Vandenberg, and the improbability of a deadlock at the Republican Convention. Publication of the correspondence not only required the General's withdrawal, it also illuminated a fatal political letter writing tendency to Republican Congressmen that would surface again seven years later during the Korean War. In fact a direct line may be drawn from the Miller-MacArthur correspondence to the General's letter to House Republican Minority Leader Joseph Martin dated March 20, 1951, which criticized limiting the war to Korea. The letter to Martin (also released to the public), was his "last public challenge" to President Harry Truman and less than one month later on April 10th, the Commander in Chief dismissed MacArthur from all of his commands.[58]

General MacArthur's political responsibilities in the Southwest Pacific during World War II must stand in contrast to the more purely military concerns of Admiral Nimitz at Pearl Harbor. For instance, as the New Guinea campaign was about to open in 1942, MacArthur conversed with Philippine President-in-exile Manuel Quezon and Australian Prime Minister Curtin. Quezon asked the General: "Tell me the frank truth. Can you liberate my country and free my people?" MacArthur responded in typically dramatic fashion: "I intend to do just that. And when I stand at the gates of Manila, I want the President of the Commonwealth at my right hand and the Prime Minister of Australia at my left . . . so help me God."[59]

MacArthur's experience therefore conforms closely with a statement by Morris Janowitz in his 1960 volume, *The Professional Soldier*. Janowitz noted: "Since the outbreak of World War II, career experiences and military indoctrination at all levels have resulted in much broader perspectives—social and political—than had been the tradition." This change was certainly exhibited by the Southwest Pacific Commander during World War II and especially during the presidential election year of 1944. MacArthur's broader political and social perspectives were clearly a major contributing factor in his differing strategic position to that of the Navy.[60]

The relationship between the military and electoral politics reached its high-water mark in the post-World War II period when former Supreme Allied Commander in Europe Dwight Eisenhower was nominated by the Republican Party and elected president in 1952, then re-elected in a landslide victory in 1956. The Vietnam War did not produce a similar result. In fact, as James Clotfelter has noted in his 1973 volume, *The Military In American Politics*, the "American experiences in Indochina can be compared to those of the French military there and in Algeria; both military forces suffered declines in public respect as a result."[61]

However, as the Vietnam experience continued to recede from the public's collective memory, the recurring pattern of successful generals being considered for the Presidency quickly reemerged during the 1991 Gulf War. Even before the coalition forces achieved victory, the name of General Colin L. Powell, Chairman of the Joint Chiefs of Staff, was mentioned in the press as a possible presidential or vice presidential candidate.[62] Indeed, looking beyond 1992 the press continues to so view him.

The American Presidency, therefore, has witnessed a succession of successful generals who have eventually reached the highest political office. That distinction was not to be achieved by General MacArthur, but his experience is instructive for our understanding of the military road to the White House.

Notes

1. On the number of generals elected to the presidency see James Clotfelter, *The Military in American Politics* (New York: Harper & Row, 1973), p. 26.
2. *The Private Papers of Senator Vandenberg*, ed. by Arthur H. Vandenberg, Jr. with the collaboration of Joe Alex Morris (Boston: Houghton Mifflin Company, 1952), p. 76.
3. U.S., War Department, *Army Regulation 600-10*, Political activities of persons in military service, No. 2 (1943).
4. 89 *Congressional Record* 3125, 3127 (1943).
5. *Ibid.*, pp. 3127–28.
6. See Roosevelt letter to Robert E. Hannegan, Chairman of the Democratic National Committee, July 11, 1944, in *The Public Papers And Addresses Of Franklin D. Roosevelt*, vol. 13: *Victory And The Threshold Of Peace 1944–45*, compiled with special material and explanatory notes by Samuel I. Rosenman (New York: Russell & Russell, 1969), pp. 197–8; 89 *Cong. Rec.* 3128 (1943).

7. Vandenberg, *Private Papers*, p. 77.
8. See Rover's "Stassen of Minnesota," *The Nation* (June, 1944): 646.
9. Dwight D. Eisenhower, *The White House Years*, vol. 1: *Mandate For Change 1953–1956* (New York: Doubleday & Company, Inc., 1963), p. 4 and footnote 1, p. 5.
10. Vandenberg, *Private Papers*, p. 77–8.
11. *Ibid.*, p. 78.
12. William Manchester, *American Caesar: Douglas MacArthur, 1880–1964* (New York: Dell Publishing Co., Inc., 1978), pp. 356–8. Richard Harding Davis was a dashing correspondent during World War I.
13. *A Soldier Speaks: Public Papers And Speeches Of General Of The Army Douglas MacArthur*, ed. by Major Vorin E. Whan, Jr., USA, with an Introduction by General Carlos P. Romulo (New York: Frederick A. Praeger, 1965), p. 126.
14. Manchester, *American Caesar*, pp. 359–60.
15. Vandenberg, *Private Papers*, p. 6.
16. *Ibid.*, for Vandenberg quote.
17. *Ibid.*, pp. 7, 78.
18. *Ibid.*, p. 78, for Vandenberg's view.
19. As quoted by Russell F. Weigley, in *Pearl Harbor As History: Japanese-American Relations 1931–1941*, ed. by Dorothy Borg and Shumpei Okamoto with the assistance of Dale K. A. Finlayson (New York: Columbia University Press, 1973), p. 181; MacArthur mentions his non-invitation to attend any of the big conferences in his *Reminiscences* (New York: McGraw-Hill Book Company, 1964), p. 196.
20. Whan, *A Soldier Speaks*, p. 112.
21. On Vandenberg's role see my "Congress and Collective Security: The Resolutions of 1943," *World Affairs* (March 1970): 332–44.
22. On the bipartisan precondition see my "Senator Vandenberg, Bipartisanship and the Origin of U.N. Article 51," *Mid-America* (October 1978): 167; on passage of the resolutions see my "Congress and Collective Security," *World Affairs*, pp. 332–44.
23. As quoted in Mary Earhart Dillon, *Wendell Willkie, 1892–1944* (New York: Da Capo Press, 1972), p. 325.
24. *Ibid.*, p. 334.
25. Robert E. Sherwood, *Roosevelt And Hopkins: An Intimate History* (New York: Harper & Brothers, 1948), p. 380.
26. Howard Teichmann, *Alice: The Life And Times Of Alice Roosevelt Longworth* (Englewood Cliffs, N.J.: Prentice-Hall, Inc., 1979), p. 189. Teichmann notes that: "Many Americans still credit Alice with personally causing the defeat of Thomas E. Dewey." *Ibid.*
27. The disagreement between Willkie and Stassen is discussed in Dillon, *Wendell Willkie*, pp. 332–3.
28. Warren had promised to remain in office a full term while running for governor in 1942. See Leon Friedman "Election of 1944" in *History of American Presidential Elections 1789–1968*, ed. by Arthur M. Schlesinger, Jr. (New York: McGraw-Hill Book Co., 1971), p. 3022.
29. Donald R. Matthews refers to Senators Bricker and Barkley as examples of Professional Politicians in his *U.S. Senators and Their World* (New York: W. W. Norton & Company Inc., 1973), pp. 63–4; Longworth comment in Teichmann, *Alice*, p. 179; see Bradford Westerfield, *Foreign Policy and Party Politics: Pearl Harbor to Korea* (New York: Octagon Books, 1972), pp. 162–3, for relative position of various candidates on foreign policy.
30. *New York Times*, March 11, 1944.
31. See text of agreement, *Ibid.* For full text of subsequent Army regulation change see U.S., War Department, *Army Regulation 600-10*, No. 4 (1944).
32. John McCarten, "General MacArthur: Fact And Legend," *The American Mercury* (January, 1944): 7–18.
33. See Vandenberg's comments and letter to Stimson in 90 *Cong. Rec.* 2411 (1944); Vandenberg, "Why I Am For MacArthur," *Collier's Weekly* (February 12, 1944): 14, 48–9.

34. See Stimson's letter reply in 90 *Cong. Rec.* 2485–6 (1944).
35. Vandenberg, *Private Papers*, p. 83; See reference to 'home' by MacArthur in his acceptance statement for an honorary degree given in absentia from University of Wisconsin, June 1, 1942, in Whan, *A Soldier Speaks*, p. 121.
36. Vandenberg, *Private Papers*, pp. 83–4.
37. Manchester, *American Caesar*, p. 417.
38. *Ibid.*, p. 418, for percentages.
39. As quoted in I. F. Stone, "MacArthur's Political Foray," *The Nation* (April, 1944): 466–7.
40. *Ibid.*
41. MacArthur, *Reminiscences*, p. 184.
42. See Sgt. Charles Pearson's story in *Yank The Army Weekly* (May, 1944): 5; MacArthur, *Reminiscences*, p. 191.
43. Vandenberg, *Private Papers*, pp. 84–5; MacArthur, *Reminiscences*, p. 185.
44. MacArthur quote and Vandenberg's analysis in *Private Papers*, p. 84.
45. *Ibid.*, p. 86.
46. Fleet Admiral William D. Leahy, *I Was There* (New York: McGraw-Hill Book Company, Inc., 1950), p. 237.
47. See reference to MacArthur-Hart discussion in Jim Bishop, *FDR's Last Year: April 1944–April 1945* (New York: Pocket Books, 1975), pp. 89–90.
48. See John Toland, *Infamy Pearl Harbor And Its Aftermath* (New York: A Berkeley Book, 1982), pp. 126–29.
49. Vandenberg, *Private Papers*, pp. 88–9.
50. On Vandenberg's role in the development of the foreign affairs plank see remarks by John Foster Dulles in *Private Papers*, pp. 87–8; Republican Platform in *National Party Platforms*, vol. 1: *1840–1956*, compiled by Donald Bruce Johnson (Urbana: University of Illinois Press, 1978), pp. 407–13.
51. MacArthur, *Reminiscences*, pp. 196–7.
52. On Roosevelt's health see James MacGregor Burns, "FDR: The Untold Story of His Last Year," *Saturday Review* (April 11, 1970), pp. 12–15, 39; D. Clayton James, *The Years Of MacArthur*, vol. 2: *1941–1945* (Boston: Houghton Mifflin Company, 1975), p. 530.
53. As quoted in Courtney Whitney, *MacArthur His Rendezvous With History* (New York: Alfred A. Knopf, 1956), p. 125. Debate amongst the Joint Chiefs of Staff on Pacific strategy continued until October 3rd when MacArthur was formally directed to invade Luzon. See James, *The Years Of MacArthur*, vol. 2, pp. 540–2.
54. *Ibid.*, p. 534.
55. Samuel P. Huntington, *The Soldier And The State: The Theory and Politics of Civil-Military Relations* (Cambridge: The Belknap Press Of Harvard University Press, 1964), p. 344.
56. C. Wright Mills, *The Power Elite* (New York: Oxford University Press, 1959), p. 205.
57. Secretary of War Edwin M. Stanton was not sure McClellan would allow himself to be removed from command, but his fears were unfounded. See Bruce Catton, *The Centennial History Of The Civil War*, vol. 2: *Terrible Swift Sword* (New York: Doubleday and Company, Inc., 1963), pp. 477–8.
58. On MacArthur's dismissal see John W. Spanier, *The Truman-MacArthur Controversy And The Korean War* (Cambridge: The Belknap Press Of Harvard University Press, 1959), pp. 202–5.
59. MacArthur, *Reminiscences*, p. 160. Both Quezon and Curtin died before the Philippines were liberated.
60. Morris Janowitz, *The Professional Soldier: A Social and Political Portrait* (New York: The Free Press, 1960), p. 12.
61. Clotfelter, *The Military In American Politics*, p. 230.
62. See Michael Barone and David Gergen, "Tomorrow," *U.S. News & World Report* (February 4, 1991), p. 57.

Shattering the Myth About President Eisenhower's Supreme Court Appointments

MICHAEL A. KAHN
Partner
Folger & Levin, Attorneys at Law

One often-repeated and commonly held myth about Dwight Eisenhower's presidency is that Eisenhower was surprised by the behavior of his appointments to the Supreme Court (especially Earl Warren and William Brennan) and that his appointees rendered decisions completely contrary to Eisenhower's expectations. Detractors of Eisenhower have seized upon this myth to deny Eisenhower credit for the progressive civil rights decisions of the Warren Court and have cited Eisenhower as an example of the futility of a president attempting to predict judicial behavior while selecting justices for the Supreme Court.

The truth, however, is that in the area of civil rights Eisenhower got exactly what he bargained for. Indeed, there is no doubt whatsoever that Eisenhower consciously steered the Supreme Court along the path of entrenching *Brown* v. *Board of Education* and laying a foundation for the Court's broad expansion of civil rights in the 1950's and 1960's.[1]

The burden of this article is to demonstrate through a discussion of each of Eisenhower's five appointments to the Supreme Court that with respect to the critical social issue facing the United States in the 1950's — the establishment and subsequent expansion of equal rights for Blacks — Eisenhower clearly and undeniably attempted to influence the Supreme Court in the direction of entrenching *Brown* v. *Board of Education* and enforcing its terms.

This analysis is particularly appropriate with the retirement of Justice Brennan (thus closing the 36-year span of service of Eisenhower's appointments beginning with Warren in 1954 and ending with Brennan in 1990) and the furious national debate about the appointment of Justice Souter which centered on the abortion issue. The Souter episode contains several ironic aspects which are worth reflecting upon in discussing Eisenhower's appointments to the Supreme Court. First, during the Souter hearings, Souter's supporters (like Bork's two years earlier[2]) complained bitterly that the selection process had become overtly political. Second, many commentators observed that the proponents and opponents of abortion rights were so vociferous that they uniquely dominated the discussion of Souter's suitability. Third, Souter was widely applauded for his supposed discretion in refusing to comment upon the continuing viability of *Roe* v. *Wade*, the controversial Supreme Court decision announcing universal abortion rights which was less than a decade old.

A review of Eisenhower's four appointments to the Court after *Brown* v. *Board of Education*—unquestionably a more important and controversial decision than *Roe* v. *Wade*—demonstrates a strength of character and a fealty to judicial precedent of Eisenhower and his appointees that seems to have been lacking in the nation's recent experience with Bush and Souter.

Brown v. *Board of Education* resulted in a firestorm of criticism of the Supreme Court and an outbreak of civil disobedience and civil strife that dominated the social and political landscape of the United States[3] for the remainder of the 1950's (and thereafter). Not surprisingly, therefore, the main senatorial agenda in the confirmation hearings of each of Eisenhower's four appointees after Warren was the willingness of the nominee to affirm or overturn *Brown*. Indeed, upon careful reflection it appears that the Supreme Court appointment process if anything was *more* politicized in the 1950's than it was in 1988 or 1990.[4]

In that supercharged political environment, Eisenhower, unlike Bush, did not select neutral appointees who refused to express their views on the central judicial political issue of the time. Rather, each of Eisenhower's appointees unequivocally asserted either in prior Court decisions or during the confirmation process, their commitment to *Brown* v. *Board of Education*. These pronouncements were made in the face of a hurricane of political activity and in the face of violent unrest in the South, all designed to overturn, neutralize or resist *Brown* v. *Board of Education*. In short, this article will demonstrate that President Eisenhower's Supreme Court appointment record was exemplary in its civil rights leadership and that it stands in proud contrast to Bush's refusal to take a leadership position on the major political issue facing the Supreme Court in his day. There is no doubt that Eisenhower is the chief architect of the judicial edifice that withstood Southern and conservative efforts to undermine *Brown* v. *Board of Education*, and it would appear appropriate for history to give Eisenhower just notice and credit for his contribution to American life in that respect.

The Appointment of Earl Warren

Eisenhower had his first opportunity to nominate a Supreme Court Justice after only nine months in office when Chief Justice Fred Vinson died of a heart attack on September 3, 1953. There is no doubt that Eisenhower recognized the symbolic importance of selecting the Chief Justice of the United States. Eisenhower wanted a man of "national stature" "worthy of the high esteem of the American people."[5] He also wanted a man "who had such recognized administrative ability as to promise an efficient conduct of the affairs of the court, and who could be expected to provide a leadership that would be favorably received by all the courts of the land."[6]

Though Eisenhower "wanted to think long and hard before making what probably would be the most important appointment of his presidency"[7], his first inclination was to elevate one of his closest advisors, John Foster Dulles, the Secretary of State.[8] Dulles, however, eliminated himself "instantly and unequivocally."[9]

Eisenhower then engaged in a methodical process which resulted in Attorney General Brownell compiling a list for Eisenhower's consideration.[10] Most of the persons on the list were eliminated because of age or unsound health and the leading candidate rapidly became Earl Warren, the third-term Governor of California.[11]

Eisenhower was very familiar with Warren, who had run as the GOP's vice presidential candidate in 1948 and who had contested Eisenhower for the presidential nomination in 1952. Moreover, Eisenhower had discussed the possibility of a cabinet post with Warren[12] in 1952 and, it is also clear that prior to assuming office, Eisenhower had discussed with Warren the possibility of nominating Warren to the Supreme Court.[13] Indeed, it has been reported that Warren turned down a cabinet post, indicating that he was interested in "that other post".[14]

Eisenhower sent Attorney General Brownell to California to meet secretly with Warren and to investigate Warren's record as a lawyer.[15] There was a lot to investigate; Warren had been a district attorney and California's Attorney General before becoming Governor of California.[16] In his autobiography Eisenhower strenuously denies that Warren was nominated in repayment of a campaign debt.[17] Though Eisenhower's protestations have been viewed skeptically,[18] Stephen Ambrose, in his thoughtful biography of Eisenhower, has sensibly concluded from the process Eisenhower engaged in that Eisenhower "felt free" to select someone other than Warren for the Chief Justice vacancy even if he had promised Warren ultimate elevation to the high court.[19]

Attorney General Brownell had been a close advisor of Governor Thomas Dewey of New York who ran for President in 1948 with Warren as his running mate and he was extremely familiar with Warren's reputation as a liberal-progressive Republican from the 1948 and 1952 campaigns. Brownell reported back to Eisenhower that Warren was a man of sound constitutional views who "stood for civil liberties."[20]

Earl Warren's political and legal record was sufficiently liberal that in 1938 he was able to cross-file for Attorney General on the Republican, Democratic and Progressive party tickets and win all three.[21] His subsequent three campaigns for Governor also witnessed substantial liberal and progressive support. Indeed, his record was so clearly progressive that Eisenhower's brother Edgar denounced Warren as a "left winger."[22]

In sum, there can be no question whatsoever that when Eisenhower and Brownell decided to make Earl Warren Chief Justice of the United States, they fully recognized the fact that they were placing the Court in the hands of a person whose record on civil rights was clearly liberal and whose stewardship on the Court would undoubtedly be progressive. Moreover, there was no question in Brownell's mind that civil rights was high on the agenda of the Supreme Court for which Brownell was helping Eisenhower select a leader. *Brown* v. *Board of Education* had been argued in the 1952–53 term and one of the final decisions of the 1953 Court was to set the decision down for rehearing. Thus, Brownell realized that he was selecting a liberal justice who would face as one of his first tasks rendering a landmark civil rights decision. Eisenhower, too, was well aware of the situation as in the Summer of 1953, Brownell and Eisenhower had discussed the Justice Department's position on this impending *Brown* decision and Eisenhower knew that the Justice he selected would have a voice in determining critical civil rights issues.[23]

If there was any doubt in Eisenhower's mind about the ideological orientation of his nominee Earl Warren, it was dispelled during the confirmation process. The most vigorous opposition to Warren came from the right wing, which criticized the selection of Earl Warren because he was an "ultra-liberal."[24] Eisenhower defiantly reacted to this criticism by writing in his diary that "[if the] Republicans as a body should try to repudiate [Warren] I shall leave the Republican Party. . . ."[25]

The personal and public record of Eisenhower's appointment of Earl Warren is, thus, unequivocal: When President Eisenhower selected Earl Warren to be Chief Justice of the United States, Eisenhower recognized that civil rights was a high priority for the Supreme Court, and he fully recognized that he was appointing a liberal Republican (perhaps the most prominent liberal Republican in the country) to lead the Supreme Court in facing these civil rights challenges. Accordingly, when *Brown* v. *Board of Education* came down resoundingly on the side of equal rights, there can be no doubt that this decision — at least as far as it was influenced by Earl Warren — was the natural consequence of the act of Eisenhower in elevating Earl Warren.[26]

The Appointment of "The Other Justice Harlan"

It might be uncritically and cynically argued that neither Eisenhower and his advisors nor the United States Senate fully appreciated the implications of the ideology of Eisenhower's first Supreme Court appointment. Indeed, it has been suggested that Eisenhower himself seemed to criticize the selection of Warren who had never been a sitting judge by later adopting the firm principle that he would not elevate anyone to the Supreme Court who had not been a sitting judge.[27] However, after the issuance of *Brown* v. *Board of Education*, which Warren himself authored, there was no doubt in anyone's mind of the stakes in each of Eisenhower's next four Supreme Court appointments. It is difficult in retrospect to fully appreciate the pervasiveness with which the civil rights issue captured the national agenda. Southern fury against the "northern Supreme Court's" effort to impose on the South "northern values" and standards of equality was unabated throughout the 1950's in virulent racist and segregationist rhetoric and conduct. It was in this context that Eisenhower in succession appointed four Midwesterners and Northerners, each of whom pledged — in absolute defiance of southern senatorial anger and threats of reprisals — to uphold the principles of *Brown* v. *Board of Education*.

It is useful to dwell for a moment on exactly what conservatives and southerners wanted from a Supreme Court Justice in 1954 through 1960. Southern partisans demanded the appointment of a man who would vote to overturn *Brown* v. *Board of Education* or who would at the very least turn implementation (or non-implementation, as the case may be) of it solely over to state authorities. Much as conservatives urged Bush to select a Supreme Court Justice who would announce an intention to overturn the controversial *Roe* v. *Wade*, abortion decision, Eisenhower was urged to select someone who would overturn *Brown* v. *Board of Education* or at least refuse to fully implement it. Not only did Eisenhower refuse this invitation, but he declined to retreat into the safe harbor of inscrutability as Bush did with Souter. Instead, Eisenhower defiantly selected four justices who were pledged to uphold *Brown*.

When Justice Robert Jackson died of a heart attack on October 9, 1954, Eisenhower first offered the position to Attorney General Brownell. Eisenhower's choice of Brownell was hardly a repudiation of either Warren or *Brown*. Indeed, Brownell had advocated the selection of Warren after interviewing him and he was in open support of the *Brown* decision.

Throughout his four and-a-half year tenure as Attorney General, Herbert Brownell was a constant force for the expansion of civil rights for Blacks and the entrenchment and enforcement of the principles of *Brown* v. *Board of Education*. Brownell was also the principal proponent of the aborted Civil Rights Act of 1956 and the principal architect of the Civil Rights Act of 1957, the first such legislation in almost 100 years.[28]

Eisenhower knew exactly what he was doing in turning to Brownell. As one biographer commented, "The President was consciously trying to build a strong, independent judiciary that would uphold civil rights and constitutional principles even against the White House if necessary."[29] When Brownell turned down the appointment, Eisenhower selected the man recommended by Brownell—Second Circuit Judge John Marshall Harlan of New York. In doing so, Eisenhower not only refused to acquiesce in the desires of southerners and conservatives but he openly and symbolically defied them. As of 1954, no southerner sat on the Supreme Court and the Court appeared to some to be dominated by New Dealers, liberals, intellectuals and New Yorkers such as Black, Frankfurter and Douglas. Nevertheless, Eisenhower nominated an intellectual Wall Street lawyer from the progressive wing of the Republican Party.[30] Harlan was the prototypical northern elite lawyer whom southerners were blaming for the drastic and supposedly disastrous result in *Brown*.

The appointment of Harlan also had symbolic content. Harlan's grandfather, John Marshall Harlan, was the lone dissenter in *Plessy* v. *Ferguson*, which was the decision overturned by *Brown* v. *Board of Education*. Eisenhower's Harlan was intensely proud of this judicial lineage.[31] There was no doubt that he intended to uphold his grandfather's dissent as embodied in Earl Warren's *Brown* opinion.

In retrospect, of course, Harlan turned out to be the leader of the Court's conservative minority on issues such as criminal rights. But viewed from the window of October 1954, conservatives and southern senators clearly got the message that another "ultra-liberal jurist" was being shoved down their throats.[32]

Accordingly, while Southern senators had allowed Warren to go to the Court without an open fight, Harlan's nomination was resisted. Of course, in terms of the criteria commonly thought to be relevant to the Senate's confirmation process, i.e., professional competence, integrity and judicial temperament, there was no question that John Marshall Harlan was well equipped to serve on the Supreme Court. Nevertheless, the Supreme Court apppointment process had become so politicized by *Brown* v. *Board of Education* that Harlan's confirmataion was delayed for four months. Ultimately, eleven Senators voted against Harlan, despite the fact that Harlan had impeccable credentials.[33] The reason that southerners and conservatives opposed Harlan was simple and straightforward. In selecting Harlan, Eisenhower was showing unequivocally that he intended to support and further entrench the principles of *Brown v. Board of Education*.

Eisenhower Appoints A Liberal Democrat

Eisenhower's next opportunity to appoint a Justice to the Supreme Court occurred in September, 1956 when Sherman Minton resigned from the Court. There are a number of interesting aspects of this appointment, but perhaps the most fascinating aspect is the timing of Eisenhower's nomination.

In October 1956, Eisenhower was running for re-election and though he was extremely popular, the election result was far from a foregone conclusion (at least in Eisenhower's mind).[34] Adlai Stevenson was a popular and articulate opponent and Eisenhower was perceived to have the twin millstones of his health and Richard Nixon as his successor hanging heavily on his candidacy. Moreover, Eisenhower, like Stevenson, was attempting to toe an awkward line on civil rights issues: he was trying to satisfy the general national sentiment in favor of the expansion of civil rights without alienating southern voters whom Eisenhower believed to be a target genuinely available to him in the election. Civil rights was not only an important election issue but it was also high on the Congressional agenda during 1956 as a fierce battle raged over the Civil Rights Act of 1956 which eventually failed.[35]

In this environment, it would not have been surprising had Eisenhower declined in October 1956 to fill the vacancy on the Supreme Court. Indeed, Eisenhower had a choice: He could appoint someone in October 1956 when he was most vulnerable to political attack as well as senatorial delay or he could wait until after the election when (assuming he won, as he did) he would have virtually unchallenged authority to select anyone whom he pleased.

Eisenhower decided to make his selection during the election and he chose to cast his lot with liberals, Catholics, Democrats and Northerners in making the selection. In doing so, he once again defied segregationist forces and made it clear that an Eisenhower administration and an Eisenhower Supreme Court would have no part in derailing the civil rights train that was gathering momentum even as it inspired rancor and bitter divisive debate.

When William Brennan was selected by Eisenhower, he had the following characteristics: He was a Supreme Court Justice from the state of New Jersey. He was a registered Democrat with liberal decisions to his credit although he was sufficiently judicious and moderate to inspire the confidence and praise of conservative Judge Arthur Vanderbilt, whom Eisenhower greatly respected.[36] He was young, only 50 years old; and, he was a Catholic. When Eisenhower appointed Brennan to the Supreme Court, he may not have been able to define the fact that Brennan would ultimately become a symbol of liberal judicial philosophy for two generations of Americans. However, there was no question whatsoever that Brennan would uphold the tenets of *Brown* v. *Board of Education* and would vigorously implement civil rights decisions despite the objections and ire of southerners. Eisenhower thus used the appointment of Brennan not only to further his own civil rights agenda but to make an unequivocal statement to the country that he believed the Supreme Court should continue to expand the rights of Blacks despite the objections of southerners.[37]

Eisenhower Selects A Fellow Kansan

Four of Eisenhower's five appointments to the Supreme Court — Earl Warren, John Marshall Harlan, William Brennan and Potter Stewart — made their mark in a distinguished fashion. Indeed, Eisenhower's record of appointing well qualified Supreme Court Justices who served the country with vision, intelligence, integrity and character and who contributed greatly to the development of American law is unmatched by any president in the twentieth century. Unfortunately, the one time that Eisenhower allowed personal influence to guide the appointment process — he appointed fellow Kansan Charles Whitaker on the recommendation of his brother — Arthur Eisenhower — he came up short.[38]

Whitaker was a fifty-six-year-old Kansas corporate trial lawyer whom Eisenhower had appointed to the district court and eighth circuit. He was considered a conservative but was recommended by Brownell, who by this time (February 1957) was actively promoting civil rights legislation in Congress.[39]

Whitaker's selection was more significant for who he wasn't than for who he was. Despite the fact that the South still had no representation on the Court and despite the fact that civil rights issues were leading to extremely heated debates in the Senate and throughout the country, Eisenhower refused to bow to southern pressure and appoint a southerner to the Court. Moreover, though southerners and conservatives clamored for the selection of someone who would promise to retreat from *Brown* or at least not further its perceived nefarious growth, Eisenhower chose no such candidate.[40]

In selecting Earl Warren, John Marshall Harlan, and William Brennan, Eisenhower made clear his allegiance to *Brown* v. *Board of Education* and his agreement with the principles of civil rights expansion. In the election of 1956, whether it was from Eisenhower's stance toward the Supreme Court or otherwise, Blacks got the message that Eisenhower was their friend. In the election of 1956, Blacks voted for Eisenhower in a greater percentage than they have for any Republican presidential candidate since that time.[41] In selecting Whitaker after the election, Eisenhower rejected an opportunity to give Southerners representation on the Court and he selected an appointee whom everyone assumed would uphold the principles of *Brown*.

Eisenhower Stays The Course

In October, 1958 when Justice Harold Burton resigned from the Court, Eisenhower was faced with his final opportunity to make an appointment to the Supreme Court. Civil rights issues had reached a fever pitch with the advent of the 1957 Civil Rights Act and the disturbances at Little Rock and throughout the South.[42] The predominant judicial issue in the country was the nature and extent of the implementation of *Brown* v. *Board of Education*. It was in this context that Eisenhower once again was urged by southern senators to appoint someone who would at the very least be sensitive to the concerns and interests of southerners.

Eisenhower once again refused to go along with these regressive sentiments and instead he chose another moderate Republican from the Midwest. Once again the southerners' desire for a Supreme Court justice was denied and once again the southern senators were enraged.

Richard Russell of Georgia led the opposition to Potter Stewart's appointment in the Senate. Russell asserted that Stewart's appointment was "a part of a deliberate policy by the Department of Justice to perpetuate some recent decisions of the Court in segregation rulings, which decisions were partly based on amicus curiae briefs submitted by the Department of Justice."[43]

Russell's opposition and that of his fellow senators was not couched in any pretense of an attack on Stewart's competence. Indeed, Stewart was a Circuit Court judge from a top Wall Street firm with sterling academic credentials. Even Senator James Eastland, a confirmed segregation supporter from Mississippi, concluded that Stewart was an able lawyer; thus, there seemed no genuine question whatsoever that Stewart was well qualified for Supreme Court elevation in terms of intelligence, integrity, judicial temperament and other qualities.[44] The problem with Stewart in the view of the southern senators was that he was another northern liberal who would trample the segregationist desires of the South.

During the confirmation process, Stewart (like Souter after him) was asked to give his opinion of the most controversial Supreme Court decision of the day. Unlike Souter, however, Stewart did not hide the ball. He said, "I would not like you to vote for me on the assumption . . . that I am dedicated to the cause of overturning that decision. Because, I am not."[45]

Stewart's candor was rewarded with delay and vituperative debate. Ultimately Stewart's confirmation was postponed for four months and in the end, 17 southern senators voted against him because of his liberal race relations position.

Eisenhower Got The Civil Rights Court That He Wanted

The foregoing review of the appointments of Warren, Harlan, Brennan, Whitaker and Stewart demonstrates clearly that Eisenhower intentionally appointed persons to the Supreme Court who would uphold liberal civil rights philosophies and implement them throughout the country. Eisenhower did *not* accidentally select persons whose civil rights philosophies of the day were liberal; he intended to do so and he defied southerners and conservatives who passionately urged him to take another course. Unlike Nixon, who pandered to the southern prejudices,[46] Eisenhower took a stand against southern prejudice and in favor of progress. Moreover, his conduct sharply contrasts with Bush's timid foray into the Supreme Court appointment arena. Finally, there is little doubt that in the area of civil rights he was satisfied with the decisions of his appointees.[47]

Eisenhower's reputation, especially in the wake of the centennial celebrations of his birth, is on the ascendancy. It is perhaps fitting that in this new historical perspective, Eisenhower receive credit as one of the most masterful and productive presidents in American history measured in terms of the value and contribution of his Supreme Court appointments.

Notes

1. It is true, however, that later in life Eisenhower grumbled about the Supreme Court's decisions in the criminal rights and communist cases and he most assuredly did not anticipate the broad expansion by the Court of criminal rights and voting rights. S. Ambrose, *Eisenhower: Vol. 2, The President* (New York: Simon and Schuster, 1984), p. 190. However, these public statements in the 1960's about the Court in no way detract from the conduct described in this article which was unequivocal in its support of the Supreme Court's most important 1950's civil rights decisions.
2. This theme is most stridently advocated in R. Bork, *The Tempting of America: The Political Seduction Of The Law* (New York: Free Press, 1990).
3. T. Branch, *Parting the Waters: America In The King Years, 1954–63* (New York: Simon and Schuster, 1988).
4. The alternative use of the confirmation process by conservative and liberal factions for their own political purposes has been observed for over 70 years:

   The New Republic in 1916 discussing the Senate debates regarding the nomination of Mr. Brandeis made an accurate prophecy of the kind of discussion that took place in that house regarding Parker and Hughes:
   > "There is no use shirking the facts. The Court has been dragged into politics, and if at some future time an appointment is made which is as conspicuously conservative as that of Mr. Brandeis was conspicuously liberal, it will not be surprising if the radicals, throwing off the self-restraint they have shown this time, should follow the wretched example set by Mr. Brandeis' conservative enemies." *The New Republic*, June 10, 1916.

   See, also, L. Tribe, *God Save This Honorable Court!: How The Choice Of Supreme Court Justices Shapes Our History* (New York: Random House, 1985); L. Kohlmeier, Jr., *God Save This Honorable Court!* (New York: Scribner, 1972).
5. D. Eisenhower, *Mandate for Change 1953–1956; The White House Years* (Garden City: Doubleday, 1963), p. 227.
6. *Id.* p. 227.
7. S. Ambrose, *supra* p. 128.
8. S. Ambrose, *supra* p. 128; S. Adams, *Firsthand Report: The Story Of The Eisenhower Administration* (New York: Harper, 1961), p. 332; D. Eisenhower, *supra* p. 227; H. Abraham, *Justices and Presidents: A Political History Of Appointments To The Supreme Court* (New York: Oxford University Press, 1974), pp. 233–242.
9. D. Eisenhower, *supra* p. 227.
10. D. Eisenhower, *supra* pp. 226–227.
11. D. Eisenhower, *supra* p. 227.
12. H. Abraham, *Justices and Presidents* (1974) p. 237.
13. S. Ambrose, *supra* p. 128; see J. Weaver, *The Honorable Earl Warren* (Philadelphia: Curtis Publishing Co., 1966), p. 185 attempting to fix the first such discussion.
14. H. Abraham, *Justices and Presidents* (1974) p. 237.
15. D. Eisenhower, *supra* p. 228; J. Weaver, *Warren*, p. 192.
16. See J. Weaver, *Warren*, generally.
17. D. Eisenhower, *supra* p. 228.
18. J. Weaver, *supra* p. 183.
19. S. Ambrose, *supra*, p. 128.
20. M. Pusey, *Eisenhower The President* (New York: Macmillan, 1956), p. 288.
21. J. Weaver, *supra*; H. Abraham, *supra*.
22. S. Ambrose, *supra* p. 128.
23. See essay by Attorney General Brownell in *Presidential Studies Quarterly*, Spring 1991, pp. 235–242.
24. H. Abraham, *supra* p. 238.
25. H. Abraham, *supra* p. 129.
26. It has often been speculated that Eisenhower disapproved of the *Brown* decision and even attempted

to discourage Warren from enforcing it. (See S. Ambrose, *supra* p. 190.) Nevertheless, even Ambrose concludes that Eisenhower's greatest contribution in the field of civil rights was the appointment of Earl Warren (S. Ambrose, *supra* p. 624). The point Ambrose completely misses is that an equally significant contribution was the subsequent appointment of four other Justices who were willing to follow and implement rather than obstruct Warren's civil rights agenda.

27. D. Eisenhower, *supra* p. 230.
28. J. W. Anderson, *Eisenhower, Brownell, And The Congress: The Tangled Origins Of The Civil Rights Bill of 1956–1957* (Tuscaloosa: University of Alabama Press, 1964).
29. M. Pusey, *supra* p. 288.
30. H. Abraham, *supra* p. 242.
31. H. Abraham, *supra* p. 244.
32. H. Abraham, *supra* p. 247.
33. H. Abraham, *supra* p. 243.
34. S. Ambrose, *supra* pp. 348–349.
35. J. W. Anderson, *supra*; R. Morgan, *The President and Civil Rights: Policymaking by Executive Order* (New York: St. Martin's Press, 1970).
36. H. Abraham, *supra* p. 24; see Judiciary Hearing on Brennan 2/26/57 p. 3; D. Eisenhower, *supra* p. 230.
37. See *The New York Times*, Sept. 8, 12, 28, 1956, Oct. 1 and 2, 1956; A. Krock, *Memoirs: Sixty Years On The Firing Line* (New York: Funk and Wagnalls, 1968).
38. H. Abraham, *supra* p. 248.
39. J. W. Anderson, *supra*; H. Abraham, *supra* p. 247.
40. *The New York Times*, Sept. 28, 1956.
41. J. W. Anderson, *supra*; R. Morgan, *The President And Civil Rights: Policymaking By Executive Order* (1976).
42. S. Ambrose, *supra* p. 414.
43. H. Abraham, *supra* p. 249.
44. H. Abraham, *supra* p. 251.
45. H. Abraham, *supra* p. 250.
46. See, L. Kohlmeier, Jr., *supra*.
47. Ambrose observed that throughout his presidency, Eisenhower remained convinced that he made the right choice in selecting Warren. (See S. Ambrose, *supra* p. 129.) Moreover, Eisenhower was so satisfied with his pro-civil rights Attorney General and with his appointee Potter Stewart that he recommended their elevation to Chief Justice when Earl Warren resigned in 1969. (S. Ambrose, *supra*, p. 673.)

Eisenhower's Congressional Defeat Of 1956: Limitations Of Television And The GOP

CRAIG ALLEN
Assistant Professor
Walter Cronkite School of
   Journalism and Telecommunication
Arizona State University

Dwight Eisenhower's landslide victory over Adlai Stevenson in 1956 is seldom viewed as an historical turning point, but it established two important trends. It was the first election in which a political party coordinated a truly national television campaign. It was also a beginning of a long Republican winter on Capitol Hill, with Eisenhower the first victorious president in 108 years to lose both houses of Congress. The Republicans saw their last majority in the House of Representatives in 1954 and controlled the Senate only six of the thirty-five years between 1955 and 1992.

The new instrument of political television played a role in Eisenhower's Congressional defeat in 1956. Although outnumbered by Democrats and independents by two-to-one, the Republicans prospered financially and invested heavily in television, considered at the time to be an untapped political resource. Eisenhower's effective TV communication magnified the President's popular image before the millions of Democrats and independent voters the GOP had to attract. Yet, party records and materials in the Eisenhower Library, and the recollections of key participants, trace a simultaneous Republican TV strategy for the 1956 House and Senate races. Planners correctly anticipated what they termed a "big vote premise," but miscalculated that Eisenhower's enormous popularity could be transferred to other Republicans by the new medium.

Failure to sell both Eisenhower and the Republican party showed for the first time that television had limitations as a vote-getting device. Television was effective in projecting candidate personalities, such as that of Eisenhower, but it did not work well for a political party. Numerous recent scholars, including Martin Wattenberg and Jeff Fishel, have described a candidate-centered trend in political campaigns in which office-seekers no longer rely on the images and identities of their parties.[1] This trend coincided with the rise of television as a dominant factor in politics, an event with many roots in the 1956 campaign.

Republican discontent at the end of 1956 also had long-term implications. The party had high hopes of winning Congress and turning politics in a Republican direction for the first time since the 1920s. Eisenhower's popularity was the main reason for this enthusiasm; the party's advanced use of television was another. No panaceas were discovered. After 1956, Republicans better isolated their weaknesses, although they were no less formidable three decades later.

I. A Republican Numbers Problem

Although the 1950s are often considered Republican years, the Eisenhower era was not a robust period for the GOP. For tens of millions of voters that decade, the Republican party was synonymous with isolationism and the Great Depression. No event since Herbert Hoover's loss to Franklin Roosevelt in 1932 did more to ravage the party than the nation's rejection in 1948 of the all-star Thomas Dewey-Earl Warren ticket at the hands of Harry Truman, who rescued himself by reviving the call of the New Deal.[2] Only when war-hero Eisenhower was persuaded to run for president as a Republican in 1952 was the party able to break a two-decade lock on White House by the Democrats.

Eisenhower was neither naive nor reticent about the potential of his personal popularity. Truman tried to get him to run for president as a Democrat in 1952, but Eisenhower believed he had a duty and a means to rebalance a two-party system he felt was imperiled by Democratic domination.[3] Eisenhower planned to serve one term and retire, presuming four years to be sufficient for jump-starting a weak Republican party. His tack was rapid modernization of party purpose and identity. Eisenhower insisted Republicans unshackle themselves from debates of the 1930s and 1940s, become a base for moderate Republicans, and offer a new home for independents, Democrats and millions of young people he felt were without firm party allegiances in the period immediately after World War II. On numerous occasions he referred to this as "Modern Republicanism."

Although Eisenhower enjoyed seventy percent Gallup poll approval ratings, the public was unsure about Modern Republicanism. The Survey Research Center at the University of Michigan reported that only thirty percent of voters considered themselves Republicans in 1952, a number that did not change through Eisenhower's first term.[4] Eisenhower's victory in 1952 was accompanied by slim Republican majorities in Congress, but well-publicized intra-party skirmishes in 1953 and 1954 were a signal the party was still confused with Eisenhower now in office.

The anti-communist crusade of Republican Joseph McCarthy's was one thorn. In addition, the President fought hard with conservative Republicans over the nomination of Charles Bohlen, an engineer of the Yalta agreement, as ambassador to Moscow. Nothing offended Eisenhower more, though, than a proposed Constitutional amendment by Republican John Bricker to severely limit a president's treaty-making authority. The Bricker Amendment was defeated in 1954, but Eisenhower had to waffle between the conservative and moderate wings of the party. Eisenhower had other irritations with party members over his refusal to cut income taxes, his plan to increase postal rates and his proposed reductions in farm price supports.[5]

Eisenhower often had to work with Democrats to execute his legislative program, something he found distasteful. Eisenhower once criticized confidant Henry Cabot Lodge for telling him that partisanship was irrelevant when the public had unswerving trust in the President. "I earnestly wanted a Republican Congress," insisted Eisenhower.[6] Because his most consistent support in Congress did come from Republicans, Eisenhower did not believe the party was in disarray, and he sensed a public relations problem.[7] Some journalists, for example, were cynical when Eisenhower befriended Senator Robert Taft, one of the most vocal of the conservative "Old Guard," who lost the 1952 nomination to Eisenhower in 1952; Taft's death in 1953 was taken hard by the administration. Eisenhower's solution was a program "so dynamic, so forward-looking, and so adapted to the needs of the United States" that a loyal party member "would have a distinct advantage."[8]

The 84th Congress in 1955–56 provided few such advantages. The 1954 mid-term elections gave control of both houses to the Democrats, who battled Eisenhower for tax increases, farm price supports, increased postal spending and a higher minimum wage. Eisenhower's Modern Republicanism had crystallized into freer foreign trade, federal aid to education, the Interstate highway program, the 18-year-old vote and Hawaiian statehood. Parts of Eisenhower's program were approved, but his many debates with Congress, now in Democratic control, left his vision watered down.

In 1955, it was apparent that Eisenhower faced a severe Republican numbers problem, and not just in Congress. Eisenhower's plans for retirement after his first term were abandoned when he considered the array of prominent Republicans, including Vice President Richard Nixon, and concluded that none were capable of being elected president. Four weeks after the 1954 elections, Eisenhower let it be known he was planning to run again in 1956.[9]

With Eisenhower on the ticket, 1956 was an important year for the party. His reelection seemed certain, but there was uncertainty about 1960 and beyond. Eisenhower was the first president affected by the 22nd Amendment that limited White House tenure to two terms. Nineteen-fifty-six shaped up as a final foreseeable opportunity to lash fortunes of Republican office seekers to an invincible national ticket.

Although Congress and the American public were unmoved by Modern Republicanism, it was understood clearly at the headquarters of the Republican National Committee. For three decades, the antique operation of the RNC symbolized the party's languor. In the late 1940s, the party was chaired by ultra-conservative Guy Gabrielson, a zealot for Senator Taft. In 1952, Arthur Summerfield headed the party long enough to get Eisenhower elected before becoming Postmaster General. Wesley Roberts then served four months as chairman in 1953, before Eisenhower ousted him amid scandal in Roberts' home state of Kansas.

Beginning in mid-1953, though, the RNC made strides under Leonard Hall, a seven-term New York Congressman who once headed the influential Republican Congressional Campaign Committee. Hall fired many of the four-dozen staff members he inherited and reassigned others. He then obtained new offices and began a rapid expansion; 130 people were on his payroll by 1956.[10] Two of Hall's three primary functions were fundraising and organization.

Hall's third function was campaign strategy, and he was fascinated by television. Hall felt that time and effort could be saved with massive applications of the new medium, an invention mothered by necessity. To Hall, national television was a substitute for grassroots vote-getting operations the party desperately needed in many locales, especially the South and border states. Hall talked about television often, so much that in 1955, *New York Times* columnist James Reston referred to Hall as a political Milton Berle.[11]

Republican TV interests sprang from other factors. The GOP already had several years of experience with TV, notably in Dewey's successful New York gubernatorial campaign in 1950 and in Eisenhower's campaign in 1952. Eisenhower himself was greatly attuned to the new medium. His close friends included William Paley of CBS, David Sarnoff of NBC and Sigurd Larmon, head of the Young and Rubicam advertising agency. Eisenhower took steps to improve his TV communication, often at the urging of these friends and advisors who insisted a direct dialogue with Americans could silence political criticism.[12] The President hired actor Robert Montgomery as a studio consultant and expanded the role of Press Secretary James Hagerty, who organized the first TV news conferences in 1955.[13]

This interest in television was inspired by the incredible growth of television during Eisenhower's first term. Demand for television had been pent up between 1948 and 1952, when the Federal Communications Commission placed a moratorium on TV station licensing in order to untangle hundreds of applications. In late 1952, only sixty-six cities and thirty-five states had stations; TV was seen in just thirty-three percent of the nation's homes. By January 1956, however, TV was available in 243 cities in all forty-eight states and it could be received in three-quarters of the homes.[14]

Important parts of the GOP television strategy were in place more than a year before the election. The party budgeted around $3 million on TV in 1956, twice as much as in 1952. By mid-1955, much of that money had been spent on numerous choice blocks of network airtime during the fall campaign. Further, the advance airtime purchases led to an innovation: five-minute "piggybacks" appeals that played after shortened entertainment programs. Hall was pleased. These "piggybacks" were an alternative to tiring half-hour speeches used in 1952 and 1954, and they gave the Republicans an advantage over the Democrats, who did not begin serious talks with the networks until the spring of 1956.[15]

The Republican TV commitment was a clue the party was thinking inventively about the Congressional races. Although House and Senate campaigns were run by state committees and local organizations, a national headquarters was active in them, especially in presidential years. The prevailing "coattail" theory impelled presidential candidates into whistle-stop tours with the local office seekers; presidential standard-bearers conducted at least some whistle-stopping in almost every campaign since 1900.[16]

Yet Hall had reason to believe this strategy was not as effective as it once was. Eisenhower had stumped for GOP candidates in 1954 without success, and crowds were smaller than in previous years. Hall surmised that television may have been a factor, that people preferred the living room comfort of Ed Sullivan or "I Love Lucy" to crowded and noisy campaign rallies.[17] Hall also reasoned that TV could overcome inherent drawbacks in whistle-stopping. A candidate, for example, could only attract a few hundred spectators at a personal appearance, compared to millions on TV.

Moreover, a candidate could only appear in one locale at a time. An appearance with a local candidate in September might be forgotten by November, a shortcoming eliminated by continuous use of television.[18]

It was because of Eisenhower that a novel approach to the 1956 campaign became a necessity. This came on September 24, 1955, when Eisenhower suffered a heart attack at the end of a working vacation in Colorado. Eisenhower was not back in the White House until December, and it was not until the following February 29 that he formally announced he would run. The heart attack, a blow to the party and the nation, expedited the television concept. Just two days after it occurred, with the President still in critical condition, Hall unflinchingly predicted that Eisenhower would head the ticket; the chairman stood firm when a reporter said, "You're nuts."[19] Hall helped fulfill his prophecy, however, by explaining to Eisenhower, in the weeks before he decided to run, that the emerging TV plans would eliminate extensive travel.[20]

II. Channeling Modern Republicanism

During the spring and summer of 1956, while Stevenson overcame Tennessee Senator Estes Kefauver and New York Governor Averell Harriman to win the Democratic nomination, Republican campaign planners studied ways to use television for the benefit of GOP candidates across the country. Their first exhibition came at the Republican Convention in San Francisco, when dozens of House and Senate candidates were introduced one by one to a national audience just prior to Eisenhower's acceptance speech.

Subsequent steps were detailed days later, when the RNC circulated a forty-seven page campaign plan that called for "maximum utilization of television." Strategy would break "completely with past experience by placing first importance on effective use of television instead of the traditional emphasis on personal appearances."[21] Chairman Hall supervised the plan, and it was written by two other RNC figures knowledgeable about the new medium. These were Robert Humphreys, who worked his way to the RNC's No. 2 position through the public relations ranks, and Publicity Director Richard Guylay, a former advertising executive whose study of political imagery was used by Vance Packard in his 1957 best-seller *The Hidden Persuaders*.[22]

This strategy, though, was heavily influenced by a powerful Republican flank on Madison Avenue. In a year when the Democrats had few takers for their ad account, GOP efforts were guided by both the world's second and third largest agencies. These were Batten, Barton, Durstine and Osborne and Young and Rubicam. BBDO, under President Ben Duffy and Vice President Carroll Newton, produced the pioneering TV work for Dewey in 1950 and Eisenhower in 1952. Young and Rubicam entered the picture when its president, Sig Larmon, volunteered the agency to a separate GOP organization known as the Citizens for Eisenhower, a giant nationwide amalgam of volunteers. It was a shotgun marriage, but despite a rivalry, BBDO and Young and Rubicam provided some of the best television expertise then available.

The agencies were convinced that Republican House and Senate candidates would benefit if national appeals revolved around Eisenhower and targeted Democrats and independents, millions of whom were already backing the national ticket based on polling data. The massive GOP television schedule would build on Eisenhower's esteem in order to run up his vote total against Stevenson, a concept known officially as "the big vote premise."[23] It assumed that a rolling wave of support for the national ticket would transfer to other candidates.

Getting this across on TV hinged on a sort of mass reverse psychology. For more than two decades, ideological differences characterized dialogue between the two parties. As the opposition party, the GOP was known for loud, often flamboyant contempt for Roosevelt's New Deal and internationalism, at a time when print and radio were the only mass media. Now through television, they would see a different Republican party, one of compassion, vision, fortitude and patriotism. TV imagery would paint the Democratic party as cemented to the 1930s and 1940s, while the Republicans looked to the future.

In August and September, Eisenhower met often with the ad agency planners. Their strategy pleased him because it was a living room manifesto for Modern Republicanism. In 1952, Eisenhower had led the party with the combative slogan "Korea, communism and corruption," with his TV appeals, produced by hard-sell advocate Rosser Reeves, displaying this fighting spirit. The 1956 theme of "peace, prosperity and progress" put a shine on the new image Eisenhower had long sought for the party.[24]

Both Young and Rubicam and BBDO had campaign coordinators; each remembered years later the "big vote premise" of 1956 and concerns about the House and Senate races. "The Citizens for Eisenhower was there to help Ike," recalled Young and Rubicam's David Levy, "but we realized the party itself was at stake. Television was important in '56 because it was a tool the Democrats really didn't have."[25] BBDO's Carroll Newton likewise noted dual priorities. "The national committee's job was to elect the damn president, but [in 1956] it bore responsibility for the Congressional and Senatorial campaigns." According to Newton, the party's attempt to use national television in local mid-term elections in 1954 was a concept BBDO tried to perfect.[26]

The prominent role of the Congressional races in the party's TV strategy was underscored in the first appeals produced by the Republicans in 1956. It was a 15-minute film series entitled "These Peaceful, Prosperous Years," which focused on an average family "going about their daily lives under a Republican era of peace." To climax the upbeat theme, the President and Mrs. Eisenhower sang an on-camera rendition of "God Bless America," before a narrator urged voters to "Give Ike a Republican Congress." The production was rounded out when some House and Senate candidates were invited to a TV studio set up by BBDO at the Capitol to record introductions. Various versions were sent by BBDO to television stations in the candidates' home districts.[27]

"These Peaceful, Prosperous Years," which the public saw beginning in early September, was one phase of the party's cumbersome attempt to target specific races with TV. Besides its network schedule, BBDO had arranged local airtime, and many segments, some as short as twenty seconds, were filled with slick, often custom-made local appeals. One half of the $3 million the Republicans spent on TV in 1956 was disbursed locally, a very large proportion considering the Democrats used only one-quarter of their $2.3 million national TV budget for the same task.[26] The Republicans directed localized TV campaigns from national headquarters because expertise in political television was almost non-existent except at the national level or in the largest television markets. This local TV knowledge gap was evident in late 1955, when the party summoned the forty-eight state committee chairs to Washington for a week-long "campaign school." Although there were panels on time-buying and TV production techniques, most of the school dealt with speech-making and candidate cosmetics.[29]

Because Eisenhower headed the ticket, this task of isolating specific campaigns was considered doable. In the House, the party needed to retain its 203 seats and pick up fifteen more to achieve a majority; the Republicans had added twenty-two seats when Eisenhower ran in 1952. There was more hope in the Senate, where the party needed just two seats for a majority. The Republicans allocated much of their TV resource to the states of Oregon, Colorado, Washington and Pennsylvania. In Oregon, Douglas McKay was attempting to unseat GOP expatriate Wayne Morse; McKay was Eisenhower's Interior Secretary until the President convinced him he would be of more help on Captiol Hill. In Colorado, Governor Dan Thornton had been persuaded by Eisenhower to seek a Senate seat. The same was true in Washington, where Arthur Langlie was coaxed into challenging Warren Magnuson. In Pennsylvania, Senator James Duff, one of Eisenhower's most fervent supporters, sought reelection. These candidates, personally anointed by the President, were to be spear carriers for Eisenhower's Modern Republicanism in the 85th Congress.

Toward the end of September, with most of the local appeals completed, attention shifted to the national phase of the campaign. While opponent Stevenson crisscrossed the country, Eisenhower, pursuant to the campaign plan, ventured from Washington only ten times during September and October, usually to headline prime time TV rallies staged by BBDO. Each TV spectacular originated from a locale strategically important to the party's Congressional hopes.

On September 24, the nation saw the people of Peoria, Illinois, cheer Eisenhower, Illinois Senator Everett Dirksen and other GOP candidates. On October 1, another enthusiastic crowd greeted Eisenhower, this time in Lexington, Kentucky, where two Senate seats were at stake; GOP contenders John Sherman Cooper and Thruston Morton appeared on national TV with the President. On October 9, Eisenhower was seen receiving the adulation of a crowd in Pittsburgh, with Duff and some Pennsylvania House candidates in attendance. The following week, Eisenhower conducted a three-day trip to the West; his appearances with Langlie in Seattle, McKay in Portland and Thornton in Denver provided more television opportunities.[30]

Not only did these remote television rallies convey a healthy Eisenhower busily engaged in a traveling campaign. They were also designed to leave the impression that infectious support existed for the list of Republican candidates. Farmers, for example, were irate at Eisenhower for his failure to expand price supports. The Republicans traditionally struggled south of the Mason-Dixon Line. Nevertheless, if Eisenhower and the party were weak in the farm belt or the border states, it would have been impossible for the rest of the nation to tell, based on the telecasts seen from Peoria and Lexington.

Moreover, these remote appearances necessitated an innocuous political discourse that the ad agencies urged in promoting Modern Republicanism. Unlike the 1952 and 1954 campaigns, Eisenhower seldom spoke with definition on regional issues, such as farm prices or hydroelectric power, because they had little nationwide sparkle. Eisenhower made short speeches on TV. "The President should stop, talk and [then] go to the main stage," stated a BBDO campaign directive. "The whole idea is to bring the President's conversation a little closer to the public".[31]

The use of subtle, emotional messages and the apolitical "peace, prosperity and progress" theme, apparent in Eisenhower's remote appearances, was even more integral to the Young and Rubicam productions for the Citizens. These were directed by David Levy. While earlier BBDO productions were tailored to geographic locations, Young and Rubicam used national TV to isolate key demographic groups. Young people comprised one such group, and Levy designed five-minute programs that focused on college life, in which students took turns praising Eisenhower's leadership.[32] Women inspired an appeal that highlighted Mamie Eisenhower. "Women will decide the election," began a female announcer, "and they like Ike. . . . and here's something else they like—Ike's beloved Mamie."[33] The President himself had suggested the Mamie spot, figuring it would help voters to recall Stevenson's 1949 divorce.[34]

These programs were seen beginning October 15; single appeals, if they followed popular programs such as "The $64,000 Question" and "I've Got A Secret," drew twenty-five percent of the nation's TV homes.[35] The viewing public also saw Eisenhower affirm Modern Republicanism in a mock TV news conference, in which average people asked the President rehearsed questions.[36] A television party celebrating Eisenhower's 66th birthday was hosted by Helen Hayes and James Stewart, who joined other Hollywood celebrities in urging Republican votes.[37] A daytime TV coffee klatsch featured Eisenhower mixing with women at the White House; he told them a Republican Congress would be sensitive to needs of the American family.[38] Young people and women were not the only groups made to feel comfortable; blacks appeared prominently in almost every TV appeal.

III. Portents of Congressional Defeat

Mid-October brought the first indications that TV was not working in the Congressional phase of the campaign. Local polling showed several key Republican candidates, including Duff and Thornton, falling behind Democratic opponents. In every region, meanwhile, support for Republican House and Senate candidates lagged behind that for Eisenhower.[39] This was confirmed in weekly tracking research conducted by BBDO through its field offices, as well as an RNC progress report that pointed to growing apathy in the campaigns of many GOP House candidates who were trailing badly.[40]

More noteworthy, though, were the dozens of Republicans locked in close races who were visibly restless with the TV effort. Requests poured into Washington from almost every state organization pleading for Eisenhower visits. "We cannot emphasize too strongly the importance of having President Eisenhower stop at Phoenix," wrote the Arizona committee. From Louisiana, "We have worked with all our hearts [and] respectfully request you appear no matter how briefly." From South Carolina, ". . . we are still part of the United States."[41]

Eisenhower was aware of this. It was his decision, not that of the national committee, to undertake a series of one-day airport tours to bolster several local campaigns. Nevertheless, international developments negated this brief diversion from the electronic strategy. Eisenhower was midway through his first tour, into Florida and Virginia, when he learned that British and French forces were invading Egypt to regain the Suez Canal, which Egypt had seized in July. As this happened, rebel factions were attempting to oust pro-Soviet leadership in Hungary; within days, thousands of Hungarians were killed as 200,000 Soviet troops rolled toward Budapest. Personal appearances that Eisenhower planned with GOP candidates in Oklahoma, Missouri, Texas, Georgia, Tennessee, Connecticut, and Massachusetts were cancelled.

These foreign hostilities, long anticipated by the administration, were not a blessing to Republican strategists. Because his military background was unmatched by Stevenson, Eisenhower benefitted from the deteriorating international situation, but this was a negative dimension and one not easily transferred to the party by television. The public, in fact, knew the Republican party was split over foreign policy, with sentiment ranging from that of isolationist John Bricker, still in the Senate, to others on Capitol Hill who insisted Eisenhower send troops to Hungary and the Middle East. Stevenson, not making headway in the campaign, nonetheless underscored these divisions in numerous speeches.

With Eisenhower now preoccupied with diplomatic maneuvers in Washington, television became more important than ever to the campaign. Hall remained confident. Still to come in the closing phase was the GOP's long-awaited living room blitz of appeals and appearances. The final week of the TV campaign got off to a good start for the party, when Eisenhower used free airtime on October 31 to address the nation and affirm his decision not to intervene in the foreign conflicts; a disjointed response by Stevenson the following night may have cinched Eisenhower's victory.

Millions of people witnessed the October 31 address, as well as a parade of partisan prime time messages that followed in the final six days before the election. Mamie and the college students were seen again and again. The Republicans tried as best they could to profit from the world crises, with additional spots that played up the "peace" component of "peace, prosperity and progress." One juxtaposed the horrors of the Korean War with a buoyant scene at a football game, emphasizing how Eisenhower's commitment to world peace touched average Americans.[42] Another featured a Washington, D.C., taxi driver walking his dog at night in Lafayette Park. Pausing by a lamppost, the cabbie spied a lighted window across the street at the White House. "A neighbor of mine lives there. Yep, Dwight Eisenhower, a man with the most important job in the world." Ominous scenes faded into pictures of happy and productive workers, farmers and homemakers, who enjoyed the fruits of Modern Republicanism and had few worries about war with Eisenhower on watch. Importantly, every filmed production ended with an appeal to "all thinking voters — regardless of party."[43]

Updated research offered a tiny bit of hope. Republican pollster George Gallup reported approval of Eisenhower's handling of the Middle East crisis; the President's margin over Stevenson soared from ten to eighteen points (52–42 to 57–39).[44] A survey conducted by Paul Gary Hoffman indicated that independent voters in several regions were starting to move to the Republican column, and that they needed some final "assurance" from Eisenhower.[45]

Yet, there continued to be little assurance from the national organization anywhere but on television. Eisenhower made a quick trip to Philadelphia for a final BBDO remote spectacular November 1. Then on November 5, he and Nixon appeared in an hour-long election eve program from the White House that was telecast on all three networks. The program took viewers to cities coast to coast, where reporters detailed crescendos of support for Eisenhower and local House and Senate candidates, as if the returns were already coming in. To enhance the effect, Young and Rubicam recruited NBC newsman John Cameron Swayze to host the program.[46]

Over seven million homes tuned to the election eve broadcast, part of the 120 million per-household impressions the Republicans made on television during the final week of the campaign. In advertising terms, this was a substantial showing because there were only 45 million total TV homes; the Democrats had made only half as many impressions.[47] The selling job, however, proved only half successful.

IV. We Still Have Much to Learn . . .

Although Eisenhower carried forty-one states and claimed fifty-eight percent of the popular vote, the sixth-largest presidential landslide up to that time, the President was deeply dismayed by the Congressional results. It had actually been a standoff; the Democrats kept their 49–47 margin in the Senate and gained only two seats in the House, increasing their majority to 231–201. Eisenhower's bewilderment was not simply the realization he was not only the first winning president in more than a century to yield both houses of Congress. He was perturbed because numerous Republican moderates, including Senate candidates Duff, McKay, Langlie and Thornton, were defeated. In a spasm of frustration on election night, Eisenhower reportedly spoke of advancing Modern Republicanism in a new political party.[48]

Eisenhower was slow to realize he had not been a savior to the Republicans, unable to repeat, for example, what Franklin Roosevelt accomplished for the Democrats in the 1930s. In 1958, the bottom fell out of Modern Republicanism as the party lost forty-seven seats in the House and thirteen more in the Senate.[49] Eisenhower continued to blame his woes on faulty public relations. A week after the 1956 election, he wrote CBS president and close friend William Paley, "The selling to the American public of this conversion has not been so well done."[50]

Yet, the 1956 campaign showed that Eisenhower had overestimated his electoral influence and underestimated his party's true shortcomings. Heavy use of TV had not been a mistake; it proved necessary because of Eisenhower's limited personal role in the campaign. What failed was the assumption that the new medium had the power to perform a partisan quick fix. Eisenhower accepted this assumption, and by centralizing the campaign through television, the party traded expedience for a careful diagnosis of underlying problems.

The party's most severe problem was weak, unresponsive grassroots organization. In 1956, the GOP tried to recruit new members through television appeals, sidestepping precinct, district, county and state committee that could have done this more effectively. Television likewise failed to correct a candidate recruiting problem. Twenty-two House contests had no Republican candidates; in many other races, GOP contenders were enlisted virtually off the street and were easily defeated by familiar Democrats.

It was largely because of television preoccupations that the national committee made a severe mistake: not capitalizing on the Citizens for Eisenhower organization. The Citizens handled television duties, but it also attracted thousands of volunteers. The professionals at national headquarters had little serious interest in the amateurs who ran the Citizens; RNC indifference to several turf conflicts left many Citizens leaders alienated. Eisenhower regretted that he did not encourage better cooperation, especially after his brother Edgar reported from his home in Washington state of disunity between the Citizens and the state committee.[51] Had the RNC extended a hand, the Citizens could have provided significant grassroots potential. Instead, the party's major interest was the national level, where the Citizens controlled half of the television activities and its agency, Young and Rubicam, was a rival of BBDO, the firm retained by the RNC.[52]

The election was a bitter lesson for Leonard Hall, who resigned as party chairman only weeks later. He was replaced by Meade Alcorn, a Connecticut lawyer with little TV background, who would learn that numerous local committees, and even some state organizations in the South, had been close to cut off from national headquarters in 1956.[53] Hall eventually conceded that TV had been incorrectly conceived as a political cure-all. "We still have much to learn about how best to use [television] in a national campaign," wrote Hall in a 1960 *Life* article. "Important as television and new transportation methods are, they don't replace the local organization. There is no substitute for this vital element, and there is no substitute for door-bell ringing and shoe leather."[54]

Uncertainties may have lingered, but 1956 marked a turning point in political television. Not only did 1956 demonstrate for the first time that a sustained and national campaign could be waged over television, it also produced the revelation that TV, ideal for projecting the strengths of candidates, was ineffectual in selling a political party. This helped explain why the influence of national parties began to wither in a television age that saw politicians run their own campaigns.

Many experts foreshadowed this trend in the 1950s, a time when television was helping preserve Eisenhower's popularity. According to the Survey Research Center, the public in 1956 perceived Eisenhower as a better leader and more likable than in

1952, key dimensions of the TV strategy. More revealing was that the Republican party, for all its self promotion, was perceived more negatively, something witnessed not just in empirical voting studies but also in actual votes.[55] Eisenhower, for example, outpolled GOP candidates in ninety percent of the House districts.[56] This challenged the conventional wisdom, including E. E. Schattschneider's influential 1942 *Party Government*, which offered that a president with fifty-eight percent of the popular vote, as with Eisenhower, would enjoy a sixty-five percent margin in the House.[57] The Republicans pulled only forty-six percent of the House seats. This classic "coat-tail" theory gave way to a concept of candidate-party divergence that keyed new political realities. As Michigan State's Charles Press wrote in 1958, the "important element that remains is the candidate's ability to campaign hard and win district votes by his own efforts."[58]

Ironically, given their commitment to television, the Republicans may have won more seats had they deemphasized linkages between Eisenhower, the national party and the Congressional candidates. Things were different than in 1952, when the Republicans swept Congress during widespread dissatisfaction with the Truman administration. By 1956, as the GOP showed time and again on television, the nation was content and back to normal. Tens of millions of comfortable Democrats "liked Ike," but came back to their party in the Congressional contests.[59]

It was also ironic that television, the domain of the national GOP in the 1950s, would stymie the party in many later Congressional elections. In the 1960s and 1970s, television was vastly more integral to House and Senate campaigns than in 1956. It was also enormously expensive, especially in House campaigns, where budgets were often very small. Incumbents, most of which were Democrats, had immediate advantages in accessing television, while superior Democratic grassroots organizing often converted into better local campaign cash flows. By the 1980s, however, the Republicans were raising and spending more money locally than Democrats; some attribute GOP gains in Congress that decade to heavy spending in races that had Democratic incumbents.[60]

The RNC continued to use national television to help House and Senate candidates in situations reminiscent of 1956, in which party-based TV messages dovetailed with powerful national candidates. As in 1956, results were not definitive. During Ronald Reagan's 1980 campaign, the RNC hired the ad agency of Humphrey Browning MacDougall for a series of spots, one featuring a look-alike of House Speaker Tip O'Neill, that attacked irresponsible spending of Congressional Democrats. This "Vote Republican" campaign was reprised during Reagan's reelection in 1984. Although these spots may have helped the GOP win the Senate in those years, the party made no headway in the House. In 1986, the Democrats once again controlled both sides of Congress, as they did in 1988, despite a sizable victory by George Bush and another supplemental television effort by the national committee. These later efforts to sell a Republican party identity marked no return to the TV "coattail" concept. By then, it was clear that any partisan TV campaign had to be peripheral to those of individual candidates.

The 1956 campaign had been pivotal in establishing this direction, even though the television-minded Republicans were trend-setters in defeat. Nineteen-fifty-six was both the first occasion in which a political party tried to sell itself through a well-orchestrated television campaign, and it was also the last. Although voters bought the standard-bearer and rejected the rest of the line, 1956 had been an important learning experience. Out of it came important insights about the political shortcomings of a bold new medium and a grand old party.

Notes

1. See Martin P. Wattenberg, *The Decline of American Political Parties* (Cambridge, Mass.: Harvard University Press, 1984) and Jeff Fishel, ed., *Parties and Elections in an Anti-Party Age* (Bloomington, Ind.: Indiana University Press, 1978).
2. See Alonzo Hamby, *Liberalism and Its Challengers* (New York: Oxford University Press, 1985), pp. 60–70.
3. Dwight Eisenhower, *Mandate for Change* (Garden City, New York: Doubleday, 1963), pp. 43, 45–46.
4. SRC figures appear in Erik W. Austin, *Political Facts of the United States Since 1789* (New York: Columbia University Press, 1986), pp. 387–388.
5. See Emmet Hughes, *The Ordeal of Power* (New York: Atheneum, 1963), pp. 142–146.
6. *Mandate*, p. 517.
7. Eisenhower considered a "Board of Strategy" to deal with his perceived public relations problem. This is detailed in a letter he sent to his staff Nov. 23, 1953; see DDE Diaries, Box 3, Eisenhower Library. This board was never created because of the increasing trust Eisenhower placed in Press Secretary James Hagerty and Hagerty's rise as a public relations coordinator.
8. *Mandate*, pp. 516–517.
9. See Hagerty Diary, Dec. 20, 1954, James C. Hagerty Papers; and C. D. Jackson to Henry Luce, Dec. 21, 1954, C. D. Jackson Papers, Eisenhower Library.
10. L. Richard Guylay, Eisenhower Oral History Project, Columbia University, p. 64; and Cabell Phillips, "Party Chairmen: Study in Feuds and Funds," *New York Times Magazine*, July 1, 1956, pp. 10–11, 28.
11. James Reston, "The Busy Republicans," *New York Times*, Sept. 15, 1955, p. 19.
12. Lodge and Presidential Assistant Sherman Adams had encouraged Eisenhower to establish a television dialogue with the public. See Lodge to Eisenhower, Oct. 30, 1953 and Nov. 12, 1953; Lodge to Wilton Persons, Nov. 12, 1953; and Charles Willis to Sherman Adams, Dec. 5, 1953, Box 415, Official File, Eisenhower Library.
13. James Hagerty, Eisenhower Oral History Project, Columbia University, pp. 176–178.
14. Federal Communications Commission figures from *Radio Annual and Television Yearbook 1957* (New York: Radio Daily Corporation, 1957), p. 73.
15. Richard Guylay to Leonard Hall, Aug. 9, 1955, Box 103, Records of the Republican National Committee; and National Citizens for Eisenhower-Nixon Summary Report, Box 6, Young and Rubicam Records, Eisenhower Library.
16. See "What Ike Will Do in the Campaign," *U.S. News and World Report*, Mar. 2, 1956, pp. 19–21.
17. RNC guide for 1955 Campaign School, Box 2, Robert Humphreys Papers, Eisenhower Library.
18. Leonard Hall, "Hall Hails the Revolution wrought by TV and Airplanes," *Life*, April 21, 1960, pp. 126–134.
19. *Ibid.*
20. Meeting transcript, Eisenhower and Richard Nixon, Feb. 7, 1956, DDE Diaries. Also see diary entries Feb. 8; Feb. 9; Feb. 22; Feb. 27 and Feb. 29, 1956, DDE Diaries, Eisenhower Library.
21. RNC Campaign Plan, Box 11, Robert Humphreys Papers, Eisenhower Library.
22. Guylay oral history, p. 9.
23. RNC Campaign Plan.

24. "Peace, prosperity and progress," first proposed by Young and Rubicam, was inspired by an Eisenhower speech in April 1956. Eisenhower's eight principles of presidential leadership were sifted into the three-word slogan, based on visual possibilities. See David Levy to Thomas Lapham, May 11, 1956, Box 5, Young and Rubicam Records, Eisenhower Library.

25. David Levy interview with author, Jan. 26, 1988.

26. Carroll Newton interview with author, Sept. 3, 1988.

27. "Film Has Duet With Eisenhowers," *New York Times*, June 24, 1956, p. 42.

28. A comprehensive summary of 1956 campaign spending appears in *Congressional Record*. 85th Cong., 1st sess., 1957. Vol. 103, pt. 4:4773–4795 and 5588–5606.

29. Guide for 1955 Campaign School.

30. Transcripts of these appearances are found in Speech Files, Box 78, James C. Hagerty Papers, Eisenhower Library. Films of the Pittsburgh and Washington state appearances are housed in the library's audio-visual holdings.

31. BBDO Campaign Plan, Sept. 21, 1956, Box 711, Central Files, Eisenhower Library.

32. Film, Young and Rubicam "College" spot, Oct., 1956, audio-visual holdings, Eisenhower Library.

33. Film, Young and Rubicam "Mamie" spot, Oct., 1956, audio-visual holdings, Eisenhower Library.

34. Levy interview.

35. A. C. Nielsen figures from John Runyon, Jennefer Verdini and Sally Runyon, *Source Book of American Presidential Campaigns and Elections 1948–1968* (New York: Frederick Ungar, 1971).

36. Kinescope, "The People Ask the President," NBC, Oct. 12, 1956, audio-visual holdings, Eisenhower Library.

37. Kinescope, "Ike Day," CBS, Oct. 13, 1956, audio-visual holdings, Eisenhower Library.

38. Kinescope, Eisenhower coffee klatsch, CBS, Oct. 24, 1956, audio-visual holdings, Eisenhower Library.

39. J. R. Wiggins, "1956 Election Could Repeat Unique Split of 1848," *Washington Post*, pp. E-1, E-5 and Burns W. Roper, "The Public Pulse: GOP Seen Leading in Presidency Alone," appearing in Box 714, Official File, Eisenhower Library.

40. RNC campaign progress report, Oct. 15, 1956, Box 104, Records of the Republican National Chairman, Eisenhower Library.

41. Trip Files, Box 29, Thomas Stephens Papers, Eisenhower Library.

42. Film, Young and Rubicam "Korea" spot, Oct., 1956, audio-visual holdings, Eisenhower Library.

43. Film, Young and Rubicam "Taxi Driver" spot, Oct., 1956, audio-visual holdings, Eisenhower Library.

44. Gallup polls Oct. 10, Oct. 26 and Nov. 4, 1956.

45. Campaign report, Paul Hoffman, Oct. 29, 1956, Box 714, Central Files, Eisenhower Library.

46. Kinescope, "Four More Years," Nov. 5, 1956, audio-visual holdings, Eisenhower Library.

47. Nielsen figures.

48. Richard Nixon, *RN: The Memoirs of Richard Nixon* (New York: Grosset and Dunlap, 1978), pp. 180–181.

49. Eisenhower felt his pleas in 1956 for Modern Republicanism were mistakenly interpreted as a "schism" in the party. He also labeled as "exaggeration" the widespread belief that these supposed divisions led to the 1958 defeats. Eisenhower blamed the poor Republican showing in 1958 on a recession and a resounding defeat in several states of right-to-work legislation which numerous Republicans supported. See Eisenhower, *Waging Peace 1956–1961* (Garden City, New York: Doubleday, 1965), pp. 374–376.

50. Eisenhower to William Paley, Nov. 14, 1956, DDE Diaries, Eisenhower Library.

51. Edgar Eisenhower to Eisenhower, Sept. 13, 1956, DDE Diaries, Eisenhower Library.

52. Guylay oral history, p. 78.

53. Meade Alcorn, Eisenhower Oral History Project, Columbia University, pp. 89–92.

54. Hall.

55. Donald Stokes, Angus Campbell and Warren Miller, "Components of Electoral Decision," *American Political Science Review* (June 1958): 367–387.

56. Charles Press, "Voting Statistics and Presidential Coattails," *American Political Science Review* (Dec., 1958): 1041–1050.
57. E. E. Schattschneider, *Party Government* (New York: Farrar and Rinehart, 1942), pp. 75–76.
58. Press.
59. Some Democratic candidates refrained from attacking Eisenhower, including Idaho's Frank Church and Ohio's Frank Lausche, who unseated Republican senators. See Charles Thomson and Frances Shattuck, *The 1956 Presidential Campaign* (Washington: Brookings Institution, 1960), p. 358.
60. Gary Jacobson, "Party Organization and Distribution of Campaign Resources: Republicans and Democrats in 1982," *Political Science Quarterly* (Winter 1985–86): 603–625.

A Step in the "Right" Direction: Conservative Republicans and the Election of 1960

MARY C. BRENNAN
Assistant Professor of History
Southwest Texas State University

Presidential election years frequently serve as convenient benchmarks for charting changes in partisan, political or societal behavior. By examining the elections of 1896 and 1936, for example, historians and political scientists discovered emerging coalitions among voters which reflected new ideological and economic motivations, as well as their new political goals. The quadrennial race also exposes intraparty divisions, increasing factional tensions as groups struggled to win the nomination, and thus, control of the party. Because of the interplay of ideology and personality surrounding any campaign, presidential elections reveal much about the evolution of political parties.

The race for the Republican presidential nomination in 1960 offers a good example of how such a campaign shapes the development of political parties. The campaign mirrored existing tensions and changes that had already developed in the party's internal power structure; more than that, by reflecting them, it acted as a prism, focusing attention on which group had control and thus intensifying the disputes. The election itself did not cause a shift within the party, but without the forum of the election, the developments within the party might have taken a different turn or remained sterile.

Because it gave political life to these new party forces, the presidential election campaign of 1960 marked a significant step in the evolution of conservatism within the Republican party. To begin with, conservative factions were driven for a variety of reasons to resolve their differences. This phenomenon combined with the discovery of a viable right-wing candidate invigorated the Right and provided the inspiration and personnel for a concerted attack on liberal control of the GOP.

Contemporaries overlooked these developments almost entirely, and instead tended to contrast the complacency of the Eisenhower administration with the youthful energy of John F. Kennedy. Historians, on the other hand, have tended to study the implications of Kennedy's narrow victory over Richard M. Nixon or focused on the subsequent decline of liberalism. Few have taken note of the emergence of a powerful conservative movement during the 1960s. Even scholars who did investigate postwar conservatism have tended to examine the Right over a longer time span or concentrate on extremist elements. The result has been to underemphasize the importance of the 1960 campaign to the overall development of conservatism within the United States as a whole and in the GOP in particular.[1] Even though the divisions within the conservative movement and the Republican party during the 1950s have been studied, it is necessary to view these developments again in light of the 1960 campaign: It is how these developments came together and reacted with one another that was the crucial ingredient in shaping the future of conservatism.

Immediately preceding and during the 1960 presidential campaign, the actions and reactions of conservatives signaled the emergence of a more organized, astute, and determined Right. By 1960, right-wing intellectuals had begun to work with one another and with a maturing conservative press to overcome the philosophical differences and to articulate their perspective. Around the nation, citizens dissatisfied with the predominance of liberalism had formed local organizations or joined national committees to voice their concerns and demand action. The development of this constituency strengthened the resolve of conservative party leaders long unhappy with the "modern Republicanism" of the Eisenhower administration, frustrated by the liberal domination of their party, and embittered by the loss of the presidential nomination in 1948 and 1952. Increasing the underlying tension was the tendency of party liberals to underestimate conservative strength and to misunderstand, or ignore, the real differences that divided one wing of the party from the other. Taken together, these factors galvanized the conservatives into an active, coordinated campaign to seize control of the party.

The dissatisfaction of the conservatives with the seemingly popular Republican administration was just one indication of the discontent lurking beneath the surface calm of the 1950s. The image of a homogeneous society of consumers trying desperately to conform to the stereotypical ideals of television contrasted sharply with the growth of dissident youth, black, and artistic subcultures. The prosperity enjoyed by most Americans hid poverty as well as problems of automation.[2] Despite the "happy days" image, the American people, and especially the intellectuals, worried about the structure of American society. They wondered if a nuclear holocaust would annihilate the world in a millisecond. They worried about the impact of "momism," suburbia, and rock-n-roll on family life. They read in disbelief the accounts of the rise of juvenile delinquency. They feared that corporate America and mass culture were swallowing up individualism.

This frustration and anxiety constantly threatened to shatter the myth of a contented population enjoying the fruits of an expanding economy and a stable political system. As a result, liberal and conservative intellectuals, corporate executives and government officials worked to maintain the illusion by explaining away the discontent as deviance and by urging greater participation in the consumer culture as cure. The problem, these "experts" assured the population, was not in society but in the individual. Consequently, the dissatisfaction remained vague and undefined, making it difficult to dispel, to articulate, and to recognize.[3]

This partly explains why many Republicans were puzzled by the vehemence and alienation of the conservatives and by the bitter factionalism within their party. Agreeing with sociologist Daniel Bell, and with much of the country, that the age of ideology was over and that a consensus existed on basic political issues, leaders of the GOP assumed the "liberal"/"conservative" disagreements involved the mere details of policy, not basic issues.[4] Reinforcing this assumption was the notion, articulated by historian Louis Hartz, that a right-wing movement, in the European sense, could not emerge in a country that lacked a feudal past.[5] Such ideas led to the conviction that in America conservatism amounted to little more than the desire of businessmen and the upper classes to maintain the status quo. The Eisenhower administration seemed to epitomize this belief. With what appeared to be widespread support from the GOP, the administration tried to hold the line on social welfare programs, limit government regulation, and pursue pro-business policies, all of which convinced much of the country that Eisenhower was a conservative. Republican National Committee Chairman Meade Alcorn summarized the feelings of many when he proclaimed that ideological conflict within the party was "more mythical than real."[6]

Alcorn's assertion was overly simplistic. Although most Republicans supported a broad philosophy of local control, free enterprise, and anticommunism, they often disagreed over how this philosophy should be interpreted and applied. Conservatives desired a more literal implementation of their beliefs than their liberal counterparts who were willing to allow the federal government more room to maneuver. Conservatives wanted to eliminate or significantly decrease most New Deal programs; moderates were willing to continue but not expand them; and liberals frequently contemplated new programs. All factions were anti-Communist—as were most Democrats—but conservatives advocated any and all means of destroying communism inside and outside the country while liberals and moderates showed more restraint. Classification along ideological lines, then, depended more on comparative than on specific terms.

Party factionalization did not stem solely from philosophical disagreements, however, but was also derived from geographic and socioeconomic differences. Predominantly members of what the conservatives saw as the "Eastern Establishment," Republican liberals shared a common background of Ivy League schools, exclusive club memberships, and financial success. Many of these wealthy businessmen embraced New Deal-style social and economic programs in the belief that such policies would alleviate class conflicts, lead to economic stability, and keep governmental control in their hands. They envisioned what historian Robert Griffith has called a "corporate commonwealth," a vision that Eisenhower shared but one that infuriated those businessmen who were excluded from this "Eastern Liberal Establishment."[7] Principally from the West and South, these conservatives stressed individual initiative over welfare programs, preferred free enterprise rather than government regulation, and felt the economic and demographic expansion of their region reflected the decreasing importance of the East. Along with leftover opponents of the New Deal, these western and southern business leaders began to coalesce into something Arizona Senator Barry Goldwater thought resembled a new populist movement.[8] By joining with intellectual conservatives, these "populists" became an increasingly strong and vocal element of the GOP.

Despite their growing influence, the Right lacked the tools to pose a serious threat to the established order. Throughout the 1950s, and especially after the death of Robert A. Taft in 1953, conservative Republicans were an amorphous group lacking definite leadership, specific goals, and effective organization.[9] Bitter from the battles for the presidential nomination in 1948 and 1952, increasingly resentful of the liberal wing's assumption of their loyalty to the party, and isolated from positions of control within the GOP, conservatives struggled to retain their identity and regain leverage in the party. In the meantime, they complained about the Eisenhower administration's espousal of "modern Republicanism" and questioned the effectiveness of the party's leadership. This discontent reverberated throughout the ranks of the GOP and, combined with distaste for liberal society and dissatisfaction with their lack of power, caused a significant portion of the American population to formulate a vaguely defined counterrevolution.[10] Waging a solitary battle on college campuses throughout the country and through political and educational foundations, conservative intellectuals laid the groundwork for the resurgence.

Conservative thought in the postwar era was extremely diverse but had three basic strains: classical liberalism which emphasized free enterprise and limited government, traditionalism which looked to a more ordered and authoritarian past, and anticommunism, which sought to fight the red enemy both at home and abroad. *National Review* editor Frank Meyer and other classical liberals, many of whom were also civil libertarians, often clashed with traditionalists such as intellectual Russell Kirk. On a purely philosophic level, the various theories could not successfully be fused together. But, on a more practical level, as conservatives of all stripes became more interested in the world of politics, they realized that allowances had to be made for differences within the movement. Most significantly, their mutual anticommunism and solid support for the efforts of Senator Joseph McCarthy forged a strong link uniting the disparate right-wing groups and offering them an acceptable path to accommodation. The extent of this reconciliation became increasingly evident in the late 1950s when the contending factions set aside their ideological differences to gain power on a national level.[11]

The revitalization of the conservative press and the growth of a conservative youth movement also helped to invigorate and unify the Right. William F. Buckley's *National Review* acquainted the American public with the philosophic and practical tenets of conservatism and with conservative politicians and platforms.[12] Together with such journals as *Human Events*, *The Freeman*, and *American Opinion*, the right-wing press chronicled and encouraged the conservative intellectuals and nurtured the growth of a conservative youth movement. The Intercollegiate Society of Individualists and the Young Republicans began preaching a more avowedly conservative line during the late 1950s.[13] These organized young conservatives, by supporting conservative candidates on a national level, spreading right-wing literature, and setting up groups such as the National Student Committee for the Loyalty Oath, proved that there existed an active, informed conservative constituency on college campuses throughout the country.[14]

A similar type of constituency began to develop at a grass-roots level throughout the nation. Reacting against liberal dominance of culture and education as well as liberal politics and economics, citizens in various parts of the country formed local and, in some cases, national groups to combat whichever aspect of liberalism particularly offended or outraged them.[15] On a local level, there were anti-integrationist, anti-black, anti-Semitic, anti-Catholic, anti-Communist, and anti-fluoridation, as well as libertarian and free enterprise groups.[16] Many of these organizations published their own newsletters or journals in an attempt to spread their message, build support, and pressure their legislators to stop the growth of liberalism. Although they often reported political events and usually encouraged political participation, most of these groups despaired over the lack of differentiation between the national parties.

In addition to these local groups, a number of national committees and organizations formed during the late 1950s and early 1960s. Some of these, such as the Committee of One Million, concentrated solely on foreign policy issues.[17] Others had a broader appeal. The most significant of these was the John Birch Society, founded in 1958 by Robert Welch.[18] Discounted as fanatics by many Democrats and Republicans, members of the society used slick propaganda techniques and publications, particularly *American Opinion*, to build a significant following that would not be silenced and eventually could not be ignored. These increasingly vocal groups offered conservative leaders in the GOP a ready-made constituency, provided the groups involved could be convinced that the Republican party was *the* conservative party.[19]

Partly as a result of exposure to this grass-roots sentiment and with the encouragement of the conservative press, Goldwater and other conservative Republicans became bolder in their criticism of the Eisenhower administration and the concept of "modern Republicanism." Although they might admire Eisenhower as a general, they sometimes found him useless as a president. The editors of *National Review* sarcastically called him the Republican Party's "Pride and Joy" and believed his administration confused "intellectually-minded folks." A letter to the editor printed in their pages expressed the opinion that Eisenhower "doesn't know anything about the principles upon which our government was founded." *Human Events* recorded the growing disgust and distrust that resulted from "Ike's" golfing while the government took care of itself. Even Barry Goldwater, who came to the Senate on Eisenhower's coattails, believed that the president was not in control of his administration and did not care about his party.[20] He was not alone in this belief. In his travels around the country as chairman of the Republican Senatorial Campaign Committee, Goldwater learned that party workers "didn't look upon [Eisenhower] as the type of leader they had hoped he would be." They were "growing increasingly critical" of the "lack of party responsibility being shown at a national level."[21]

Goldwater also joined other conservatives in rejecting the "faulty premises" of Eisenhower's modern Republicanism.[22] Although he blamed Eisenhower's staff rather than the president himself, Goldwater's tone became progressively more strident during the last years of Eisenhower's second term. By early 1960, Goldwater was accusing the administration of practicing "dime-store New Dealism" and publicly advocating a much tougher foreign policy.[23] Senator John Bricker of Ohio felt that the country was "in worse shape today than at the depths of the New Deal." Senator

Styles Bridges denounced the president's policy on "Meet the Press" and even former President Herbert Hoover felt compelled to protest the infection of the Eisenhower administration with the "Karl Marx virus."[24] As conservatives within the party expressed their discontent, the right-wing public applauded and hoped that the 1960 election would bring a change for the better.

Republicans of various ideological stripes were ready for the challenge of a presidential campaign. The front-runner was Eisenhower's vice president and heir apparent, Richard M. Nixon.[25] In some ways, he was the perfect compromise candidate for Republicans, acceptable to both the liberal and conservative wings of the party. He had supported many aspects of Eisenhower's modern Republicanism, including the expansion of social security, foreign aid projects, and the administration's "road of peace, prosperity and progress." He felt it was a "privilege to participate in the great decisions of [Eisenhower's] administration."[26] While these stands helped shore up his credentials among the party's liberal wing, conservative Republicans could look to the Nixon who was not a member of the Eastern elite, who had first been elected to the Senate as a rabid anti-Communist, and who won a national reputation for his role in the Alger Hiss trial. Further, Nixon had added to his national reputation as an experienced and tough diplomat — and to his conservative laurels — by courageously facing anti-American mobs in South America and standing up to Nikita Khrushchev in the "kitchen debate" in Moscow, where he and the Soviet premier vigorously argued the merits of American materialism before television cameras.[27] Nixon himself considered his philosophy somewhat conservative in 1960. "I carried the banner of constructive postwar Republicanism," he would write later in his memoirs, "bred of conservative beliefs that a healthy private sector and individual initiative set the best pace for prosperity and progress."[28]

Nevertheless, Nixon's mixed political legacy led most conservatives to wonder who controlled his "political soul."[29] Barry Goldwater believed the vice president to be "basically conservative," but still felt compelled to tell him that the party needed to move to the right during the election year.[30] Prominent conservative Alfred Kohlberg worried in 1957 that the favorable publicity about Nixon in the liberal press might alienate the vice president's "natural supporters." In 1960, he warned Nixon that his support for administration policies had generated a "lack of enthusiasm for you" among conservative Republicans.[31] Ronald Reagan, still a registered Democrat but increasingly interested in Republican affairs, expressed concern that Nixon might commit a "fatal" mistake by accepting the advice of those who wanted to "outliberal" the Democratic candidate, John F. Kennedy.[32] The conservative press resounded with similar fears about Nixon's commitment to conservatism. As one National Review reader put it, "genuine conservatives are weary of false or unlettered promises in the language of conservatism." L. Brent Bozell, William Buckley's brother-in-law, advised conservatives to give up waiting for Nixon to show his "true conservative colors." They were further discouraged because Nixon was apparently ignoring their warnings of a conservative boycott and continuing his "soft-shoe" march to the "excluded middle." Human Events editors, who had warmly supported the "new Nixon" of 1958, were questioning his reliability by 1960.[33]

One reason conservatives were so reluctant to accept Nixon at face value was that they finally had a nationally known leader in Barry Goldwater. Neither a lawyer nor a member of a famous political family, Goldwater epitomized the successful western businessman and community leader. Elected to the Senate in 1952, he made his name as a conservative by voting against the censure of Joseph McCarthy and, as he recalled, by "consistently voting against spending programs" and criticizing the administration's budget policy.[34] His service on the Senate Labor Committee pitted him against labor leaders, especially Walter Reuther, who, according to Goldwater, actively campaigned against him in 1958. Despite union opposition, Goldwater won re-election by a 35,000-vote majority, and attracted national press coverage in the process.[35] *Human Events* hailed him as the "Man of the Hour" and welcomed the return of leadership to Washington. Thereafter his name or his picture appeared in almost every issue of that journal through 1960.[36] Goldwater bolstered his national reputation by criticizing Eisenhower's policies and by writing a column, "How Do You Stand, Sir?", which was syndicated to 140 newspapers.[37] As chairman of the Republican Senatorial Campaign Committee, he visited "every state in the union, almost every district and precinct, not once, but many, many times," building up his national reputation and his relationship with party workers.[38]

Goldwater's work with the committee solidified his position within the party machinery, but it was the publication of his book, *The Conscience of a Conservative*, that propelled him to the forefront of the movement.[39] With the help of Bozell, Goldwater drew on many of his earlier speeches to set forth a credo that redefined conservatism in twentieth-century terms. Rejecting the common misconception that conservatism concentrated solely on economic theory, he insisted instead that conservatism "puts material things in their proper place." A true conservative, according to Goldwater, "believes that man is in part, an economic, an animal creature; but that he is also a spiritual creature with spiritual desires." Although conservatives emphasized freedom, Goldwater explained, they also realized that "the practice of freedom requires the establishment of order." The necessity for order, however, posed the twin dangers of excessive government controls and the use of that power for illicit purposes. In addition to domestic concerns, Goldwater discussed the dangers caused by the Soviet Union, urged the withdrawal of recognition from all Communist countries, and advocated the use of nuclear weapons to liberate "captive nations."[40]

Goldwater's straightforward language spoke for a broad range of conservatives who previously had no voice in Republican councils, influenced many young people who were searching for a philosophy to express their discontent, and ignited the fires of a grassroots campaign to place the Arizonan on the party's national ticket. Here, finally, was an *electable* conservative Republican.[41] Conservative journals began to note the "Goldwater for Vice President" endorsements emanating from numerous Young Republican and College Republican groups, a trend that adults increasingly joined throughout the summer of 1960, but that neither Nixon, Goldwater, nor any Republican political advisers seriously considered.[42]

Meanwhile, "Goldwater for President" groups began to develop in the spring of 1960 and scored a stunning success when the South Carolina Republican convention pledged its delegates to the nomination of Goldwater for President in 1960.[43] Although Goldwater explained that he did not want the nomination, South Carolina chairman G. D. Shorey refused to change his mind. Instead he went to work and by 11 July was able to inform Goldwater that he had at least sixty-three delegate votes for president.[44] Shorey encouraged Goldwater to combine the "7 or 8 organizations all over the country" into "a real campaign organization and staff." These groups generally originated in Arizona but claimed to have branches in a number of states.[45] Their leaders urged volunteers to circulate petitions, to write to Nixon and the Republican National Committee with their opinions, and, if possible, to attend the national convention in Chicago.[46] Although Goldwater had not authorized anyone to use his name or to set up such organizations on his behalf, these groups believed that "if the people speak loud enough, Senator Barry Goldwater will be nominated and be the next president of the United States."[47]

Neither Nixon nor subsequent historians attached much significance to the Goldwater boomlet that developed after March 1960. By ignoring these grass-roots organizations, the leaders of the Republican party displayed their tendency to discount the power and potential of citizens' groups and their unwillingness to recognize conservatives as legitimate members of the party. Ironically, F. Clifton White, who headed "Volunteers for Nixon-Lodge," and who was a catalyst in the "Draft Goldwater" movement, recognized this shortcoming and encouraged Nixon to take "full advantage of citizens' and volunteer groups."[48] Had Nixon and other party leaders paid more attention to these groups, they might have co-opted conservatives into the party instead of alienating them. They also might have spared their party the divisive and disastrous election of 1964.

In 1960, however, Nixon was more concerned with the challenge mounted from the left of his party by Nelson Rockefeller, governor of New York.[49] A popular figure from a wealthy and well-connected family, Rockefeller posed a serious threat to Nixon's dream of a united Republican party. To conservatives, Rockefeller's willingness to implement New Deal-style programs, his ardent advocacy of civil rights, and his upper-class northeastern background epitomized the "Eastern Liberal Establishment." Although Rockefeller was philosophically similar to Eisenhower, in the late 1950s he became increasingly critical of the Republican administration and, by implication, of the vice president. Milton Eisenhower, looking back, felt that Rockefeller had done this "in order to forward his candidacy, to take positions different from those of the Vice President."[50] The governor particularly angered many staunch Eisenhower backers with his demand for increased defense spending, a position Nixon secretly agreed with but could not admit without angering Eisenhower.[51]

After testing the primary waters, which were decidedly chilly, Rockefeller announced on 26 December 1959 that he would not be a candidate for either the presidency or the vice presidency.[52] Conservative Republicans took him at his word, but were dismayed that Nixon would be left without any competition for the nomination.[53] They underestimated Rockefeller. Despite his formal declaration of noncandidacy, he continued to make statements and to act in ways that made it look as though he awaited a draft. On 9 June 1960 he released a statement criticizing both the Eisenhower administration and the "leading Republican candidate" for their failure "to make clear where this Party is heading" and enumerating the problems he felt ought to be addressed.[54] Two days later, he tried to get Eisenhower's endorsement to re-enter the race; what he got was a lecture and a warning that his prospects were not very good.[55]

Even though his nomination was all but assured, Nixon sought a method of securing the support of the Rockefeller wing and decided that the best solution was to have Rockefeller sign on as his running mate. Rockefeller resisted all such suggestions, however, and Nixon realized that he would have to make the effort to go to the governor.[56] The meeting took place secretly in Rockefeller's home on the very day that the press reported Rockefeller's dissatisfaction with the platform and his threat to "take a walk" and "just be Governor of New York" during the Nixon campaign.[57] In a long meeting, the two men worked out a mutually acceptable statement concerning the contents of the platform. Which man compromised most was of little importance in the long run; both men claimed victory.[58]

Nixon's gesture in making concessions to Rockefeller sent shock waves throughout the rest of the party. Insulted by the apparent repudiation of his policies, Eisenhower angrily phoned Nixon, who agreed to make the language in the platform more general. The platform committee, which had almost completed its work, was similarly displeased and it took all of Nixon's diplomatic skills, as well as some arm-twisting by platform committee members Melvin Laird and Charles Percy, to get the changes accepted.[59]

The loudest cry, however, came from the conservatives, who saw the Rockefeller-Nixon pact as a "surrender."[60] Goldwater felt that he had been deceived and manipulated, and he labeled the meeting and the resulting pact the "Munich of the Republican Party." If liberal Republicans "alienate the Conservatives — as the party is now in the process of doing," Goldwater warned, "the handful of Liberal militants that are seeking to take control over the Republican Party will inherit a mess of pottage."[61] The announcement of the Nixon-Rockefeller pact strengthened the resolve of those Republican delegates already committed to Goldwater and prompted many others to see him as "the only legitimate spokesman among National Republican leaders for true Republican principles." Finally, it convinced the senator to let his name be placed in nomination.[62]

Arizona Governor Paul Fannin's nominating speech contained all the normal political rhetoric, except for his explanation that he was making his nomination against the wishes of the candidate. In his memoirs, Goldwater explained that this was a deliberate subterfuge to allow him to make a speech withdrawing his name.[63] Goldwater's speech was remarkable in at least two respects. First, considering the anger that he felt toward Nixon, Goldwater was generous in telling conservatives to go out and work for the vice president's election. He followed his own advice tirelessly, making 126 speeches in 26 states during the campaign. Although unhappy with Nixon's performance at the convention, Goldwater still urged conservatives to support Nixon because the Democratic alternative was unacceptable, because Nixon was a conservative on foreign affairs, and because once he became president, Nixon's underlying conservatism would reemerge.[64]

Second, and more important, the Arizonan used his speech to issue a challenge to conservatives for the future: to "grow up" and work if they wanted to set the party back on track.[65] Nixon, who thought it a "particularly effective speech," missed the significance of that challenge. He and other Republicans assumed that the conservative wing of the party would fall in line as it always had.[66] To an extent, as Goldwater's behavior proved, they were right. The challenge, however, did not go entirely unnoticed. Young conservatives joined together not long after the convention to form the Young Americans for Freedom, and shortly after the election a group of concerned conservatives met to discuss their future within the party. Six months later, political scientist F. Clifton White, *National Review* editor William Rusher, and Ohio Congressman John Ashbrook decided to form a committee to nominate a conservative in 1964.[67] Even *The New York Times* commented on the depth of support Goldwater had developed at the convention.[68]

Those events were overshadowed by the initial flush of excitement that followed Nixon's nomination, by the intense campaign that ensued, and by the dramatic photo-finish that brought the Democrats into the White House with a limited mandate.[69] America's New Frontier soon captured the public imagination, however, and as Camelot liberalism took shape, conservatism was forgotten by all but the conservatives, who began to work slowly, and often secretly, toward their goal of the White House.

Nineteen sixty proved to be a pivotal year in the conservative effort to develop an effective political movement. Building on a widespread but unarticulated public dissatisfaction with government and society, a resurgent intellectual movement, and a mushrooming network of grass-roots groups, conservative Republican politicians began to develop their own organization within the party. Unlike Taft, who scorned the conservative intellectuals, the new Right enjoyed intimate financial and personal ties with these savants, as well as with the burgeoning conservative press. The result was to give voice to long-existing, but previously inchoate sentiments. Conservatives soon discovered that they were not alone. But they also confronted a wide diversity of opinion on the Right, and it was their willingness, albeit grudging at times, to tolerate the breadth of the developing movement that helped to unify the factions in their assault on the "Eastern Liberal Establishment."

This trend toward unity and the emergence of Barry Goldwater are the two most important events in the early development of the conservative movement. The integration of various right-wing groups during the late 1950s occurred on several levels. Philosophically, intellectuals of diverse beliefs realized the value of concentrating on their similarities rather than their differences in the common fight against the liberals. Politically, conservatives of all stripes and all socioeconomic backgrounds rallied around the cause of anti-communism, willingly overlooking disagreements in their efforts to support McCarthy. Once the precedent of working together had been set, it was easier to continue the process. Moreover, many borderline conservatives were frightened into a more open espousal of right-wing views by the increasingly visible civil rights movement, the successes of the Soviets in the space and arms races, and dissatisfaction with Eisenhower's "stop-go" economy, his continuation of New Deal "handouts," as well as his failure to follow a hard-line foreign policy. Helping to articulate and enumerate these vague feelings of discontent, right-wing journals such as *National Review* provided its audience with specific arguments and causes, in the process creating an image of conservatism that was neither stodgy nor old-fashioned but witty, bold, and attractive.

Eventually Goldwater came to represent that image. He spoke to and for many members of the middle class who viewed him as a champion of hardworking businessmen frustrated by governmental controls, parents concerned about their children's education, and patriots worried by the spread of Communist ideology at home and abroad. Even those who found him intellectually limited and oratorically crude realized that he was the first attractive and popular right-wing Republican in the postwar era. He excited people in a way Robert Taft had never managed and he did not suffer from a loser image. Goldwater's performance at the 1960 convention confirmed conservative faith in him and raised hopes for the future.

The 1960s held promise for the conservatives. After years of frustration as a minority faction ignored and abused within the party, they were determined to heed Goldwater's advice and seize control of their party. Liberal and moderate Republicans, like the rest of the country at that time and like historians since, continued to view the conservatives in the old one-dimensional mold. In the face of Goldwater's popularity, the successful conservative press, and the right-wing takeover of the Young Republicans, the party majority continued to discount the growing conservative pressure. Consequently, while Nixon and liberal Republicans ignored the complaints and assumed the cooperation of the right wing, the conservatives were left alone to start building support within the party structure and in the voting public. Though on a limited scale in 1960, it was a definite beginning to the conservative takeover of the party four years later.

Notes

1. David H. Bennett, *The Party of Fear: From Nativist Movements to the New Right in American History* (Chapel Hill, 1988); David N. Reinhard, *The Republican Right Since 1945* (Lexington, Ky., 1983); Michael W. Miles, *The Odyssey of the American Right* (New York, 1980); Jonathan Martin Kolkey, *The New Right. 1960–1968 With Epilogue 1969–1980* (Washington, DC, 1983); Richard H. Pells, *The Liberal Mind in a Conservative Age* (New York, 1985); George H. Nash, *The Conservative Intellectual Tradition in America since 1945* (New York, 1976).
2. For a general introduction to the 1950s see James Gilbert, *Another Chance, Postwar America, 1945–1968* (New York, 1981), 7–191; William L. O'Neill, *Coming Apart: An Informal History of America in the 1960s* (New York, 1971), 3–25; Frederick F. Siegel, *Troubled Journey: From Pearl Harbor to Ronald Reagan* (New York, 1984), 86–130. Eric F. Goldman, *The Crucial Decade and After: America, 1945–1960*, rev. ed. (New York, 1960). For Eisenhower's presidency see Alexander, *Holding the Line*; and Fred I. Greenstein, *The Hidden-Hand Presidency: Eisenhower as Leader* (New York, 1982).
3. See Gilbert, *Another Chance*; O'Neill, *Coming Apart*; Siegel, *Troubled Journey*; and Pells, *The Liberal Mind*; Marty Jezer, *The Dark Ages: Life in the United States 1945–1960* (Boston, 1982); Philip Wylie, *Sons and Daughters of Mom* (Garden City, N.Y., 1971); and Christopher Lasch, *The Culture of Narcissism* (New York, 1979), 267–320.

4. Daniel Bell, *The End of Ideology* (New York, 1960), 393, 402–403.
5. Louis Hartz, *The Liberal Tradition in America* (New York, 1955).
6. Meade Alcorn, interview, 5 June 1967, Columbia Oral History Project, Dwight D. Eisenhower Presidential Library, Abilene, Kansas. See also Charles C. Alexander, *Holding the Line: The Eisenhower Era 1952–1961* (Bloomington, Ind., 1975).
7. Robert Griffith, Dwight D. Eisenhower and the Corporate Commonwealth," *American Historical Review* 87 (February 1982): 88. For a discussion of the composition of the liberal faction see the rest of the Griffith article and to Theodore H. White, *America in Search of Itself* (New York, 1982), 55; Thomas Ferguson and Joel Rogers, *Right Turn: The Decline of the Democrats and the Future of American Politics* (New York, 1986), 50–53; and Barry Goldwater, *Goldwater* (New York, 1988), 115–16.
8. Goldwater, *Goldwater*, 116. Goldwater apparently is not referring to the historical movement of the 1890s. He uses the word populist to mean a grassroots movement challenging an established institution. For years liberals attempted to link the postwar conservatives to the agrarian radical movement. Michael Paul Rogin conclusively refutes this theory in his book, *The Intellectuals and McCarthy: The Radical Specter* (Cambridge, Mass., 1967).
9. William Knowland was suggested as Taft's replacement but his failure to win the California gubernatorial race and his lack of strength ended all such plans. See Reinhard, *The Republican Right*, 142–44; and William Rusher, *Rise of the Right* (New York, 1984), 66.
10. William F. Buckley, Jr., among others, thought of himself as a counter-revolutionary. John B. Judis, *William F. Buckley, Jr.: Patron Saint of the Conservatives* (New York, 1988).
11. Nash, *Conservative Intellectual Tradition*, 3–35, 38–84, 84–131.
12. For information on the impact of the conservative press see Nash, *Conservative Intellectual Tradition*, 27–28, 124, 125, 148–53, among others. See also Reinhard, *The Republican Right*, 171–72.
13. For a brief description and history of these groups see Edward Cain, *They'd Rather Be Right* (New York, 1963), 156–77; *History of the Young Republicans*, [1972?] box 7, Republican National Committee Library, National Archives, Washington.
14. The loyalty oath, part of the National Defense Act of 1958, was required of students who wished to qualify for student loans. Many students, particularly those at Yale and Harvard, strongly opposed this provision. William F. Buckley, "Please Note Our Highmindedness," *National Review*, 5 December 1959, 513–14. See "The Week," ibid., 16 January 1960, 28 for sketchy details of the committee for the oath.
15. See Miles, *Odyssey of the American Right*, 222–41, for a discussion of conservative reaction to the perceived liberalization of American culture.
16. The quickest way to grasp the breadth and number of these grass-roots movements is to look at *The Guide to the Right-wing Collection of the University of Iowa Libraries, 1918–1977* (Iowa City). This collection, which contains almost 200 reels of microfilm, catalogs a wide variety of conservative/radical groups. Many of these had publications with a very small audience, but their existence indicates the strength of anti-liberal feeling in the country.
17. The Committee of One Million fought to keep Communist China out of the United Nations. Many prominent politicians of varying ideological beliefs were members, including Paul Douglas, Walter Judd, and Kenneth Keating. Many of the papers of the Committee are in the Papers of Marvin Liebman Associates [MLA], Hoover Institution on War, Revolution and Peace, Stanford, California.
18. Robert Welch, *The New Americanism* (Boston, 1966), 115–52. See also Seymour Martin Lipsett and Earl Raab, *The Politics of Unreason: Right-wing Extremism in America, 1790–1970* (New York, 1970), 248–50.
19. Goldwater, interview by Ed Edwin, 15 June 1967, Columbia Oral History Project.
20. "The Week," *National Review*, 30 January 1960, 60; Max Eastman, letter to the editor, *National Review*, 9 April 1960, 244; "Can Nixon Assume Taft's Mantle?" *Human Events*, 6 October 1958, 1; Goldwater interview, 34–35. Goldwater explained to Richard Nixon: "I cannot detect any evidence of interest in politics or frankly, any evidence of interest in the future of our party [in

Eisenhower]." Goldwater to Nixon, 16 December 1958, Richard Nixon Vice Presidential Papers (hereafter Nixon VP Papers), National Archives, Los Angeles, California, Branch (NALA).

21. Goldwater interview, 34–35.

22. William Hines, "Republicans Close Ranks to Deny Rift in Party," *Washington Evening Star*, 10 April 1957.

23. Goldwater, speech on Senate floor, *Congressional Record*, 86th Cong., 2d sess., 6 May 1960, 106, pt. 7:9524. "GOP Rift Widened by Goldwater Speech," *Washington Evening Star*, 16 March 1960.

24. Bricker to Nixon, 20 November 1958, "Bricker, Hon. John," box 102, series 320, Nixon VP Papers; "Fresh Leadership," *Human Events*, 31 March 1958, 1; Herbert Hoover, [20 February 1960?], as quoted in "The Week," *National Review*, 27 February 1960, 124.

25. Biographies of Nixon are numerous and varied. In addition, his memoirs are an invaluable source of information. See, for example, Fawn Brodie, *Richard Nixon, The Shaping of His Character* (New York, 1981); Richard Nixon, *RN: The Memoirs of Richard Nixon* (New York, 1978); and Richard Nixon, *Six Crises* (Garden City, N.Y., 1962).

26. Nixon, "The Economy," [1st television talk], 1 November 1960, "RN's copies [#2]," box 2, series 45, Nixon to Nelson Rockefeller, 15 January 1957, "Rockefeller, Nelson A. 1955–1959," box 650, series 320, Nixon statement in Fresno, California, 4 November 1960, "RN's Copies [#1]," box 2, series 45, all located in Nixon VP Papers.

27. Nixon, *RN*, 185–93, 203–14.

28. Ibid., 214, 215.

29. Reinhard, *The Republican Right*, 152.

30. Goldwater to Nixon, 16 December 1958, "Goldwater, Barry 1953 thru 1959," box 293, series 320, Nixon VP Papers.

31. Kohlberg to Nixon, 5 December 1957 and 17 February 1960, "Kohlberg, Alfred," box 423, series 320, Nixon VP Papers.

32. Reagan to Nixon, 15 July 1960, "Reagan, Ronald, Mr and Mrs," box 621, series 320, Nixon VP Papers. This is the famous letter in which Reagan states that under JFK's "tousled boyish haircut is still old Karl Marx."

33. Robert J. Needles, letter to the editor, *National Review*, 16 January 1960, 53; "The Week," *National Review*, 18 June 1960, 380; L. Brent Bozell, "Mr. Nixon's Moment of Truth," *National Review*, 8 October 1960, 204; "Can Nixon Assume Taft's Mantle?" *Human Events*, 6 October 1958, 1.

34. Goldwater, *With No Apologies: The Personal and Political Memoirs of United States Senator Barry M. Goldwater* (New York, 1979), 62. There is no scholarly biography of Goldwater at this time. Most are campaign biographies or other such propaganda. Goldwater's memoirs offer his side of the story and, especially for his early life, are extremely helpful.

35. See Goldwater, *With No Apologies*, 62–63, 88–95. Goldwater details the most famous incident in which a pamphlet with no endorsement was distributed saying that Stalin would approve of Goldwater. The circumstances surrounding this, including the supposed investigation by the Senate Select Committee on Elections and Privileges, were never fully explained, but the story made many of the national papers.

36. "Man of the Hour," *Human Events*, 1 December 1958, 1.

37. Goldwater, *With No Apologies*, 74–77, 95–100.

38. Goldwater notes to diary, 25 June 1976, box 3, Alpha File, Barry Goldwater Papers, Arizona Historical Foundation, Arizona State University, Tempe, Arizona. Meade Alcorn was one who saw Goldwater's handling of the chairmanship as an attempt to gain the nomination. See Alcorn interview #2, 146. Goldwater himself admitted that "this is where you really get into the party, where you get on a first name basis." Goldwater interview, 32; and Goldwater, *Goldwater*, 118–19.

39. Goldwater, *The Conscience of a Conservative* (Shepherdsville, Ky., 1960). Though the original print order was for ten thousand copies, the book ultimately sold more than 3.5 million copies and made the *The New York Times* nonfiction bestseller list. Goldwater, *With No Apologies*. 100; "For the Record," *National Review*, 18 June 1960, 379.

40. Goldwater, *Conscience of a Conservative*, 18, 21, 97–134.
41. Goldwater, "Face the Nation" transcript, [19 April 1960?], "Goldwater, Barry, 1953 thru 1959," box 293, series 320, Nixon VP Papers. See also "How Goldwater Won," and "Man of the Hour," *Human Events*, 24 November and 1 December 1958, both on p. 1.
42. See "For the Record," *National Review*, 23 April 1960, 251; ibid., 2 July 1960, 411; "The Week," ibid., 21 May 1960; letter to the editor, ibid., 7 May 1960, 310–11; 18 June 1960, 405; 16 July 1960, 29; Mr. and Mrs. Ronald Reagan telegram to Nixon headquarters, 23 July 1960, "Reagan, Ronald, Mr. and Mrs," box 621, series 320, Nixon VP Papers; and "He Says 'Would Accept If Offered' Goldwater for Vice President?" *The American Statesman* (Salt Lake City, Utah), 27 November 1959. None of Nixon's biographies mention Goldwater as a possibility for the vice presidential nomination.
43. Goldwater, *With No Apologies*, 101–103.
44. Shorey to Goldwater, 11 July 1960, box 3H493, Goldwater Collection, Barker Texas History Center, Austin, Texas. Goldwater did not want the nomination but viewed it as an opportunity to show the Platform Committee that rank-and-file Republicans "were not particularly happy with Richard Nixon." Goldwater, *With No Apologies*, 101–103.
45. I found evidence of three groups besides Shorey's: Aubrey Barker's "Goldwater for President Committee," Frank Cullen Brophy's "Americans for Goldwater," and Kent Courtney's "Goldwater for President Clubs," in the Goldwater Collection, box 3H497, Barker Center.
46. Barker to Paul Talbert, 2 July 1960, "Goldwater Clubs, California," box 3H498, Goldwater Collection, Barker Center.
47. Goldwater to Barker, 12 July 1960, box 3H497, Goldwater Collection, Barker Center; Barker to "Fellow American," 3 June 1960, "Goldwater, Barry, Clippings—1960," box 293, series 320, Nixon VP Papers.
48. White to Bob Finch, 8 September 1959, "White, F. Clifton," box 812, series 320, Nixon VP Papers.
49. For a brief comparison of the two men see White, *1960*, 65–68.
50. Milton Eisenhower, 21 June 1967, OH 292, 48, Columbia Oral History Project.
51. William Robinson to Dwight Eisenhower, 10 February 1959, "Eisenhower—January—February 1959," box 3, William Robinson Papers, Eisenhower Chronological Series, Eisenhower Library. For a discussion of Nixon's views on Rockefeller's defense policy see Stephen Ambrose, *Nixon: The Education of a Politician 1913–1962* (New York, 1987), 536.
52. See White, *1960*, 67–77.
53. See *National Review*, 2 January 1960, 5; 16 January 1960, 30–31; 30 January 1960, 63–64.
54. Rockefeller text of statement, 9 June 1960, *The Washington Post*.
55. Ambrose, *Nixon*, 540.
56. Nixon, *Six Crises*, 314.
57. Rockefeller, as quoted in John Dreiske, "Rockefeller Blasts Hopes of Unity," *Chicago Sun-Times*, 23 July 1960.
58. Rockefeller, in his statement the morning following the meeting, said that "these [statements] constitute the basic positions for which [he] had been fighting." Nelson Rockefeller, text of statement, 23 July 1960, "Rep Party Platform, July 1960," box 1, Robert Merriam Papers, Eisenhower Library. On the other hand, Nixon's staff reported that "on no single substantive issue did you retreat from, drop, or significantly alter a prior position or program or policy recommendation." [Chuck Lichenstein], "Memorandum on the Joint Nixon-Rockefeller Statement of July 23, 1960," 15 September 1960, "1960 Election Chapter," box 1, series 258, Nixon VP Papers.
59. Ambrose, *Nixon*, 552; Robert Finch interview, 1967, Columbia Oral History Project, Eisenhower Library.
60. W. H. Lawrence, "Pact Opens Way for Party Amity," *The New York Times*, 24 July 1960; Russell Baker, "Goldwater Hits Platform Accord," *The New York Times*, 24 July 1960.
61. Goldwater, *With No Apologies*, 109–17; Goldwater, "Goldwater Calls Nixon-Rockefeller Meeting

a Republican Munich," press release, 23 July 1960, "Sen. Barry Goldwater," box 29, MLA, Hoover Institution.

62. Goldwater for President Coordinating Committee, press release, 24 July 1960, box 3H493, Goldwater Collection, Barker Center.

63. Fannin, nominating speech, 27 July 1960, box 3H493, Goldwater Collection, Barker Center; Goldwater, *With No Apologies*, 115.

64. Goldwater telegram to Nixon, n.d., "Goldwater, Barry, Clippings—1960," box 293, series 320, Nixon VP Papers; Goldwater, "Conservatives Should Support Nixon," n.d., box 3H493, Goldwater Collection, Barker Center.

65. Goldwater, speech withdrawing name from nomination, 27 July 1960, reprinted in *The New York Times*, 28 July 1960.

66. Nixon, typed transcript of Tape 4 for *Six Crises* manuscript, n.d., "[unlabelled #1]," box 1, series 258, Nixon Pre-Presidential Papers, NALA.

67. Rusher, *Rise of the Right*, 89–91; F. Clifton White, *Suite 3505: The Story of the Draft Goldwater Movement* (New Rochelle, N.Y.), 25–36.

68. "Republican Old Guard Rallying to Goldwater As Its Last Hope," *The New York Times*, 23 July 1960.

69. Ambrose, *Nixon*, 605–606.

Religious Periodicals and Presidential Elections, 1960–1988

JAMES D. FAIRBANKS
Professor of Political Science
University of Houston-Downtown

JOHN FRANCIS BURKE
Assistant Professor of Political Science
University of Houston-Downtown

The secular print media has long been recognized as an important determinant of political behavior, but contemporary political science has paid little attention to the political cues found in religious periodicals. Interest in the political influence of the religious media has largely been limited to the more flamboyant television evangelists.[1] While many religious publications are like many of the television ministries in focusing on the personal spiritual development needs of the laity, some strive to apply religious principles to a wide range of social problems.

The purpose of this paper is to examine the way in which four of the nation's leading religious periodicals — *Christianity Today, Christian Century, America,* and *Commonweal* have covered national presidential elections since 1960. *Christianity Today* is conservative and evangelical in orientation while *Christian Century* is a mainline, liberal Protestant journal. *America* is a Jesuit publication while *Commonweal* is independent of formal Catholic Church ties.

The basic questions this paper explores are:

1. How extensive is each journal's coverage of presidential elections and political affairs? Has it changed over time?

2. Does each journal suggest that its readers (conservative evangelicals, liberal Catholics, etc.) have or should have their own public policy agenda which reflect that group's distinguishing theological orientation? Have the priority items of this agenda changed over time?

3. How does the evidence regarding what the concerns are of those Christians targeted by the journal compare/contrast with other types of evidence or theories of what their concerns are or have been?

No claim is made that these journals directly shape the views of large numbers of voters. Indeed, they all have modest circulations: *Christianity Today* — 185,000, *Christian Century* — 35,000, *America* — 35,000, and *Commonweal* — 20,000. As "journals of record," however, they are politically significant in at least four ways:

1. Political information is often spread through a "two-step" process. The views

expressed in editorials and columns are read by a relatively small number of "opinion leaders" who then relay what they have learned to friends and co-workers.[2] Those who read magazines like *Christian Century*, *Christianity Today*, *America*, and *Commonweal* tend to be the "opinion leaders" of their respective religious communities.

2. Because of their standing as a voice for major constituencies of the Christian community, policy makers interested in cultivating these constituencies (or who personally identify with them) will sometimes look to these journals for policy guidance.

3. Each journal represents an important religious tradition and reflects the politically relevant values and assumptions of that tradition. The political material published in these journals manifests a richness and complexity of thought which stands in sharp contrast to many of the stereotypes regarding church positions which exist in the literature, be it survey research or voting analysis.

4. Journals such as *Christian Century*, *Christianity Today*, *America*, and *Commonweal* not only illuminate church political stands and their underlying value premises, but also provide insights into the deliberative process through which these stands came into being.

Editorials and articles in every issue of *America*, *Christian Century*, *Christianity Today*, and *Commonweal* appearing during the presidential election years from 1960 to 1988 were reviewed to determine if they were political in nature. Editorials and articles dealing specifically with the campaign were also identified as were pieces on religion as a campaign issue. Generally, whatever the publication listed as an "article" in the table of contents was included in its articles count and whatever was given an "editorial" heading as included in its editorial count. Discretion had to be used when the table of contents was incomplete.

Christianity Today

The publication having the greatest influence within Evangelical Christianity is *Christianity Today*. The magazine was founded in 1956 by a group of evangelical leaders including Billy Graham, Graham's father-in-law, L. Nelson Bell, and theologian Carl F. H. Henry who were interested in bringing greater intellectual respectability to conservative religion. Henry served as editor until 1968 when he was succeeded by the more conservative Harold Lindsell. Henry set forth that the new magazine would stir evangelical Christians to get more actively engaged in crucial social movements and political events:

> We intend to proclaim Christ's Gospel with passion and to apply the ethical teachings of the Bible to the contemporary social crisis. We will resolutely declare what we believe God's revelation and its implications are in such problem areas as war, youth, race, relations, poverty, the environment, lawlessness, over-population, drugs, and pornography.

Striker and Strober have charged that despite this commitment, very little appears in its pages which would "disturb the most conservative defenders of wealth and privilege."[4] In 1978, newly appointed editor Kenneth Kantzer acknowledged

TABLE 1
Editorials on Presidential Campaigns and on Other Political Topics: 1960–1988

Year	Total Editions	% on Any Aspect of Campaign	% on Religion in the Campaign	% on All Political Topics
1960				
Christ. Today	109	5%	3%	46%
Christ. Cent.	444	11%	6%	65%
America	190	15%	10%	72%
Commonweal	234	28%	16%	59%
1964				
Christ. Today	153	5%	1%	50%
Christ. Cent.	428	10%	3%	71%
America	178	6%	5%	69%
Commonweal	166	13%	1%	68%
1968				
Christ. Today	150	5%	0%	41%
Christ. Cent.	277	6%	1%	72%
America	144	10%	0%	71%
Commonweal	97	20%	0%	58%
1972				
Christ. Today	199	5%	1%	50%
Christ. Cent.	183	6%	1%	63%
America	83	8%	0%	86%
Commonweal	57	40%	2%	51%
1976				
Christ. Today	121	6%	3%	41%
Christ. Cent.	94	15%	5%	72%
America	47	17%	4%	68%
Commonweal	27	37%	11%	41%
1980				
Christ. Today	46	9%	4%	54%
Christ. Cent.	96	14%	9%	73%
America	129	22%	2%	71%
Commonweal	41	27%	2%	68%
1984				
Christ. Today	18	11%	11%	61%
Christ. Cent.	167	12%	5%	60%
America	131	22%	5%	70%
Commonweal	40	30%	15%	40%
1988				
Christ. Today	36	14%	8%	69%
Christ. Cent.	147	8%	3%	53%
America	59	22%	2%	64%
Commonweal	60	12%	2%	75%

Percentages are based on the total number of editorials published in each periodical for the time period indicated.

that Biblical instruction regarding a Christian's obligation to the poor and disfranchised was unequivocal and indicated he would welcome contributions from those who would encourage the church to be more politically and socially active. The evidence remains mixed, however, regarding *Christianity Today*'s commitment to exploring fully the social implications of the Gospel.[5]

Campaign Coverage

Prior to the 1976 campaign, *Christianity Today* gave the least attention to presidential campaigns of the four journals examined. There were virtually no feature

TABLE 2
Articles on Presidential Campaigns and on Other
Political Topics in Four Religious Periodicals

Year	Total Articles	% on Any Aspect of Campaign	% on Religion in the Campaign	% on All Political Topics
1960				
Christ. Today	121	0%	0%	16%
Christ. Cent.	149	8%	7%	52%
America	261	18%	5%	48%
Commonweal	186	14%	10%	52%
1964				
Christ. Today	133	1%	0%	19%
Christ. Cent.	127	6%	5%	50%
America	268	15%	1%	40%
Commonweal	248	10%	0%	57%
1968				
Christ. Today	119	0%	0%	17%
Christ. Cent.	136	1%	1%	53%
America	239	9%	0%	52%
Commonweal	278	16%	0%	60%
1972				
Christ. Today	104	0%	0%	22%
Christ. Cent.	120	5%	2%	52%
America	241	8%	0%	48%
Commonweal	194	20%	2%	57%
1976				
Christ. Today	102	2%	2%	25%
Christ. Cent.	98	5%	2%	52%
America	182	9%	5%	51%
Commonweal	148	20%	4%	57%
1980				
Christ. Today	97	2%	2%	27%
Christ. Cent.	111	3%	2%	37%
America	188	3%	0%	48%
Commonweal	127	19%	2%	61%
1984				
Christ. Today	78	6%	3%	41%
Christ. Cent.	109	2%	1%	54%
America	169	7%	4%	56%
Commonweal	127	22%	8%	49%
1988				
Christ. Today	63	5%	0%	22%
Christ. Cent.	114	1%	1%	44%
America	170	2%	2%	54%
Commonweal	128	13%	1%	52%

Percentages are based on the total number of articles published in each periodical for the time period indicated.

articles on campaign-related topics and only occasional editorial comment, but more general political concerns were addressed quite regularly. With the rise of the Religious Right and the growing political self-consciousness of Evangelicals, *Christianity Today* has been devoting more space to campaign-related material. In 1988, 14 percent of all editorials run were on the campaign, nearly triple the percent run in 1960 and more than double the 1988 percentage of the more liberal *Christian Century*. The magazine's increased attention to national elections does not represent increased partisanship. Recent editorials have emphasized the complexity of political issues and cautioned readers against simplistic "scorecard" judgments on candidates.

TABLE 3
Candidate Endorsements and Other Indications of
Editorial Preference: 1960–1988

Year	Formal Endorsement	No Endorsement But Sympathetic	Negative Endorsement or Critical Coverage of Aspects of Campaign
1960			
Christ. Today		Nixon	"Reverse bigotry"
Christ. Cent.		Stevenson, Rockefeller	Catholic Bloc Voting
America			
Commonweal		Kennedy	
1964			
Christ. Today			Rel. Pronouncements
Christ. Cent.	Johnson, Scranton (M. Eisenhower for VP)		Goldwater
America		Johnson	
Commonweal			Goldwater
1968			
Christ. Today		Nixon	
Christ. Cent.		R. Kennedy	Wallace, Reagan
America			Wallace
Commonweal	McCarthy		
1972			
Christ. Today		Nixon	
Christ. Cent.			Press Coverage
America			
Commonweal	McGovern		
1976			
Christ. Today			Religious Coverage
Christ. Cent.		Carter	Reagan (Primaries)
America			
Commonweal	Carter (after McCarthy)		
1980			
Christ. Today			
Christ. Cent.		Carter	
America			Reagan Social. Pols.
Commonweal	Need for "Third Way"		
1984			
Christ. Today			
Christ. Cent.			Lack of Issues
America			
Commonweal			
1988			
Christ. Today			Lack of Leadership
Christ. Cent.			Campaign Tactics
America			
Commonweal			Campaign Tactics

At no time has *Christianity Today* formally endorsed a candidate for the presidency, though at times its position on issues has shown it to be clearly closer to one candidate than to another. In the 1960's and 1970's, anti-communism and conservative economics were the journal's major political concerns and its editorial themes often echoed those of the Republican campaign. In 1960, it cited the expansion of big government and the "inordinate power of labor leaders" as among the major problems with which the next president would have to contend. It also expressed the hope that any "intimation that the [presidency] can be obtained by inordinate ambition or excessive use of personal funds" be firmly rebutted.[6] In 1968, the journal urged its readers to ask themselves which candidate would better safeguard Judeo-Christian values and be more likely to nominate Supreme Court Justices "who will close the door on pornography and not coddle criminals."[7] And in 1972 the journal's campaign assessment seemed heavily weighted in Nixon's favor: "let us take pains to try to judge the candidates for public office on how biblical their views are on such matters as abortion, pornography, homosexuality, drugs, and prostitution. . . ."[8]

Editorials and articles since 1972 have had a less pronounced Republican bias as the magazine began to move away from its once predictable conservative positions on both foreign and domestic policy, positions which had become official policy in Reagan's Washington. Contrary to the conventional wisdom that evangelical political interests were limited to a few narrow moral issues prior to the late 1970's when the New Right began an unprecedented mobilization of evangelicals on behalf of conservative economic policies, *Christianity Today* is now devoting much more space to moral issues than it did previously, while its attention to economic and defense issues has declined.

Religion as a Campaign Issue

The religious issue of 1960 was, of course, John Kennedy's Catholicism. While never claiming that Kennedy's faith should disqualify him from the presidency, *Christianity Today* did see Catholic political power as posing a real threat to traditional American liberties: "opposition to political Romanism is not unreasonable because a Catholic in the Presidency would be torn between two loyalties as no Protestant has ever been." According to the editors, to suggest that opposition to a Catholic presidency "is bigotry is itself a smear."[9] The journal featured a number of articles on protestant persecution in Catholic controlled governments and ran several articles on the Catholic Church's claims of ultimate authority. In a post-election analysis, the journal pointed to Kennedy's support among big city "bosses" and Catholic, union, and Negro "bloc voting" as the key to his victory.[10]

Religion as a campaign issue practically disappeared until Jimmy Carter's born-again candidacy of 1976. Carter was the subject of several favorable articles and editorials in both 1976 and 1980 but the editors gave few clues as to who their actual choice for president was in either election. A 1976 editorial acknowledged that it was wrong to vote for Christians just because they are Christians, but did argue that evangelicals had the right to demand that candidates "respect the perpetuation of that [evangelical] ethos that has always pervaded American life."[11] During the Reagan campaigns, the journal backed away from the strict separatist position on church-state issues it had espoused in 1960. In an editorial endorsing parochial school aid, the editor confessed that this position represented a "radical. 180-degree reversal in his thinking."[12]

The largest number of editorials on religion and electoral politics appeared during the campaigns of the 1980's. While endorsing a Christian's civic responsibility, *Christianity Today* did not give its blanket support to the type of political involvement the Religious Right seemed intent on promoting. In response to claims that the evangelical turnout had led to the 1980 Republican victory, an editorial cautioned:

> politically conservative evangelicals against taking too much credit for the outcome of the election . . . as a minority in a pluralistic society, conservative evangelicals must neither expect nor encourage Mr. Reagan to adopt a dogmatic, uncompromising stand on all positions of deep concern to them.[13]

Similarly, early in the 1988 race, the editors declared that "leadership, know how. and honesty rank above faith on our presidential wish list."[14]

Christian Century

The *Christian Century* evolved from the Disciples of Christ periodical, the *Christian Oracle*, founded in Chicago in 1884. Its name was changed to *Christian Century* in 1900; then, in 1908 it was purchased by Charles Clayton Morrison, who cut its ties to the Disciples and built it into "Protestantism's leading interdenominational journal."[15] International peace and justice have since been the priority political concerns of the *Century*.[16]

Morrison retired as editor in 1947 but remained a strong influence at the *Century* until his death in 1966. Since 1960, there have been four editors: Harold E. Fey (1956–1964), Kyle Haselden (1964–68), Alan Geyer (1968–1972), and James Wall.

Reflecting Morrison's ecumenical commitments, the magazine has given extensive and sympathetic coverage to the Council of Churches, the World Council of Churches, and the assemblies of the major mainline denominations. Once militantly protestant, the journal's ecumenical vision became more inclusive in the 1960's as seen by the appointment of prominent Catholics like Michael Novak to editorial positions.

Under Haselden and Geyer, the *Century* was aggressively involved in the civil rights struggle and anti-war movement and was frequently criticized by more conservative publications like *Christianity Today*.[17] The journal suffered financially in the early 1970s because, according to Martin Marty, old readers found it too far to the left in its opposition to the Vietnam War while a new generation of "should-be subscribers" found it "too stodgy, too pacific, too nonviolent, too antirevolutionary, too theistic. . . ." Wall, Marty adds, through cost-cutting and less "semisecular meanderings" has led the journal "toward a more self-consciously churchly posture."[18]

Campaign Coverage

Christian Century's most direct involvement in a presidential campaign was in 1964 when the editors pledged to do whatever "we can to contribute to [Goldwater's] defeat."[19] To its critics who urged the journal to be more evenhanded and present both sides, *Christian Century* asked rhetorically: "Is it Christian responsibility to fabricate another side on issues about which we are as intellectually and morally certain as we can ever become?"[20] In several editorials, "Goldwaterism" was compared to fascism and its influence in Germany in the early 1930's.[21] In view of the journal's partisanship, the Internal Revenue Service suspended the magazine's tax exempt status for a year.

While studiously avoiding endorsements after 1964, the journal's editorials generally were disposed toward the policy positions of the political liberal candidates, though not as completely as the journal's liberal reputation might suggest. In 1968, the *Christian Century* (which is published in Chicago) was outraged by the "armed camp politics" of Mayor Daley at the Democratic Convention and was "Plaguing Both Houses" as the formal campaign got underway. Early in the year, the candidates receiving the most sympathetic editorial coverage were Robert Kennedy and Nelson Rockefeller. Aside from bemoaning the fact that Nixon's nomination was as "inevitable as death and taxes," the journal virtually ignored the Republican nominee.[22] In 1972, Nixon was attacked in several post-election pieces, but little appeared during the campaign that was specifically critical of Nixon or supportive of McGovern.

While its difficulties with the IRS taught it to avoid overt partisanship during campaigns, *Christian Century* has not been reluctant to reveal its preferences after the votes have been counted. After the 1972 election, an editorial lamented that McGovern had represented a "Morality That Did Not Communicate."[23] The magazine's sympathies were also hinted at in post-election analyses comparing the Nixon campaign to those run by Georgia's Gene Talmadge in the 1930's and another which urged McGovern supporters to "keep faith and hang on."[24]

Editor Wall took a leave of absence during 1976 to work for the Carter campaign and wrote several pieces about this experience on his return. Making clear that he was expressing his own views, not the *Century*'s, Wall wrote a "personal opinion" column after the 1980 election in which he praised Carter and admitted to being "deeply saddened" by the election's outcome.[25] In a 1984 editorial entitled "Requiem for a Dream," an obviously disappointed editor accented the American voter's willingness to "bury the peculiarly American dream of protecting the rights of the oppressed."[26]

Religion as a Campaign Issue

In the 1960 campaign, *Christian Century*, like *Christianity Today*, argued that many of the concerns about a Catholic president were legitimate and that the burden of proof was on Kennedy to demonstrate that he would not allow Rome to dictate his policies. (In 1928, the magazine had openly and aggressively opposed Al Smith on religious grounds.) Likewise, it accused many of Kennedy's defenders of being themselves bigots for not respecting the honest concerns voters had about the candidate's religion. After Kennedy's appearance before the Houston Ministerial Association, the editors acknowledged that they were comfortable that the candidate was committed to separation of church and state, but expressed concern that the Church itself had yet to repudiate its claim to ultimate obedience from all its members.

During the Carter campaigns, Wall vigorously defended the Georgian Baptist from charges appearing in the secular media that he was mixing religion and politics. Several editorials charged that many in the secular press seemed to think that religion was fine as long as it was not taken too seriously. To the question posed in the editorial, "Presidential Piety: Must It Be Kept Private," the *Christian Century* answered with a resounding "no."[27] In a surprisingly spirited defense of Reagan's right to talk about his religious faith, this editorial also made clear that it disagreed emphatically with the policy directions in which Reagan's faith was taking him. A 1984 editorial underscored that Jesse Jackson was suffering as had Carter from "a strong journalistic resistance to political figures who explain their motivations in religious terms."[29] Of the religious publications examined, the *Century*, has consistently been the most critical of the secular press's coverage of the role of religion in political campaigns.

The *Century* has also been quick to condemn any perceived exploitation of religion. Its highest editorial coverage of "Religion in the Campaign" — 9% — was in 1980: the New Right was criticized — not for introducing religion into politics — but for celebrating a "self-righteous greed, not a sacrificial gospel" and for using "diversionary tactics" like the prayer amendment to detract attention from the real issues.[29] The magazine was quite willing to endorse "a politics rooted in religion" but wanted nothing to do with "religion that played politics."[30] In comparing the public statements of the presidential candidates in 1984, the *Christian Century* concluded that Reagan was right in principle but wrong in practice while Mondale was wrong in principle but right in practice.[31]

America

The inaugural edition of *America* was published by the Jesuit Order of North America on April 17, 1909. It succeeded *The Messenger*, a monthly publication at Fordham University. The initial editor, J. Wynne argued there was a need for a weekly Catholic journal on public affairs:

> *AMERICA* will take the place of the monthly periodical, *The Messenger*, and continue its mission. It is in reality an adaptation of its precursor to meet the needs of the time. Among these needs are a review and conscientious criticism of the life and literature of the day, a discussion of actual questions and a study of vital problems from the Christian standpoint. . . .[32]

This journal, he continued, would both articulate the Catholic outlook on political, literary, and religious matters and reach out in a cosmopolitan spirit to non-Catholics.

Catholic social thought, culled from the political philosophy of Thomas Aquinas and the positions of the papal encyclicals, accents the roles of Christians, religious institutions, and government in providing for the common good. Ninety years hence, *America* continues to be true to this tradition and remains nonsectarian in its discussion of the intersection of religion and politics. In the words of a more recent editor, Joseph O'Hare: "To identify authentic religious faith with a particular world view, or a set political agenda, or a specific political party or program, is to reduce religious faith to political options, whether of the right or the left."[33]

Campaign Coverage

During the U. S. presidential campaigns from 1960 through 1988, *America* has had four editors: Thurston Davis (1960, 64, & 68), Donald Campion (1972), Joseph O'Hare (1976, 80, & 84), and George Hunt (1984 & 88). The reason the percentage of articles devoted to the campaign is highest during the 1960 and 1964 campaigns is that these articles are primarily featured in a weekly section titled "Washington Front". These articles focus on the strategies and platforms of the candidates and their parties. In 1968, the column alternates week to week with a new section, Social Front. In 1972, WF only appears periodically and by 1976 disappears entirely.

Another weekly section, "Cross Currents," is a set of 10–20 news stories a paragraph long which appears in *America* from the 1960 through the 1980 campaigns. Frequently CC features information about the primaries and other factual information related to the campaign; because of the brevity of these entries they have not been included in the back tables. After 1980, it is retitled "In Sight" and becomes much more apolitical in orientation. With the diminishing role of both WF and CC in the 70's and 80's, *America* shifts its coverage of the campaigns to the editorial page.

America in each campaign strives to give a fair hearing to both candidates: the journal reserves the right to state its view on policy issues, but consistently refuses to endorse candidates or parties in a partisan fashion. In both 1960 and 1976, in successive October issues, the cover stories featured one candidate and then the other. In 1964, several WF articles glowed with praise for the Johnson administration, but the journal never endorsed him. In at least one instance, the journal gives a "negative endorsement": a 1968 editorial states that the Wallace-LeMay ticket lacks the insight requisite for the nation's highest two offices.[34]

In terms of Vietnam, *America* supports administration policy in 1968, but then withdraws it in 1972 under a different editor. In 1976, Joseph O'Hare uses the prefatory "Of Many Things" column as much as the editorial page to comment on the campaign. In 1980 he editorializes against rising U.S. militarism in response to Iran and the Soviet invasion of Afghanistan and in his final six months as editor in 1984 against Reagan's social policy.[35] That year O'Hare was named President of Fordham University. In contrast to the strict scrutiny *America* paid to each step of the 1960's campaigns, by 1988, George Hunt in a March editorial questions the very value of campaign "marathons," proposing as an alternative a September national primary to be followed by the November general election.[36]

Religion as a Campaign Issue

In the 1960 campaign, *America* devotes 10% of its editorials and 5% of its articles to the famed "religious issue." In its September 24th editorial, *America* states that there is nothing either in the First Amendment or in Catholic doctrine which would suggest that if a Catholic became president that they would not respect the religious pluralism of America.[37] What follows in this issue is a symposium between Catholics and non-Catholics which reinforces this editorial stance. After the election, avoiding a sectarian outlook, the journal affirms that the electoral process weathered whatever bigotry appeared in the campaign.[38]

In 1964, this same religious issue reappears, except in reverse: can either party win the White House without a Catholic on the ticket? Indeed, William Miller, Goldwater's eventual running mate, was a Catholic and a graduate of Notre Dame. *America* in a January editorial quickly puts this issue to rest:

A candidate's Catholic faith should not become a qualification for office. . . . If the old "religious issue" was shameful, its new version is "ridiculous."[39]

From 1976 through 1988, three issues share the "religion spotlight": abortion, the extent to which churches should engage in partisan politics, and the role a candidate's religious views should play both in their run for the presidency and policy views. *America* consistently argues that voters should make their choice for president on more than one issue and that the entire scope of Catholic stands on moral and social issues should be brought to bear on a campaign. Nevertheless, in a 1976 editorial, the journal flirts with a Catholic "litmus test" when in evaluating Carter's relationship to Catholics, it suggests that Carter needs to address federal aid to private education and the empowering of church-related organizations to deal with social problems in the cities.[40]

Akin to its editorial stance on partisanship in campaigns, *America* insists whether it be the evangelical right in the 1980's or Afro-American churches in relationship to the Jackson campaigns of 1980 and 1984, churches should refrain from active support of particular parties or candidates.[41] Finally, be it Carter's faith or the fact that Robertson and Jackson are members of the cloth, *America* maintains in a 1984 editorial that each voter should take into account "at least as much about a candidate's skill in governing wisely . . . as about a candidate's theology."[42]

Commonweal

The inaugural edition of *Commonweal* was November 12, 1924. Similar to *America*, it introduced itself as a journal committed to a Christian perspective on public affairs, especially from the standpoint of Catholic social thought. But in contrast to its Jesuit counterpart, the introductory editorial characterizes its orientation as "the independent, personal product of its editors and contributors, who, for the most part, will be layman."[43] [11/12/24, 5] Furthermore, this independence would be fortified by including writers of other Christian and non-Christian beliefs.

For the past eighty-five years *Commonweal* has engaged religious and political issues in this spirit of independence and ecumenism. Over the years, as James O'Gara — a more recent editor — relates, the "*Commonweal* Catholic" has come to mean "The commitment . . . to a church that was open and pluralistic, not rigid and authoritarian, a church that was the visible manifestation of Jesus's presence in the world."[44]

As much as the reforms of the Second Vatican Council cultivated openness and pluralism within Catholicism, *Commonweal*, for years had promoted social and racial justice, arms control, and ecumenism — defying critics within and without Catholicism. And although these progressive stances become *passe* in the wake of Vatican II and the Great Society, the journal remains committed to the longstanding Catholic lay responsibility to manifest the Christian message in one's worldly activities.

Campaign Coverage

During the U.S. presidential campaigns from 1960 through 1988, *Commonweal* has had four editors: Edward Skillen (1960 & 1964), James O'Gara (1968, 1972, 1976, 1980, & 1984), Peter Steinfels (1984) and Margaret O'Brien Steinfels

(1988).[45] The campaign articles in *Commonweal* between 1960–1988 fall into three categories: 1) what the editors term liberal-left assessments of the candidates and the issues and 2) historical or political behavioral analyses by scholars such as Walter Dean Burnham, and 3) in 1976 and 1980, partisan features on each candidate.

In contrast to *America*'s nonpartisan, "above-it-all" editorial stance, *Commonweal* does disclose political preferences. In 1960, though *Commonweal* does not formally endorse either candidate, its editorials are more critical of Nixon; even when the journal is critical of Kennedy, the back cover features a picture of Kennedy paid for by the New York State Democratic Committee.[46]

Commonweal depicts the 1964 race as "A Sorry Campaign": "the shallowness of [Goldwater's] grasp of his own ideas" versus Johnson's inability to be more specific on civil rights than Goldwater.[47] When it comes to the GOP, *Commonweal* and *America* throughout the 1960's campaigns lend favorable coverage—not endorsements—to Republican moderates such as Rockefeller, Scranton, and Romney during the primaries.

Under O'Gara, *Commonweal* in 1968 and 1972 becomes very passionate regarding the prospect of liberal-left politics. The excitement of the McCarthy-Kennedy contest in the spring 1968 issues of *Commonweal* gives way to gloom, for it becomes apparent in the wake of JFK's assassination that Humphrey, "the pleader of platitudes and the defender of policies that have split the country and left it morally bankrupt before the world," will gain the party nomination over McCarthy.[48] In the end, the journal calls for a transformation of protest politics into a programmatic political movement.[49]

In 1972, *Commonweal* insists upon an end to the war in Vietnam: a May editorial pointedly states "The enemy is Nixon."[50] O'Gara places hope upon hope for a McGovern victory, but the Nixon landslide again leads him to beckon Democrats, Liberals, and "disgruntled Republicans" to congregate and consider what "life, liberty, and the pursuit of happiness mean today."[51]

Disenchantment sets in with the subsequent campaigns. In 1976, the journal reservedly endorses Carter in view of the hopelessness of the McCarthy campaign.[52] This guarded faith in Carter gives way in 1980 to the editorial lament—which candidate do you distrust least?[53] At the end of the 1984 race, Peter Steinfels offers "the third way" of Catholic social thought as an alternative to the major party packages.[54] By 1988, Margaret O'Brien Steinfels laments "Our politicians have taken the lead in depoliticizing the electorate. . . ."[55]

Religion as a Campaign Issue

Commonweal, even more so than *America*, gives a great deal of attention to the "religious issue" of the 1960, 1976 and 1984 campaigns. In a January 1, 1960 editorial, *Commonweal* states in no uncertain terms: "Here is a certain fact which cannot be repeated too often: American Catholics wholeheartedly support the Constitution, including the First Amendment. . . ." But the editorial continues that a Catholic running for president is still a symbolic issue for most Catholics: are we to have "a pluralistic society with a strong Protestant tradition rather than a Protestant society with a pluralistic tradition?"[56] This "emergence from the cultural ghetto" motif leads *Commonweal* on three occasions to challenge editorials or articles from the *Christian Century* either encouraging the "religious issue" as a voting criterion or misconstruing the Catholic view on ecumenism.[57]

In terms of other moral issues which arise amid the 1976 through 1988 campaigns, *Commonweal* echoes *America*'s insistence that voting should not be tied to one issue, namely abortion, but rather reflect the "seamless garment" of Catholic moral and social issues—including arms control, the blight of capital punishment, and economic justice. In 1976, the journal prophetically warns that an insistence upon the abortion issue alone will in the end distract the church from pursuing all the issues of traditional Catholic thought.[58] In 1984, five editorials and six articles within eight issues (July 13–November 30) are devoted to the American bishops and abortion in relation to the campaign. In 1988, although both Catholic journals focus on AIDS, *Commonweal* also covers the moral dilemmas posed by care for the elderly, the caliber of health care, surrogate contracts, and organ transplants.

Throughout the campaigns, *Commonweal* insists that churches focus their political energies on issues of economic justice and the empowerment of individuals to engage in the political process—such as the American Catholic bishops' pastoral letters on nuclear arms and on the economy—rather than participate in campaigns in a partisan fashion. In 1976, in comparing the respective "religiosity" of Carter and Jerry Brown, *Commonweal* only faults Carter's faith-in-action for not provoking people to pursue social justice enough.[59] On the other hand, at the conclusion of the 1988 campaign, *Commonweal* balks at the idea of Bush as the "Catholic candidate"—again, the full panorama of Catholic social thought must be brought to bear upon the debate of a presidential campaign.[60]

Discussion and Comparisons
Extent of Campaign and Political Coverage

In the election years studied, with the exception of 1964 and 1988, the Catholic journals give more editorial space to campaign coverage than do their protestant counterparts. In fact, *Commonweal*, again with the exception of 1988 gives the highest editorial coverage, averaging 27% over the eight campaigns. With regard to campaign articles the Catholic-protestant contrast is even more striking: neither protestant journal devotes more than 8% of its articles to any campaign whereas *America* averages 9% and *Commonweal* 17% over the eight campaigns. When there were salient religious issues—1960, 1976, 1980, 1984, & 1988—the attention paid to the campaign tended to be slightly above average in each journal.

In terms of each journal's attention to religion in these campaigns, editorially the Catholic journals give more coverage in 1960 and *Commonweal* gives the highest coverage when abortion is a key campaign issue. On the other hand, from the 1976 campaign onward, *Christianity Today* steps up its editorial coverage, reflecting the rise of the evangelical movement in American politics; in fact, both protestant journals give more coverage than their Catholic counterparts in 1980 and 1988. Articles on religion in the campaign fluctuate over the campaigns for each journal: again, attention in the Catholic journals is highest in 1960 and the "abortion" campaigns — 1976 and 1984.

The percentage of space devoted to overall political material has remained about the same in *Commonweal* and *America* while *Christian Century* has shown a slight decrease and *Christianity Today* a modest increase, at least on its editorial pages. Furthermore, unlike the coverage of campaigns, the average level of editorial coverage of all political topics among the journals is comparable: *Christianity Today* 52%, *Christian Century* 66%, *America* 71% and *Commonweal* 58%. In average article coverage of all political topics, *Christianity Today* lags well behind the other three: 24% as opposed to *Christian Century* 56%, *America* 50%, and *Commonweal* 56%.

Policy Agendas in View of Theological Standpoint

Both *America* and *Commonweal* are unequivocally committed to evaluating the stance of candidates on public policy issues from the standpoint of Catholic social thought. For instance, in 1984, both journals endorse the seamless garment approach which links all pro-life issues together — abortion, opposition to capital punishment, and arms control — and oppose attempts by sectarian groups within or without the church to ground partisan support on a single issue. Catholic social thought, furthermore, encompasses not only the preceding issues but a longstanding commitment to social and economic justice: for either journal, suggestions of a "Catholic candidate" mock the depth and legacy of this tradition.

Although *America* insists that religious institutions have an obligation to comment on the pressing policy issues of the day, the journal draws the line at partisan entanglements. *Commonweal*, by contrast, feels no trepidation in its mobilization of the citizenry around peace and justice issues, though this engagement was tainted in the 1980's by a despair over how candidates and parties were depoliticizing the electorate. *Commonweal*'s passion as opposed to *America*'s reserve, even after Vatican II, still reflects the distinct institutional venues of the laity and clergy in Catholicism.

In contrast to *America* and *Commonweal*, *Christianity Today* and *Christian Century* lack strong ties to any one particular church. *Christian Century* comes out of the social gospel tradition which emphasizes the church's role in promoting social and economic reform; *Christianity Today* comes out of the evangelical tradition with its more pessimistic appraisal of the potential for human institutions to better society and its greater emphasis on the conversion of the individual. Neither of those traditions manifest a "seamless garment" constellation of political concerns which provides an explicit policy agenda rooted in religious principles.

Christian Century links theology and public policy primarily in the area of foreign policy. While recent editors have not embraced pacifism to the extent that founder Morrison did, *Christian Century* has continued to emphasize Christian teachings on peace and to condemn military actions undertaken in pursuit of nationalistic aims. Except in the area of civil rights, it has not systematically applied Christian teachings to domestic policy. *Christianity Today* relates its core religious beliefs to politics with the least consistency. The journal's accent in campaign coverage has shifted during the period studied from an endorsement of laissez-faire economics and militant anti-communism to a sober appraisal of the political and moral platform of the evangelical movement. Its recent advocacy asks only that readers be responsive citizens.

"Church Issue Stereotypes"

The political concerns of these religious periodicals do not always fit "church issue" stereotypes. Within *America* and *Commonweal*, abortion is not the overriding Catholic concern, as conveyed by the right-to-life movement. *Christianity Today* does share some of the concerns of Jerry Falwell and the "Religious Right" but there is little in its political commentary to suggest that a new marriage has taken place between religious conservatives and the secular right. On the other hand, *Christian Century* is placing increased emphasis on evaluating politics by religious criteria—a practice which places it out of step with the secular political left. Consequently, *Christianity Today* and the *Christian Century* exhibit more similarities than their conservative and "liberal" labels would suggest.

In terms of religion as a campaign issue, only in 1960 was there a sectarian split between the journals in terms of their coverage: the commentary on the Kennedy candidacy by the protestant journals was remarkably similar whereas the Catholic journals saw no incompatibility between a Catholic as president and the First Amendment. *Commonweal* amplified the controversy by insisting it entailed the symbolic issue as to whether Catholics would now gain their rightful place in a genuinely pluralistic America. But apart from some tensions between the Carter campaign and the Catholic community regarding aid to parochial schools in 1976, the parameters of American pluralism remained an undeveloped issue in all four journals after 1960.

Especially in the presidential campaigns from 1976 to the present, each journal has attested to the role of religion in politics. *Christianity Today* has cautiously assessed the import of the rise of the evangelical movement. *Christian Century* has upheld the legitimacy of political stances grounded upon religion while castigating those who manipulate religion for politics' sake. Giving the abortion controversy its due, *America* and *Commonweal* have been steadfast in their articulation of the relevance of Catholic social thought for public policy.

Distinct from the secular media, the claims these religious journals make on the political order are rooted in the transcendent ethic of a sovereign deity. It must be noted that none of these journals, whatever their particular accent in covering presidential campaigns, claims that political leadership can be evaluated strictly in terms of religious criteria. Nevertheless, their religious dimension provides an insight otherwise absent in contemporary analyses of political campaigns.

Notes

1. See Jeffrey Hadden and Charles Swann, *Prime Time Preachers* (Reading, Massachusetts: Addison-Wesley, 1981) & Jeffrey Hadden and Anson Shupe, *Televangelism: Power and Politics on God's Frontier* (New York: Henry Holt and Company, 1988).
2. Elihu Katz, "The Two-Step Flow of Communication: An Up-to-Date Report on an Hypothesis," *Public Opinion Quarterly* 21 (Winter 1956): 61–78.
3. "Statement of Purpose," *Christianity Today* 15 (9 October 1970): 24. At the time, Henry also

indicted evangelicals for their preoccupation with "individual sin rather than social evil." Hadden and Swann, 153.

4. Lowell Streiker and Gerald Strober, *Religion and the New Majority* (New York: Harper and Row, 1972), 114.
5. See James D. Fairbanks, "The Politics of *Christianity Today*" in *Religion and Political Behavior in the United States*, ed. Ted Jelen (New York: Praeger Publishers, 1989), 243–48 & James Hunter, *Evangelicalism: The Coming Generation* (Chicago: University of Chicago Press, 1987).
6. "Political Anxieties Rise as Party Conventions Approach," *Christianity Today* 4 (4 July 1960): 22.
7. "A Country at the Crossroads," *Christianity Today* 11 (11 October 1968): 27.
8. "Judging the Candidates," *Christianity Today* 16 (15 September 1972): 34
9. "Bigotry or Smear," *Christianity Today* 4 (1 February 1960): 20.
10. "Another Era Underway in the American Venture," *Christianity Today* 5 (21 November 1960): 21.
11. "Should Christians Vote for Christians?," *Christianity Today* 20 (18 June 1976): 20.
12. "Tax Support For Christian Colleges: Balancing the Ledger." *Christianity Today* 24 (7 November 1980): 10.
13. "Just Because Reagan Has Won." *Christianity Today* 24 (12 December 1980): 14.
14. "The Vision Test: Leadership, Know How, and Honesty." *Christianity Today* 32 (8 April 1988): 15.
15. William Katz and Linda Katz, *Magazine For Libraries* (New York: R.R. Bowker, 1986), 114.
16. During the 1930's, Morrison was a near pacifist whose refusal to support any type of aid to the British led contributing editor Reinhold Niebuhr to launch *Christianity and Crisis*, because he found the *Century*'s foreign policy positions as far too optimistic and idealistic. Martin Marty, *Righteous Empire: The Protestant Experience in America* (New York: Dial Press, 1970), 57.
17. Martin Luther King, Jr. began writing for the *Century* in 1956 and quickly rose to the position of editor-at-large. The *Century*, in 1963, was the first nationally distributed periodical to publish his "Letter from Birmingham Jail" in its entirety. See *Christian Century* 80 (12 June 1963): 767–73.
18. "How It Looks in the Moonlight," *Christian Century* 93 (3 November 1976): 947–48.
19. "Goldwater? No!," *Christian Century* 81 (1 July 1964): 851.
20. "On Presenting Both Sides," *Christian Century* 81 (23 September 1964): 1163.
21. "The 1964 Religious Issue." *Christian Century* 81 (7 October 1964): 1227 and "The Nation: Move Toward A Good Society," *Christian Century* 81 (11 November 1964): 1387.
22. "Plaguing Both Houses," *Christian Century* 85 (28 August 1968): 1071.
23. "Morality That Did Not Communicate," *Christian Century* 89 (15 November 1972): 1143.
24. "A Personal Word From A New Editor," *Christian Century* 89 (29 November 1972): 1207 and "Hang On." *Christian Century* 89 (6 December 1972): 1235.
25. "God Help Me I Love It," *Christian Century* 97 (26 November 1980): 1150.
26. "Requiem For A Dream." *Christian Century* 97 (5 December 1984): 1140.
27. "Presidential Piety: Must It Be Kept Private," *Christian Century* 101 (22 February 1984); 187.
28. "Jesse Jackson: Rescue of U.S. Flyers." *Christian Century* 101 (18 January 1984): 35.
29. "The New Right," *Christian Century* 101 (10 October 1984): 915 and "Ban Neutrality From Campaign Talk," *Christian Century* 101 (12–19 September 1984): 819.
30. "Getting Into Another Political Year," *Christian Century* 97 (2 February 1980): 211.
31. "Religion and Politics: Fireworks in a Fog," *Christian Century* 101 (24 October 1984): 973.
32. "Editorial Announcement," *America* 1 (17 April 1909): 5.
33. "Communications in the Church," *America* 150 (23–30 June 1984): 470.
34. "Your Vote and the Next President," *America* 119 (2 November 1968): 394–96.
35. "Midsummer Militarism," *America* 143 (2–9 August 1980): 44; "The President's Budget," *America* 150 (18 February 1984): 102; "Wishing Away the Deficit," *America* 150 (31 March 1984): 229; and "Harassed Are the Poor," *America* 150 (19 May 1984): 370.
36. "Is This Marathon Necessary?," *America* 158 (5 May 1988): 227.

37. "The Voice of the Church in America," *America* 103 (24 September 1960): 695–96.
38. "The People's Choice," *America* 104 (19 November 1960): 257.
39. "Catholic on the Ticket?," *America* 110 (18 January 1964): 73.
40. "Candidate Carter and the Catholics," *America* 135 (7 August 1976): 42.
41. "Churches and Political Candidates." *America* 143 (5–12 July 1980): 4; "The Christian Vote in 1980," *America* 143 (13 September 1980): 105; and "Jesse Jackson: Church and State," 150 (4 February 1984): 63.
42. "The Politics of Religion," *America* 151 (15 September 1984): 117.
43. "An Introduction." *Commonweal* 1 (12 November 1924): 5.
44. James O'Gara, "By Way of Farewell: A Personal Note," *Commonweal* 111 (23 March 1984): 165.
45. The total number of editorials and articles in *Commonweal* drops with the 1976 campaign because the journal shifts from publishing weekly to every other week; however, the percentage of its articles on the campaign actually increases in the 1970's and 1980's, with the exception of 1988. The closest feature in *Commonweal* like the Washington Front column of *America* is a section in the 1960's titled Washington Report. Parallel to *America*'s Current Comment, *Commonweal* features a weekly section in the 1968–1976 campaigns titled "News and Views," but these news bits are fewer in total and also more humorous than those in CC.
46. "The Loyalty Issue," *Commonweal* 73 (7 October 1960): 27–28; "The Big Issue," *Commonweal* 73 (28 October 1960): 107–08; and "Heating Up The Campaign," *Commonweal* 73 (4 November 1960): 140–41.
47. "Goldwater's Thirty Days," *Commonweal* 79 (14 February 1964): 585 and "A Sorry Campaign," *Commonweal* 81 (6 November 1964): 179–80.
48. "A Candidate Ill-Served," *Commonweal* 88 (10 May 1968): 221.
49. "Thinking About November," *Commonweal* 89 (18 October 1968): 75–76.
50. "Students, Arise," *Commonweal* 96 (5 May 1972): 203.
51. "Beginning Again," *Commonweal* 97 (24 November 1972): 172.
52. "The Election," *Commonweal* 103 (22 October 1976): 675–76.
53. "The Politics of Distrust," *Commonweal* 107 (29 August 1980): 451–52.
54. "Faith and the Economics of Inequality," *Commonweal* 111 (2–16 November 1984): 582.
55. "The Day of Reckoning," *Commonweal* 115 (4 November 1988): 580.
56. "Catholics and the Presidency," *Commonweal* 71 (1 January 1960): 384.
57. "Bigotry and Responsibility," *Commonweal* 72 (6 May 1960): 140–41; "When Is An Issue?," *Commonweal* 72 (2 September 1960): 435–36; and "Freed From Logic," *Commonweal* 72 (9 September 1960): 460–61.
58. "Politics and Abortion," *Commonweal* 103 (27 February 1976): 131–32.
59. "Carter, Brown, and God," *Commonweal* 103 (9 April 1976): 227–28.
60. "Et Cetera: More Election Afterthoughts," *Commonweal* 115 (16 December 1988): 677.

Scenario for a Centrist Revolt: Third Party Prospects in a Time of Ideological Polarization

EDWARD N. KEARNY
Professor of Government
Western Kentucky University

ROBERT A. HEINEMAN
Professor of Political Science
Alfred University

Abstract

This paper explores the implications of the impact of the ideologically specific candidacies of Pat Robertson and Jesse Jackson in the 1988 presidential nominations campaigns. The possibility of polarized parties led by prophetic rather than pragmatic candidates is examined. The paper concludes with a description of how the political center might organize to protect itself and its tradition of flexible leadership in times of crisis. *

In recent years political scientists have spent much time discussing whether the American electorate has undergone or is undergoing a critical realignment of voting preferences.[1] It is generally conceded that such realignments occurred because of the Civil War and the Great Depression. The current argument is that beginning with the 1964 presidential election an enduring shift toward the Republican Party may have materialized. There are, of course, a number of problems with this thesis. One of these is that the Democrats remain strong in Congress and in many states. Another is that there has been no national catastrophe of the scope of the Civil War or the Great Depression to activate a fundamental change in voter allegiances. Nonetheless, since the New Deal, something has been happening to voter partisanship. What was once seen as a Democratic stranglehold on a majority of the electorate has become at least a draw between Republican control of the presidency and Democratic control of Congress.

We shall suggest here that focusing on the question of a critical realignment has distracted attention from changes in the presidential nominating process that raise important electoral possibilities other than a realignment in two-party partisanship. Our concern is not voter preferences *per se* but the potential that trends in the nominating process may have for moving the nation toward the emergence of a viable third party. From this perspective, the interesting questions in light of the 1988 presidential campaign are: Has the nominating process worked to moderate the demands of special interest groups and ideologically extreme factions and in what direction might the nominating process take the electoral process and the nation in the next several presidential elections?

It is our thesis that structural and dynamic changes in the nomination of presidential candidates in conjunction with socioeconomic events that can be reasonably expected to occur could conspire to produce for the first time in the twentieth century a viable third party of the ideological center in reaction to capture of one or both of the parties' presidential nominations by ideologically polarizing candidates. Hints of this possibility now exist. In the past twenty years, two serious third party efforts at the presidency have been mounted by George Wallace and John Anderson, respectively, and strongly ideological candidates in the persons of Barry Goldwater, George McGovern, and Ronald Reagan have captured their party's nomination.[2] Everett Carll Ladd has noted that in the 1976 Republican nominating process, won by the moderate Ford, Reagan, although consistently behind in the polls, managed an almost even split in the party primaries.[3]

Of particular importance to our thesis are the structural changes in the nomination of presidential candidates. These structural changes have been seen as reforms of the process but have encouraged the power of special interests and ideological factions that do not represent the mass of voters. At the same time, special interests have increased tremendously in their capacity to manipulate the system.[4] As Theodore Lowi has indicated, interest groups impact heavily on the electoral process as well as the formulation and implementation of policy.[5] In this they have been aided by the use of political action committees that allow them to direct financing toward individual candidates and to ignore the parties, encouraging candidates in turn to do the same to a degree. The effects of interest groups have been exacerbated by the emergence of the so-called single issue group. These groups are characterized by their fanaticism and by their attachment to non-economic principles. In a political system built on compromise they are a seriously disruptive element.

A major concern about the nomination process has been that it does almost nothing to moderate the demands of special interests. Indeed, it activates these groups and intensifies their pressure on presidential candidates. The result is that coalition building—which involves the moderation of group demands in order to build an electoral majority for the general election and to govern effectively afterwards—is weakened. The kind of strong party leader who three decades ago helped to build coalitions is a rare commodity in today's presidential nominating process.[6] As this type of party leader becomes less influential in the nominating process, the movement toward ideologically less flexible candidates gains in momentum.

In his recent book, *The Citizen's Presidency*, Bruce Buchanan makes a persuasive case for the pragmatic type leader in preference to the more ideological type. The pragmatist, Buchanan observes, "does not merely believe his ideas are right in the manner of an ideologue; he tests them by their consequences."[7] Because of this attentiveness to actual consequences, the pragmatic leader has a greater ability to manage the emotional undercurrents in his or her own thinking. These forces play a larger and less disciplined role in the thought of the ideological leader.[8]

Buchanan concludes that the pragmatic leader is preferable to the ideological leader as a crisis manager. This person has a greater ability to "directly address the system-threatening problems likely to arise in a chaotic world."[9] The pragmatic president can recognize the need to act flexibly to meet crises and to bring together public actors from across the ideological spectrum to work together.

When coalition building was the dominant feature of the presidential nominating process, the two parties hovered close to the political center, where the party leaders believed most of the votes were. Replacement of coalition oriented party leaders as key power brokers in the nominating process by representatives of special interests and ideologically fixated factions of the parties has contributed to polarization of the two major parties. This polarization is creating a void in the political center even though polls continue to indicate that the center is where most Americans position themselves.[10]

In effect the presidential nominating process tends to skew the selection process away from centrist leaders representing the views of the majority of Americans. This discrepancy becomes more serious as the separation of powers between executive and legislature at the national level becomes reinforced by long-term partisan political division that has the Republicans controlling the White House and the Democrats controlling Congress.[11]

Charles Krauthammer has observed that democracies are drawn toward extremes in times of crisis. Yet, he notes, 1988 with its "low unemployment, low inflation, peace abroad, and no acute social crisis at home" was not a time of crisis. Krauthammer contends that the rise of extremes in both parties is a result of changes in the presidential nomination process and in the political process generally. Recent party polarization has been the "result of changes in political procedure rather than of changes or crisis in the underlying conditions of American life."[12]

Krauthammer's analysis is persuasive and, taken in the context of American history, more troubling than perhaps he recognizes. His preliminary observation — that times of crisis encourage the rise of extremes — is especially noteworthy. If the 1990's decade produces an economic, international, social, or political crisis or combination of crises, the resulting upheaval in conjunction with existing nominating procedures could propel the polarization process far beyond what now seems likely.[13] If history is any kind of meaningful guide, the American nation either domestically or internationally will be faced with serious crises over regular intervals. Political scientists from Walter Dean Burnham to Samuel Huntington have argued that periodic crises that have serious political ramifications are a characteristic of American culture.[14] Concluding his recent study of the growth of American government in the twentieth century, Robert Higgs asserts that "in one form or another, great crises will surely come again."[15] Although it is unlikely, the Bush Administration may escape such a crisis, but almost certainly its successor will not. The country has already established a record for peacetime prosperity, and at this writing in 1989 its last major military effort is now sixteen years past.

When Krauthammer's and Buchanan's observations are combined, the outline of an ominous political paradox begins to take shape. That is, crisis conditions tend to engender prophetic-ideological leaders who are emotionally incapable of assessing the realities of a crisis. If a crisis were to unfold within the next decade, the configuration of the nominating process might render the two major parties incapable of nominating pragmatic candidates who could be flexible and creative in their approaches. Changes in the nominating process intended to provide greater participatory democracy have, in fact, increased the power of special interests and ideological factions. This development has decreased the flexibility of the political parties to respond constructively to national crises. Instead of the likelihood that they will produce pragmatic, experienced political leadership at such times, they now constitute structures that will facilitate the campaigns of those who can arouse strong, committed emotional attachments with concomitant ideological and policy rigidity.[16]

A superficial assessment of the nomination process in 1988 might lead to the conclusion that concern over the power of special interests in that process has been greatly overstated. Pat Robertson, the leader of the evangelical faction, did not do as well in the Republican nomination race as many had expected. His campaign floundered early enough for George Bush to unify the Republican party in the process of winning the nomination. Jesse Jackson, the leader of black America, mounted a lengthy campaign that worried coalition builders in the Democratic party until the party convention met in Atlanta. However, at that point, Jackson decided to support the winning candidate, Michael Dukakis, in order to promote party unity. Yet both Robertson and Jackson represent the potential for serious party splits in the future.[17] The personal organizations that Ladd notes must be assembled to win primaries are still largely intact.[18] Both candidates emerged from the 1988 campaign with stronger potential political bases.

A Robertson candidacy raises religious and social issues that can split the Republican party, which remains a promising target for evangelical Christians. Polls indicate that white born-again Christians represent 20 percent of the total electorate and that they have moved overwhelmingly toward the Republican party.[19] Robertson, perhaps in consort with other established leaders such as Senator Jesse Helms, shows every indication of being ready to lead this faction again. When his presidential campaign closed, he had a mailing list with seven million names, the Christian Broadcasting Network, and an army of religious activists who had tasted considerable success in Republican state and local politics.[20] Although his 1988 presidential campaign was short-lived, Robertson has established himself as an important force in Republican presidential politics.

Like Robertson, Jackson emerged from the 1988 presidential campaign with a stronger base in his party. By the end of the campaign, Jackson had achieved virtually complete command of the black vote. In 1984, he received slightly more than half of the black vote in the early primaries, then improved sharply to obtain about 80 percent of the black vote in the later primaries of that year. In the 1988 campaign, he was able to command 90 percent of the black vote on a consistent basis.[21]

Jackson also strengthened his base in the Democratic party in 1988 by increasing his support among white voters. In New York, for example, he doubled his white support from seven percent in 1984 to fifteen percent in 1988.[22] This white support did not come from blue collar Democrats, as many expected, but from better educated white liberals. Jackson seems to have put himself in command of a loyal liberal-left faction in his party that is reminiscent of the staunch McGovernites of 1972. This faction proved to be very potent in the 1988 Democratic caucuses and also in the primaries, especially when more than one white candidate was competing or when turnout was low. The Michigan caucuses, for example, with very low turnout gave the Jackson forces an important lift that carried them into the Atlanta convention.[23]

In the wake of Dukakis's defeat at the hands of George Bush, Jackson seems poised to lead his faction to greater power in 1992. He remains prominent and active in state and local politics, playing an important role, for example, in the 1989 Chicago mayoral election. Within the national party, rules changes which the Jackson forces successfully advocated for adoption in 1988 should strengthen his position in 1992. The first of these reduced the number of superdelegates (uncommitted delegates who are top Democratic office holders) from 645 to 394. The second eliminated the system in Illinois, Pennsylvania, New Jersey, and some small states in which the highest vote getter in a congressional district received all of that district's delegates to the party convention.[24]

These rule changes would have enabled the Jackson forces to make a much stronger showing in 1988. They are expected to strengthen Jackson's support when they are implemented in 1992. Generally speaking, the rules changes represented a defeat for moderate Democrats who wish to diminish the power of special interests in the party and a victory for those led by Jackson who are inclined to believe that such forces are the essence of the Democratic party.

Krauthammer has pointed out the polarizing effect of the increasing power of the ideological factions within the parties. Noting that Robertson and Jackson have become major figures in their parties, he observes, "the really interesting thing about this election [1988] is not about issues or even personalities, but about the rise, in both parties, of the extremes."[25] This polarization naturally extends to party positions on issues. In the area of foreign policy, for example, Jackson's Third World perspective represents the extreme left wing of the Democratic party while Robertson's Armageddon orientation represents the extreme right wing of the Republican party. With these perspectives, these factions have clearly exerted a more extreme, polarizing influence on the foreign policy positions of the two parties.

If the ideological factions continue to gain power within their parties, the center of gravity of the Republican party could move much closer to Robertson's religious right, perhaps augmented by remnants of the more secular New Right movement. The center of gravity in the Democratic party could become dominated by left-wing elements led by Jackson and composed principally of black voters augmented by liberal-left white activists. Such parties would produce different kinds of leaders from those produced by the centrist oriented parties that have been prevalent in American politics throughout most of the post-World War II era.

Polarized parties would tend to produce a prophetic-ideological type of leader in contrast to the pragmatic type favored by centrist political parties. Pat Robertson and Jesse Jackson are clear examples of the former type of leader. Jackson's leadership style is clearly what Buchanan would call ideological. "Politicians ask, 'Will it work?'" declares Jackson. "Prophets ask, 'Is it right?'"[26] The emotional undercurrents in Jackson's thinking are so strong that they give it an absolutist tinge. Speaking to a black audience, he asserted:

> We were sent here by God to save the human race. We have this awesome burden of being prophetic. I'm God's barometer measuring the weight and worth of your soul. Our strongest weapon is that we're right. If you're right, God will fight your battle.[27]

Although the content of Pat Robertson's beliefs is radically different from those of Jackson, the prophetic-ideological style of his thinking is almost identical. The statements of Jackson quoted above are strikingly similar to many made by Robertson over the years to his evangelical constituency.

The American political system is increasingly being characterized by rigidities that limit the influence of the majority of citizens. Reference has already been made to the role partisanship seems to be playing in reinforcing the separation of powers between the executive and legislative branches. No serious student of American politics expects the House of Representatives to be controlled by the Republican party again in this century. David Mayhew has called attention to the "disappearing marginals," those congressional seats where competition still exists.[28] The 1988 election found the number of such districts to have diminished even further. The advantage of incumbent congressman was such that Ladd has called the 1988 congressional elections "the most uncompetitive in U.S. history."[29] Deep conflict between the executive and legislative branches is reflected in the increasing appeal to the Federal courts for the resolution of separation-of-powers issues. The legislative process itself seems incapable of resolving serious issues. Much of the major legislation of the Reagan Administration—the Omnibus Budget Reconciliation Act of 1981, Social Security Reform, the Gramm-Rudman Act—circumvented normal congressional procedures. These rigidities extend even to the electoral process, where, through amendments to the 1965 Voting Rights Act, Congress has enacted specific protections for blacks and Hispanics in the drawing of electoral districts where black or Hispanic officeholders have been elected.[30] By encouraging the influence of special interests and ideological factions, the national nominating process threatens to add another element of inflexibility and remoteness from popular sentiment into the system.

Given the strong possibility of the emergence of crises of some sort within the next decade, the system may have reached a level of rigidity that will necessitate the kind of fundamental change which occasions critical realignments.[31] Pendleton Herring observed many years ago that such a realignment might engender the rise of a third party. In his words: "The rise of a third party to any position of influence would be a portent of serious rigidities in our political system. It would not indicate a movement to be frowned upon but would suggest rather that our party leaders had failed in their task of harmonizing and adjusting the economic and social forces of their communities."[32] If this context is not already in existence, a serious national challenge, either domestically or internationally, could rapidly bring it into being.

We are suggesting that current trends favoring special interests in the national nominating process may in the appropriate circumstances encourage, perhaps force, the emergence of a centrist third party.[33] The inability of the government to resolve a serious crisis could encourage the emergence of leaders urging drastic solutions at either or both ends of the ideological spectrum. The national nominating process at this time seems particularly vulnerable to manipulation by intensely committed and well organized factions. Victory in the nominating process by such forces would leave the political center unrepresented. In these circumstances a third party, unlike many previous third parties, would not be rigidly ideological or oriented toward a single issue. It would derive much of its strength from the fact that it appealed to the center of the political spectrum.

A significant possibility for such a party is represented by the Democratic Leadership Council (DLC), formed in 1985. Although it remains within the Democratic party, the DLC is a political organization avowedly centrist and ideologically independent of those forces pulling the party to the left. By February, 1986, DLC membership had grown to about 110 elected officials, led by influential members of Congress and state governors.[34] Initially, its members have no intention of starting a third party, but the DLC, or an organization like it, could have that potential in the face of a system-threatening political crisis.

Five prominent characteristics of the DLC make it a credible source of strong, pragmatic leadership. First, its leading members and organizational credo are avowedly centrist.[35] Second, its leaders are accomplished coalition builders who wish to downplay the importance of causes in party decisions.[36] Third, its leaders are pragmatic individuals who have important experience in governing. Fourth, these people have established, viable political bases and organizations in their states. Fifth, DLC leaders exercise considerable policy control within Congress or within their states. Should the DLC choose to act independently as a political force, the two major parties would not be able to intimidate its leaders or undercut its organizational support easily. We now move to consideration of the characteristics which a third party that could draw on resources like those of the DLC would have.

What relationship would the new third party have to the two major parties? At its outset the party's primary concern would be the nomination of a strong centrist presidential ticket separate from the Democratic and Republican parties. It should not begin with the overly ambitious goal of displacing the established parties in congressional, state, and local elections. In these arenas, it could follow the strategy of the DLC and remain nominally within one or both of the two major parties. This would help to protect officeholders from effective attacks on their power bases.[37] In its effort at the national level the new party could welcome support from officeholders from both parties.

How should the new third party be constituted? The key unit in the new party should be the party convention. It is here that experienced political leaders would be able to ward off the demands of special interests.

At least one-third of the delegate votes (not necessarily delegates) at the convention should be held by U.S. Senators and state governors. Because they are elected statewide rather than locally, Senators and governors are responsive to the kind of broad constituencies that elect presidents. Their voice in the nomination process should be substantial. One-third of the delegate votes should be held by members of the House of Representatives. Together with U.S. Senators, these delegates would give the presidential candidate a base in Congress that would enable him to govern effectively if elected and limit the kind of partisan divisiveness that now exists.[38]

Finally one-third of the delegate votes should be held by the top legislative leaders of the fifty states. Together with the state governors represented, these delegates would strengthen the party's state and local perspective. They would protect the new party from charges that it was an exclusive "Washington Establishment" party.

What would be some of the disadvantages of the new third party? First, there would a sizeable risk of retaliation against its members from the adherents of key interests. For example, Democratic officeholders who joined the party might lose the support of black voters in their re-election campaigns if these voters perceived the new party as an affront to black leaders such as Jesse Jackson. However, Jackson's success in attaining the Democratic presidential or vice presidential nomination might also pose a serious threat to the power bases of elected Democrats. Faced with this possibility some officeholders might be willing to participate in a new kind of nominating process oriented toward placing avowedly centrist candidates on the presidential ticket.[39]

A second major disadvantage of the new party described above would be that its nominating procedure would not conform to the populist bias of contemporary American politics. According to the populist position, direct democracy is morally and politically superior to representative or mediated democracy. This outlook definitely dominates the presidential nominating processes of the two major parties. These processes now center on direct election of delegates in caucuses and primaries and dilute the mediating role of strong party leaders. In contrast, the convention of the new political party would not employ direct election of delegates but would draw on public officials *who have already been chosen* in general elections. This procedure conforms with the idea of representative or mediated democracy rather than the populist idea of direct democracy.

Although American voters deplore many of the side effects of presidential nominations by direct democracy (e.g., the enormous power of the media and special interests in the process), they do not associate these effects with the idea of direct democracy itself. Therefore, a new party that departs from direct democracy can expect to be criticized as being a "politician's party" instead of a "people's party." In the midst of a national crisis, however, voters could easily be more concerned about the results of the nominating process than the procedures and might vote for an able third party candidate even though he or she was nominated by a new procedure.[40]

What would be some of the major advantages of the new third party? First, candidates for the new party's presidential nomination would be spared the long marathon of primaries and caucuses that must be endured by candidates seeking the nominations

of the two major parties. During this marathon (which includes months, sometimes years, of *pre*-primary and *pre*-caucus campaigning) major party candidates must cope with prolonged and incessant pressures that both demean and compromise them. Among the most prominent of these are
  — demands and ultimatums from special interests,
  — incessant concern about the orientation of the mass media upon which the candidates slavishly depend for communicating with primary and caucus voters,
  — the continuous need to raise funds,
  — highly publicized duels to the death with other candidates in one's own party.
Although the presidential nominating procedure of the new party would not eliminate the pressures and conflicts of nomination politics, it could reduce them to human proportions. A much shorter and more deliberative process featuring Senators, congressmen, governors, and state legislative leaders as unpledged delegates to the convention would serve this purpose.

Using a representative, mediated approach to nominating presidential candidates would also relieve the physical toll exacted by the current process. *The Washington Post*, reporting on Richard Gephardt's campaign for the Democratic presidential nomination, provided a poignant description of a candidate's exhaustion.

> Gephardt's vocal cords are beginning to give out, strained by two years of making eight speeches a day. 'They're just worn down,' he says, noting his new drink of choice is hot water and lemon.[41]

The *Post* report was made in November 1987, *two months before the 1988 Democratic caucuses and primaries even began.* Although Gephardt may have subjected himself to a more grueling campaign than other contenders, his experience with extreme physical wear and tear is a common feature of the nominations marathons.

Because the new party's deliberative approach would avoid the extreme pressure and fatigue of today's nominations marathons, it would have an important third advantage. It would attract experienced and capable candidates who refuse to subject themselves to the existing process. The assertion that these lengthy battles are somehow a test of a candidate's fitness to govern is being met with increasing skepticism by both voters and scholars. Instead of helping to produce able leaders, the heavy pressures of the nominating marathons apparently discouraged many of the nation's ablest leaders from participating in 1988. Noting that such potential front-runners as New York Governor Mario Cuomo, Senator Sam Nunn of Georgia, Senator Bill Bradley of New Jersey, Senator Dale Bumpers of Arkansas, and former Virginia Governor Chuck Robb had all refused to enter the 1988 Democratic nomination contest, *Newsweek* concluded:

> Their absence from the field is still more evidence that the 18 month ordeal of incessant travel, campaign debt, and microscopic scrutiny by press and public alike is an increasingly powerful deterrent to able and experienced politicians.[42]

Although Lowi sees the emergence of a third party as important to the preservation of presidential power,[43] we argue that it could also be essential to maintaining the political center, the real fulcrum of the American nation. If polarization of the two major parties were to accelerate in a time of national crisis, a huge vacuum would be left in the center. The majority of American voters, who classify themselves as "middle-of-the-road" rather than "conservative" or "liberal," would be left adrift. Examining this possibility, Steven E. Schier has suggested that the consequences could be serious for the nation.

> If ideologically extreme process participants choose candidates largely on the grounds of ideological proximity, electoral dysfunctions—alienated voters, lower turnout—will probably result. The quality of opinion representation in nominations processes in this way fundamentally influences the legitimacy of the American electoral system.[44]

If the activists of the two major parties refused to respond to voter discomfort with the ideologies of their presidential nominees, a third party would be a reasonable vehicle for filling the political void. It might also be the only vehicle that could give the nation the option of strong, pragmatic leadership in a time of crisis.

What we have presented here is intended to be suggestive. The scenario for a centrist revolt may seem unlikely after George Bush's decisive victory of 1988. However, there are clear indications that the nominating process will inordinately reflect the strength of the ideological left and right. These forces continue to have the potential to increase their prominence within the two major parties. Our position is that the ingredients for the emergence of a viable centrist third party are available. A serious national crisis could be the catalyst to activate them in the direction that we have suggested. Pragmatic centrists would do well to ponder now their political and organizational options if party polarization trends continue. Ideological flexibility and political moderation have been the foundation stones of the American political process. When the two-party system can no longer assure their strength, other democratic options deserve consideration.

* The authors would like to express their appreciation to Professor Steven A. Peterson for his helpful comments.

Notes

1. See for example: Herbert B. Asher, *Presidential Elections and American Politics* (Fourth edition; Chicago: Dorsey Press, 1988), pp. 328–348; Larry J. Sabato, *The Party's Just Begun* (Glenview, Ill.: Scott, Foresman, 1988), pp. 151–175; Frank J. Sorauf and Paul Allen Beck, *Party Politics in America* (Sixth edition; Glenview, Ill.: Scott, Foresman, 1988), pp. 160–167, 186–190, 488–493; Martin P. Wattenberg, *The Decline of American Political Parties* (Cambridge, Mass.: Harvard University Press, 1986); John Kenneth White, *The New Politics of Old Values* (Hanover, N.H.: University Press of New England, 1988), pp. 84–102.
2. See Everett Carll Ladd, *Where Have All the Voters Gone?* (Second edition; New York: W.W. Norton, 1982), p. 50; Asher, *op. cit.*, p. 331.
3. Ladd, *op. cit.*, p. 62.
4. See Ladd, *op. cit.*, pp. 54, 58–59; Nelson Polsby, *Consequences of Party Reform* (New York: Oxford University Press, 1983), p. 140.
5. Theodore J. Lowi, *The End of Liberalism* (Second edition; New York: W.W. Norton, 1979); Theodore J. Lowi, *The Personal President* (Ithaca, N.Y.: Cornell University Press, 1985).
6. Michael Barone, after a careful survey of the 1988 party caucuses, states that it simply can no

longer be assumed "that there exists a group of party leaders who remain involved in party affairs and dominate the party structure from one election year to the next." See "Let's Make More of the Races Primaries," *Washington Post National Weekly Edition* (April 18–24, 1988), p. 23.

7. Bruce Buchanan, *The Citizen's Presidency* (Washington, D.C.: Congressional Quarterly Press, 1987), p. 67.
8. *Ibid.*, p. 73.
9. *Ibid.*
10. Barry Sussman reports a stable voter preference for the middle of the political spectrum over the years. For example, he reports the results of Gallup polls taken in 1986 and in 1976 as follows: "[in 1986] 28 percent came out right of center, 45 percent in the middle, and 20 percent on the left. Ten years ago . . . the result was virtually the same: 30 percent right, 42 percent center, 18 percent left." In these polls conservatives were described as being "right of center" and liberals as being "left of center." See "What's the Evidence for this Shift to the Right We Hear About?" *Washington Post Weekly Edition* (July 21, 1986), p. 37.
11. See Everett Carll Ladd, "The New Workings of Separation of Powers," *The Christian Science Monitor* (March 3, 1989), p. 19.
12. Charles Krauthammer, "Rise of the Extremes," *Washington Post National Weekly Edition* (March 14–20, 1988), p. 29.
13. Kenneth Dolbeare has described a plausible scenario of political polarization in which the nation could swing toward a right–wing populism focused on racial tensions and national security fears or to a left–wing populism drawing on employment and economic democracy issues. If social and moral issues, such as crime and abortion, are added to the right–wing ideological configuration, Dolbeare's political script closely parallels that of Krauthammer. See *Democracy at Risk* (Revised edition; Chatham, N.J.: Chatham House Publishers, 1986), pp. 210, 217–224.
14. Samuel P. Huntington, *American Politics* (Cambridge, Mass.: Harvard University Press, 1981); Walter Dean Burnham, *Critical Elections and the Mainsprings of American Politics* (New York: W.W. Norton, 1970).
15. Robert Higgs, *Crisis and Leviathan* (New York: Oxford University Press, 1987), p. 262.
16. See Ladd, *Where Have*, pp. 50, 54, 58.
17. William Schneider concludes: "These days religion is to the Republican Party as race is to the Democratic Party: whenever the issue comes up, it tears the party apart." See "The Political Legacy of the Reagan Years," in Sidney Blumenthal and Thomas Edsall (eds.), *The Reagan Legacy* (New York: Pantheon Books, 1988), p. 12.
18. See Ladd, *Where Have*, pp. 56–57.
19. Thomas Edsall, "Evangelical Christian Candidates Are Showing Their Strength," *Washington Post National Weekly Edition* (June 9, 1986), p. 12.
20. Jeffery Sheler, "The Resurrection of Pat Robertson?" *U.S. News and World Report* (April 18, 1988), p. 43; Fred Barnes, "Robertson Ascendent," *Louisville Courier Journal* (November 23, 1987).
21. Richard Morin, "Jackson's White Support Is the 'Peugeot Proletariat,'" *Washington Post National Weekly Edition* (May 2–8, 1988), p. 37.
22. *Ibid.*
23. In the Michigan Democratic caucuses Jackson carried 53% of the vote with less than 115,000 votes out of a total statewide voting population of 6.8 million. Rhodes Cook, "Lunch-Bucket Voters the Key in Coming Democratic Events," *Congressional Quarterly Weekly Report* (April 2, 1988), p. 855.
24. "Harmony's Price," *Washington Post National Weekly Edition* (July 4–10, 1988), p. 27.
25. Krauthammer, *op. cit.*, p. 29.
26. Walt Harrington, "The Puzzle Named Jesse Jackson," *Washington Post National Weekly Edition* (March 9, 1987), p. 8.
27. *Ibid.*
28. David R. Mayhew, "Congressional Elections: The Case of the Vanishing Marginals," *Polity* (Spring 1974), pp. 295–317.

29. Everett Carll Ladd, *The American Polity* (Third Edition; New York: W.W. Norton, 1989), p. 451.
30. See Abigail M. Thernstrom, *Whose Votes Count?* (Cambridge, Mass.: Harvard University Press, 1987).
31. See Burnham, *op. cit.*, pp. 181–182.
32. Pendleton Herring, *The Politics of Democracy* (New York: Rinehart and Company, Inc., 1940), p. 179.
33. See James L. Sundquist, *Dynamics of the Party System* (Revised edition; Washington, D.C.: The Brookings Institution, 1983), pp. 28–30.
34. Richard Cohen, "Democratic Leadership Council Sees Party Void and Is Ready to Fill It," *National Journal* (February 1, 1986), p. 267.
35. Senator Sam Nunn exemplifies the avowedly centrist views of leading DLC members. "Many of us have concluded," he has said, "that the national Democratic Party has to have leadership . . . that clearly is identified in the middle, if it's got a chance of becoming a party that can compete for the presidency." See Fred Barnes, "Flying Nunn," *The New Republic* (April 28, 1986), p. 17.
36. Senator Chuck Robb has expressed the outlook of DLC leaders regarding special interests. In his view, "the perception that the Democratic party is beholden to any group is very harmful to our chances of winning the presidency." Robb went on to assert that DLC members "don't want to do business in the old way of submitting to each organization's litmus test." See Richard Cohen, *op. cit.*, p. 268.
37. Lowi, *Personal President*, p. 200, notes that one effective way for a third party to survive at the state and local levels is to cross endorse candidates.
38. Coming at the issue from a somewhat different perspective, Lowi also believes that a third party would strengthen the presidency. *Ibid.*, pp. 203–205.
39. The formation of the DLC *within* the Democratic party in 1985 was motivated, to a large extent, by a concern among Democratic officeholders that their power bases were being weakened by the leftward drift of the national party. "Most of us had been running away from the Democratic Party for years," said Senator Lawton Chiles of Florida. "But we were beginning to see you couldn't enjoy the luxury of that anymore." In the event of a Jackson presidential or vice presidential nomination, these concerns might intensify to the point that DLC members would see their survival linked to a new presidential party outside the national Democratic party. See Fred Barnes, *op. cit.*, p. 18.
40. According to a poll reported by R.W. Apple of *The New York Times News Service*, Senator Lloyd Bentsen of Texas was more respected by voters than either George Bush or Michael Dukakis. It is significant that, as a known centrist, Bentsen could not win the presidential nomination. His popularity in 1988 might indicate, however, that a new centrist party could do very well with an experienced leader like Bentsen, even if that candidate was not a product of primary and caucus victories. See R.W. Apple, "Running on Empty," *Louisville Courier Journal* (October 11, 1988).
41. Paul Taylor, "Gephardt Has Put a Lot of Eggs in His Iowa Basket," *Washington Post National Weekly Edition* (November 23, 1987).
42. Eleanor Clift, "So Why Is the A Team Sitting on the Bench?" *Newsweek* (April 27, 1987), p. 33.
43. See Lowi, *Personal President*, pp. 195–208.
44. Steven E. Schier, "The Underexplored Nomination Process," in Ronald B. Rapoport, Alan I. Abramovitz, John McGlennon (eds.), *The Life of the Party* (Lexington, Ky.: University Press of Kentucky, 1986), p. 22.

Peak Presidential Approval from Franklin Roosevelt to Ronald Reagan

DAVID C. NICE
Associate Professor of Political Science
Washington State University

Abstract

The highest Gallup approval ratings for U.S. presidents from Franklin Roosevelt to Ronald Reagan are positively associated with the proportion of the public identifying with the president's party and negatively related to the proportion of independents in the population. Voter turnout, war, and the unemployment rate during the president's first year are unrelated to peak approval.

Introduction

Evaluations of presidents have been a major point of interest to political scientists, historians, pollsters, and journalists for many years. Concern for public evaluations of presidents grows in part from the principle that democratic government rests on the consent of the citizens. Their assessments of presidential performance are, consequently, intrinsically important. In addition, evaluations may shape presidential performance; an unpopular president may have greater difficulty gaining the cooperation of Congress.[1] Past evaluations also establish ideals and standards that subsequent presidents feel pressured to meet.[2] Finally, approval of presidents may reflect the movement of broader political currents and events. The following analysis will explore maximum public approval of presidents from Franklin Roosevelt to Ronald Reagan.

Research on evaluations of presidents has pursued two different strategies. One approach utilizes contemporary evaluations of presidents (that is, evaluations of a particular president's performance at the time) and then examines changes in those evaluations over time[3] or variations across respondents.[4] The other approach involves retrospective assessments of a number of presidents, usually all of them, and seeks to compare their evaluations. These studies typically produce rankings of presidents (from greatest to worst or most effective to least effective) and sometimes analyze influences on the evaluations.[5]

The present study draws from both of these strategies. The highest Gallup Poll approval rating for each president gives a contemporary evaluation of presidential performance. By comparing those maximum values across presidents, however, we can explore the dynamics of peak approval, for some presidents have clearly been more successful at gaining broad approval than have others. Harry Truman, for example, achieved an 87 percent approval rating, while Ronald Reagan's highest

Gallup approval rating was 68 per cent. However, in his last months in office Truman received the lowest approval rating, 23 per cent, lower than Nixon's final 24 per cent.

Because peak approval ratings typically occur early in a president's term,[6] before the incumbent has had a realistic opportunity to influence events very much, those ratings are an indicator of diffuse support — feelings of loyalty and approval that are not a function of satisfaction with individual governmental actions.[7] Diffuse support can help to foster compliance with decisions that are unpopular among some segments of the public and can help the political system endure when it is unable to satisfy specific demands.[8]

Diffuse support can also be useful to presidents in other ways. Broad public support can be used by a president to promote proposals that may or may not be individually popular with the public. The tendency for presidents to concentrate major new legislative requests in the first year of their terms,[9] when their approval ratings are highest, reflects an effort to make use of that early popularity. Peak approval, as an indicator of diffuse support, has clearly varied among recent presidents. Previous research suggests a number of possible explanations for the variations in peak approval.

Influences on Maximum Approval

Most citizens perceive the political world through partisan eyes. Party loyalties shape perceptions of candidates, officials, and issues, both by filtering political information and by serving as a substitute for information.[10] Party loyalties are not immutable, however; policy beliefs and other short-term forces can erode existing party loyalties and create new ones, especially among the young.[11] Research on contemporary evaluations of presidents indicates that members of a president's party are considerably more likely to approve of his performance than are members of the opposition party.[12] We would expect presidents who have a larger base of partisan loyalists to have higher peak approval ratings.

Partisan considerations may shape peak presidential approval in an indirect fashion as well. According to Easton:

> "[I]t is likely that whenever large aggregates of persons are involved, personal legitimizing occurs through lower echelon leaders, permeating down to the smallest groups in the political system."[13]

In a political party with more identifiers, the efforts of party workers, campaign activists, and presidential staffers to generate broad support for the new president are likely to find a more receptive audience.

Partisan forces may also affect peak approval in other ways. The Democratic party has been described as an inclusive coalition — that is, a coalition that includes people looking to government for assistance. The Republican Party has been depicted as an exclusive coalition, which excludes people seeking government benefits.[14] To the degree that Democratic presidents are more inclined to distribute governments benefits, they may have an advantage in cultivating public support in most years. Election studies from 1952 through 1984 show a consistent tendency for people to see the Democrats as more helpful to groups to which the respondents belonged or felt favorably,[15] a pattern consistent with the inclusive coalition perspective.

One other partisan influence on maximum presidential approval is likely to be the proportion of independents in the general public. Studies of contemporary evaluations of presidents indicate that independents are less supportive of the president than are members of the president's own party but more supportive than members of the opposition party.[16] The intermediate position of independents is consistent with the view that political independence often reflects neutrality toward the parties (and their leader) rather than outright hostility.[17]

The proportion of independents may also help to track the dynamics of the realignment cycle. A realignment creates a firm base of partisan loyalties in the electorate and a party in government which is organized to deal with the realigning issue. The prospects for successful presidential activity are, consequently, enhanced. As time passes, however, new issues arise and cut across the existing party cleavage, a development that reduces party unity in government. The voters whose strong party loyalties were forged by the realignment are gradually replaced by new generations of voters whose party loyalties are weaker. At both elite and mass levels, the parties have increasing difficulty mobilizing a base of support for concerted action.[18] The weakening of the parties, as indicated by the growth of political independence, should lead to lower peak approval ratings. Analysis of retrospective presidential evaluations supports this possibility; the presidents regarded as greatest generally served during or shortly after realignments.[19]

In a related vein, higher voter turnout for a president's first election may lead to higher maximum approval. Some analysts contend that low voter turnout reflects a failure of the political system to offer voters a meaningful choice.[20] Available evidence indicates that people with stronger party loyalties, more concern over the election outcome, and greater psychological involvement in politics are more likely to vote.[21] A president may have a difficult time winning the approval of people who regard the parties and their leaders as irrelevant, regarded the current president's selection as a matter of negligible concern, and have little or no interest in politics.

Peak presidential approval may also be shaped by the presence of military conflict, although the nature of the relationship is difficult to predict. On one hand, studies of contemporary presidential approval have found that war tends to reduce public approval of presidents.[22] However, because peak presidential approval typically occurs early in a president's term,[23] the impact of war for a new president may provide a short-term boost in public approval as the public rallies around the new leader, if only temporarily.[24] In this view, war may lead to higher peak approval, a finding consistent with retrospective evaluations: the most highly rated presidents tend to be war presidents.[25]

A final potential influence on peak approval is the unemployment rate during a president's first year. Studies of presidential popularity have generally found that a faltering economy leads to a loss of public support.[26] Of course, a new president may try to shift blame for a weak economy to his predecessor, but prosperity eliminates the need for any concerns regarding blame.

FIGURE 1

Maximum Gallup Approval Ratings from Franklin Roosevelt to Ronald Reagan

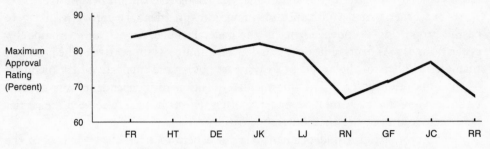

Analysis

As Figure 1 indicates, maximum presidential approval has generally declined during the period covered by this analysis. Three of the first four presidents achieved peak approval ratings of over eighty percent, and the one exception came very close. By contrast, all four of the most recent presidents have maximum approval ratings below 76 per cent. A similar downward trend has been observed for average annual approval ratings.[27]

This pattern is far from consistent, however. Of the eight presidential successions covered by this analysis, four presidents have had higher peak approval ratings than their predecessors. Accounting for the variations in a systematic way is the next step in the analysis.

The zero-order relationships between maximum presidential approval and the independent variables included in the analysis are generally consistent with the more partisan interpretations of presidential support (see Table 1). Presidential approval tends to be higher when a president has a larger base of partisan loyalists, which in turn indicates that Democratic presidents tend to draw higher peak approval ratings. An even more pronounced tendency, however, is the close association between maximum approval and the relative size of the independent group. The growth of political independence closely tracks the decline of peak presidential approval.

TABLE 1

Correlates of Maximum Presidential Approval

Percentage of Population Identifying with President's Party[a]	.76*
President's Party[b]	.77*
Percentage Independent[c]	− .84*
Turnout[d]	.16
War[e]	.20
Unemployment Rate[f]	.24

* Significant at the .01 level.
[a] At beginning of president's first term, as measured by Gallup polls.
[b] 1 = Democrat, 0 = Republican
[c] At beginning of president's first term, as measured by Gallup polls.
[d] For president's first election. Turnout in 1944 was used for Truman.
[e] Existence of war = 1; 0 = otherwise.
[f] Percentage unemployment during president's first year of office.

TABLE 2
Regression Analysis of Peak Presidential Approval

	b	Standard Error	beta	t
Percentage Independent	− .88	.35	− .60	− 2.49**
Percentage of Public Identifying with President's Party	.24	.16	.38	1.55*
Constant	89.5	13.4		6.65**
R² = .79		Durbin Watson D = 1.58		

** Significant at the .05 level, one-tailed test.
* Significant at the .10 level, one-tailed test.

By contrast, voter turnout, war, and the unemployment rate are not substantially related to peak approval. A higher mobilization of voters does not produce a more solid base of support, nor does the existence of peace or prosperity, although the latter two characteristics obviously have implications for where the president's approval rating goes from the peak.

Regression analysis of peak presidential approval indicates that partisan forces can account for most of the decline in peak presidential approval (see Table 2). The analysis indicates that a ten percentage point increase in the ranks of political independents is associated with a decline of peak presidential approval of nearly nine percentage points. As a result, the 14 percentage point growth in political independents during the period covered by this analysis accounts for just over 12 percentage points of the decline in peak approval. In addition, a ten percentage point decline in the proportion of the public identifying with the president's party is associated with a decline in peak approval of approximately two and a half percentage points. Overall the model is able to account for nearly 80% of the variation in peak presidential approval.[28]

As a safeguard against the possibility that party loyalties are a reaction to current political events,[29] the model was re-estimated using party identification and political independence data from the year before the president took office (due to data limitations, 1937 data was used for Roosevelt and 1944 for Truman). In addition, the unemployment rate for the year before the president took office and the presence of war during the previous president's term were included in order to assess the possibility that conditions preceding a presidential inauguration shape maximum presidential approval.

The results of the analysis are broadly similar to the results in Table 2, with one exception (see Table 3). Peak approval is higher among presidents who had proportionally more party loyalists in the year before they took office and among presidents who faced fewer independents in the year before being inaugurated. War, unemployment, and voter turnout have no noticeable influence, either at the zero-order level or once partisan factors are taken into account.

A noticeable difference, however, between the findings produced by partisan characteristics measured in the president's first year and measured in the year before involves the relative influence of the two partisan characteristics. When party identification and independence are measured the year before the president took office, the

TABLE 3

Regression Analysis of Peak Presidential Approval:
Prior-Year Effects

	b	Standard Error	beta	t
Percentage of Public Identifying with President's Party[a]	.42	.14	.62	2.93**
Percentage Independent[a]	−.47	.25	−.40	−1.89*
Constant	73.0	9.86		7.40**
R^2 = .79		Durbin Watson D = 1.69		

** Significant at the .05 level, one-tailed test.
* Significant at the .10 level, one-tailed test.
[a] Measured the year before the president took office, excepting Roosevelt (1937) and Truman (1944).

proportion of the public identifying with the president's party is more strongly related to peak approval than is the proportion of independents.[30] When party loyalties are measured during the president's first year, the opposite tendency occurs. A possible explanation for the divergent patterns may lie in the tendency for lopsided presidential elections to produce a temporary bulge in the proportion of the public identifying with the president's party. If deeply rooted party attachments are the key influence on peak approval, the bulge may constitute measurement error, which is avoided by using the prior-year measure.

Discussion

The preceding analysis reinforces Stimson's emphasis on the climate of expectations which develops when a president is first elected to office.[31] Peak presidential approval is a reflection of those early expectations, which appear to be largely independent of factors such as the economy or war. In a sense that finding indicates a degree of public rationality, for a newly elected president has very little ability to bring a war to an immediate halt or instantly revive a stalled economy.

As public attachments to the parties have weakened in recent decades,[32] and as public cynicism regarding government has risen,[33] the climate of expectations for new presidents has changed. The presidential candidates, as heads of their respective party tickets, have come to be judged more critically.[34] The newly elected president discovers that the public is more reluctant to grant its approval.

That early expression of approval is to a large degree an expression of faith, for the earliest approval ratings are generally taken before a president has any realistic opportunity to affect the course of the nation very substantially. Along with the erosion of party loyalties and confidence in many institutions has come an eroding of that faith. In light of the fact that presidential approval tends to decline over time,[35] our more recent presidents have begun their terms with a smaller reserve of approval. They have a smaller cushion to absorb later shocks and disappointments.

Notes

1. George Edwards, *Presidential Influence in Congress* (San Francisco: Freeman, 1980), Chapter 4.
2. On the notion of expectations, see Thomas Cronin, *The State of the Presidency*, 2nd ed. (Boston: Little, Brown, 1980), Chapter 3.
3. For examples, see John Mueller, "Presidential Popularity from Truman to Johnson," *American Political Science Review*, 64 (March 1970), 18–34; Charles Ostrom and Dennis Simon, "Promise and Performance: A Dynamic Model of Presidential Popularity," *American Political Science Review*, 79 (June, 1985), 334–358; Lyn Ragsdale, "Presidential Speechmaking and the Public Audience: Individual Presidents and Group Attitudes," *Journal of Politics*, 49 (August 1987), 704–736; James Stimson, "Public Support for American Presidents: A Cyclical Model," *Public Opinion Quarterly*, 40 (Spring, 1976), 1–21.
4. For example, George Edwards, *The Public Presidency* (New York: St. Martin's, 1983).
5. See Gary Maranell and Richard Dodder, "Political Orientation and the Evaluation of Presidential Prestige: A Study of American Histories," *Social Science Quarterly* 51 (Summer, 1970), 415–421; Robert Murray and Tim Blessing, "The Presidential Performance Study: A Progress Report," *Journal of American History*, 70 (December, 1983), 535–555; David Nice, "The Influence of War and Party System Aging on the Ranking of Presidents," *Western Political Quarterly*, 37 (Fall, 1984), 443–455; David Nice, "In Retreat from Excellence: The Single Six-Year Presidential Term," *Congress and the Presidency*, 13 (Autumn, 1986), 209–220; Dean Simonton, *Why Presidents Succeed* (New Haven: Yale, 1987).
6. Mueller, 26–27; Stimson.
7. See David Easton, *A Framework for Political Analysis* (Chicago: University of Chicago, 1979), pp. 124–125; David Easton, *A Systems Analysis of Political Life* (Chicago: University of Chicago, 1979), pp. 273, 302–303.
8. Easton, *A Framework* . . ., 125–126; Easton, *A Systems* . . ., 270–273.
9. Paul Light, "Presidents as Domestic Policymakers," in Thomas Cronin, ed., *Rethinking the Presidency* (Boston: Little, Brown, 1982), 351–370.
10. Herbert Asher, *Presidential Elections and American Politics*, 4th Ed. (Chicago: Dorsey, 1988), 61, 67; Angus Campbell, Philip Converse, Warren Miller, and Donald Stokes, *The American Voter* (abridged), (New York: Wiley, 1964), 72–83.
11. Asher, 72–73; Charles Franklin and John Jackson, "The Dynamics of Party Identification," *American Political Science Review*, 77 (December 1983), 966–968.
12. Edwards, *The Public*, 212–214; Ragsdale, 707.
13. Easton, *A Systems* . . . , 305.
14. See David Mayhew, *Party Loyalty Among Congressmen* (Cambridge: Harvard, 1966), 147–168.
15. William Flanigan and Nancy Zingale, *Political Behavior of the American Electorate*, 6th ed. (Boston: Allyn and Bacon, 1987), 142–143.
16. Edwards, *The Public* . . ., 213–214; Ragsdale, 707, 715.
17. See Martin Wattenberg, "The Decline of Political Partisanship in the United States: Negativity or Neutrality?", *American Political Science Review* 75 (December 1981), 941–950.
18. See Paul Beck, "A Socialization Theory of Partisan Realignment," in Richard Niemi and Herbert Weisberg, eds., *Controversies in American Voting Behavior* (San Francisco: Freeman, 1976), 396–411; David Brady and Joseph Stewart, "Congressional Party Realignment and Transformations of Public Policy in Three Realignment Eras," *American Journal of Political Science* 26 (May 1982), 333–360; Jerome Clubb, William Flanigan and Nancy Zingale, *Partisan Realignment* (Beverly Hills: Sage, 1980), 30–37, 162–165; James Sundquist, *Dynamics of the Party System* (Washington, D.C.: Brookings, 1973).
19. Nice, "The Influence . . . ," 449–452.
20. Walter Burnham, "The Changing Shape of the American Political Universe," *American Political Science Review*, 59 (March 1965), 7–28.
21. Campbell, Converse, Miller, and Stokes, 53–57; Margaret Conway, *Political Participation in the*

United States (Washington, D.C.: CQ Press, 1985), 44–46, 130–138; Sidney Verba and Norman Nie, *Participation in America* (New York: Harper and Row, 1972), 83–93.

22. See Mueller, 23–24; Ostrom and Simon, 348–350.
23. Mueller, 20–21, 26–27; Stimson, 1976.
24. Mueller, 21, 26–27; Ostrom and Simon, 348–350.
25. Thomas Bailey, *Presidential Greatness* (New York: Appleton-Century, 1966), 98–100; Nice, "The Influence," 450–452.
26. Henry Kenski, "The Impact of Economic Conditions on Presidential Popularity," *Journal of Politics* 39 (August 1977), 764–777; Mueller, 26–27; Ostrom and Simon, 348–350.
27. Edwards, *The Public* . . .
28. A model based on the percentage of independents and a dummy variable for the president's party has very slightly more predictive power (R^2 = .81) but has two deficiencies relative to the model in Table 2. First, the president's party variable is theoretically ambiguous, particularly when the percentage of the public identifying with the president's party is not part of the model. Second, the dummy variable model may have some autocorrelation problems (Durbin-Watson D = 1.34). Once the proportion of the public identifying with the president's party is taken into account, the party of the president has no discernible influence on peak approval, nor do turnout, war, or unemployment. The correlation between the percentage independent and the percentage of the public identifying with the president's party is − .63. Stepwise regression analysis was used to produce the models in Tables 2 and 3.
29. See Franklin and Jackson, 957–973.
30. The correlation between the percentage independent and the percentage of the public identifying with the president's party the year before he took office is − .45.
31. Stimson, 9–10.
32. See Norman Nie, Sidney Verba, and John Petrocik, *The Changing American Voter* (Cambridge: Harvard, 1976), Chapter 4; Wattenberg, 941–950.
33. Paul Abramson, *Political Attitudes in America* (San Francisco: Freeman, 1983), Chapter 13; Arthur Miller, "Political Issues and Trust in Government: 1964–1970," *American Political Science Review* 68 (December 1974), 951–972.
34. For evidence of that trend since 1952, see Flanigan and Zingale, 123; Steven Rosenstone, Roy Behr, and Edward Lazarus, *Third Parties in America* (Princeton, NJ: Princeton, 1984), 225.
35. Mueller, 26–27; Stimson, 1–21.

Selected Fiscal and Economic Effects on Presidential Elections*

ALFRED G. CUZÁN
Associate Professor of Political Science
The University of West Florida

CHARLES M. BUNDRICK
Professor and Director
Institute for Statistical and Mathematical Modeling
The University of West Florida

Abstract

In a previous article published in Presidential Studies Quarterly, *the effects of fiscal expansion and fiscal cut-back on presidential elections were examined. This article carries the analysis a step further, controlling for certain economic effects. When inflation and economic growth are taken into account, fiscal policy is the single best predictor of whether the incumbent party elects its candidate to the White House. However, inflation/deflation is the best predictor of the share of the popular vote going to the incumbent party.*

Introduction

An article published in *Presidential Studies Quarterly* several years ago presented a fiscal model of presidential elections, one "in which the re-election of presidential incumbents is a negative function of increases and accelerations in federal expenditures relative to Gross National Product" (Cuzán and Heggen, 1984: 98). This fiscal effect on presidential elections was explained with an economic analogy. Fiscal expansion was hypothesized to be equivalent to an increase in the "price" of government, prompting voters-cum-consumers to cast ballots for the opposition party candidate. On the other hand, a policy of fiscal restraint finds favor with voters, leading to reelection, much as lowering the price of most goods increases sales.

An analysis of presidential elections held between 1880 and 1980 was supportive of this view: in 21 of 26 elections, fiscal expansion was followed by defeat of the incumbent party's presidential candidate and fiscal cut-back by reelection. One of the exceptions is worth noting: in 1944 an unprecedented fiscal expansion, necessitated by World War II, did not prevent President Roosevelt's reelection to a fourth term. This exception is accounted for in the model, which allows for the "displacement" effect of war (on displacement, see Peacock and Wiseman, 1961).

TABLE 1
Fiscal, Economic, and Political Variables Used to
Analyze Presidential Elections, 1892–1988

Variable	Definition
F	$F = \dfrac{\text{Federal expenditures}}{\text{GNP}}$
F'	$F' = \dfrac{F_t - F_{t-1}}{F_{t-1}} \times 100 = \dfrac{dF}{dt}$ as a percent, where t is an election year and t−1 is a previous election year
F''	$F'' = F'_t - F'_{t-1}$
FISCAL	FISCAL = +1 if either F' or F'' or both are greater than 2 percent and neither is smaller than −2 percent
	FISCAL = −1 if either F' or F'' or both are smaller than −2 percent
	FISCAL = 0 if F' and F'' fall between −2 and +2 (no such case exists)
GROWTH	Real per capita economic growth in election year
PRICES	Absolute change in the level of prices, measured as the percent change in the GNP deflator between election year and previous year regardless of whether the change is positive or negative. This means that deflation and inflation are equally costly politically
VOTE	Percent of the popular vote won by the candidate of the party occupying the White House, i.e., the incumbent party
ELECT	Election outcome for incumbent party, coded +1 (reelection) or −1 (defeat)
PRESIDENT	Incumbent president is (+1) or is not (0) seeking reelection

A limitation of the original paper, acknowledged by the authors, is that non-fiscal variables known to influence election outcomes were left out. (For a comprehensive list of variables, see Lichtman and Killis-Borok, 1981.) In particular, economic conditions were ignored, even though it has been well-established that economic growth and inflation are reliable predictors of presidential election outcomes, with the former contributing to reelection and the latter to defeat of the incumbents. A recent demonstration is made by Fair (1988).

The purpose of this paper is to evaluate statistically the relative effects of economic and fiscal influences on presidential elections. When economic conditions are taken into account, does fiscal policy still matter? If so, what is its relative import? That is, when both economic and fiscal policy variables are included in a multiple regression model, does fiscal policy significantly affect election outcomes?

Data, Methodology, and Specification

Table 1 describes the nine variables used in the analysis. The data, displayed in the Appendix, cover 25 presidential elections held between 1892 (the earliest year for which complete data are available) and 1988.

The variable definitions are self-explanatory except in the case of FISCAL. This variable is constructed from three others, F, F' and F''. F is the ratio of federal expenditures to Gross National Product, which in 1988 stood at 21.7. Note that F is a measure of *relative*, not total spending. Government expenditures may increase absolutely without raising F, provided the added spending does not outstrip the growth in GNP. For the remainder of this paper, the words "spending" and "expenditures" are used in this relative sense.

The percent change in F between election years is F', which indicates whether spending has increased or decreased during a presidential term. In 1984, F' amounted to 5 percent and in 1988 to − 4 percent. Thus, Reagan's first term saw an increase in spending but in his second term expenditures fell.

The third fiscal variable is F'', the arithmetic change in F' between election years. It shows whether fiscal expansion is accelerating or decelerating. For example, during the first and second of FDR's administrations spending grew, but at a slower rate than during the previous presidential term, yielding a negative value in F'' in 1936 and 1940 (− 177 and − 15, respectively). On the other hand, in FDR's third term, which encompassed most of the years the U.S. fought in World War II, F shot up to an unprecedented 44.3 percent in 1944, for an F' of 281 percent and an F'' of 276 (281 − 5 = 276). In other words, while spending increased in each of FDR's terms, it did so at a decelerating rate in the first two terms, but at an accelerating rate in the third.

Following the original model, the ensuing combinations of F' and F'' define fiscal policy:

An *expansionary* fiscal policy is one in which F' or F'' is positive and neither is negative. When both variables are positive, F is growing, and at an accelerated rate. This represents a clear case of fiscal expansion, such as FDR's third term. If F' is positive and F'' is zero, spending is rising but at the same rate as in the previous administration. This, too, represents an expansionary fiscal policy. A third possibility is less straightforward: if F' is zero and F'' is positive, it indicates that whereas in the previous administration there was a cut in the ratio of expenditures to GNP, in the current administration the ratio remained constant. Having failed to cut spending, the current administration has reversed fiscal course, and it therefore is classified as "expansionary." This interpretation is open to challenge. Fortunately, the question is purely theoretical, since none of the cases falls in this category. We can, therefore, sidestep the theoretical thicket this possibility raises and take up the cut-back cases.

Fiscal policy is said to be *cut-back* when either F' or F'' is negative. If both F' and F'' are negative, then spending is falling at an accelerating rate — a clear case of fiscal cut-back, such as occurred during Eisenhower's first term. The remaining two possibilities involve what can be called *deceleration*: If F' is zero and F'' is negative, it means that whereas the previous administration had presided over an increase in expenditures, F has remained constant in the current administration. This happened in Nixon's first term. If F' is positive and F'' is negative, it means that while spending has gone up, the increase was at a smaller rate than in the previous administration as in FDR's first and second terms. In both cases, although spending has not decreased, fiscal policy is said to be "cut-back" because, compared to the preceding presidential term, expenditures either have not been allowed to increase or have been permitted to grow at a slower rate. An increase in spending, if it is smaller than that which occurred in the previous term, amounts to fiscal relief. The deciding factor is the sign of F''.

TABLE 2

Pearson Correlation Coefficients: Bivariate Relations between Electoral Outcomes and Fiscal, Economic, and Political Factors, 1892–1988

	FISCAL	GROWTH	PRICES	PRESIDENT
	(a) 1944 Election Included (N = 25)			
ELECT	−0.59***	0.31*	−0.36**	0.32*
VOTE	−0.36**	0.33*	−0.53***	0.18
	(b) 1944 election excluded (N = 24)			
ELECT	−0.66***	0.29	−0.35**	0.30
VOTE	−0.38**	0.32*	−0.53***	0.17

* Significant at .15 level.
** Significant at .10 level.
*** Significant at .01 level.
NOTE: A correlation coefficient is a number between −1 and +1 that measures the degree of linear relationship between two variables.

A final combination of F′ and F″ is possible: if both are zero (defined as either variable taking a value between −2 and +2), this represents a steady-state policy, one in which spending has remained constant for two consecutive terms. Theoretically, it is not clear what electoral outcome one should expect for the second of the two administrations. It would appear to depend on whether the ratio of spending was at or above the equilibrium point (see Cuzán and Heggen, 1984, 1985). Since the data do not include a single case of a steady-state policy, we can evade the theoretical problem this possibility presents.

The next step is to specify a statistical model to evaluate the relative effects of selected fiscal and economic variables on presidential elections. A multiple-regression equation accomplishes this purpose: it measures the concurrent effects of *several* variables (in this case fiscal and economic) on *one* variable (in this case election outcome). The following equation identifies the model to be tested:

$$\text{ELECT (or VOTE)} = a_0 + b_1 \text{ FISCAL} + b_2 \text{ GROWTH} + b_3 \text{ PRICES} + b_4 \text{ PRESIDENT} + e$$

where the variables are as defined in Table 1, a_0 is a constant term (intercept); b_1, b_2, . . . , b_4 are regression parameters; and e is a term which allows for random error.

Note that the model includes a dummy variable, PRESIDENT, which takes the value of +1 if the incumbent president is running for reelection and 0 if he is not. Fair (1988) found this variable to be of statistical significance in elections between 1916 and 1984. We shall see whether its influence extends over the entire 1892–1988 period.

Results

Table 2 presents the pairwise correlations between electoral outcomes and the exogenous predictors. Two sets of correlation coefficients are shown, one including and one excluding data for 1944, when an extraordinary fiscal expansion occurred because the U.S. was fighting in World War II. This was clearly a circumstance which obviates the normal relation between fiscal policy and election. Voters understandably discount fiscal expansion at the ballot box under such an emergency.

The first thing to notice in Table 2 is that, although not all the coefficients reach the level of statistical significance, in every case the direction of the relationship is as expected. Fiscal expansion and absolute changes in the level of prices are both associated with incumbent defeat. On the other hand, economic growth has a positive effect on incumbent electoral performance, and when the president is running for reelection the incumbent party does better than when the ticket is headed by someone other than the president.

Two sets of coefficients stand out: those of FISCAL with ELECT and VOTE with PRICES. The strongest coefficients are those of FISCAL with ELECT: The single best predictor of whether the incumbent party retains the White House for another term is fiscal policy, with fiscal expansion usually resulting in defeat and fiscal cut-back in reelection. As expected, the relation is stronger when 1944 is excluded. On the other hand, the single best predictor of incumbent vote is PRICES, the absolute percent change in the GNP deflator between election year and the previous year, with inflation and deflation both tending to cost the incumbent votes. Unlike FISCAL, there is practically no effect on the coefficients attributable to World War II.

The third best predictor of election outcome is economic GROWTH, whose effect is about the same on ELECT and VOTE, and which is virtually unaffected by World War II. Last in line is PRESIDENT: when the president himself is running, incumbents are more likely to be reelected; however, the presence of the president on the ticket has only a small effect on VOTE, and it is not statistically significant.

While these results are interesting, it remains to be seen when economic factors are controlled for statistically whether fiscal policy still has an effect on election outcome. A straightforward method for testing this hypothesis is step-wise regression analysis. This procedure selects from the predictor variables those that have an influence on the dependent variable, ranking them on the basis of the strength of this influence. The procedure works in steps. In step one, the single best predictor of the dependent variable is brought into the model. In step two, the second best predictor is added to the model based on the strength of its influence independent of that of the first predictor in the model. This model is the best two-variable combination for predicting values of the dependent variable. The procedure continues with additional steps until none of the remaining predictors meets the minimal level of statistical significance for entry into the model (usually set at 0.15).

Table 3 displays the results of step-wise regression analysis applied to the data. It shows that the single best predictor of VOTE is PRICES, while the single best predictor of ELECT is FISCAL. These results parallel those obtained in Table 3. However, there are important differences between the two tables. First, when the effect of PRICES is taken into account, neither FISCAL nor economic GROWTH exerts a statistically significant effect on VOTE. On the other hand, when FISCAL is taken into account, GROWTH still has an effect on ELECT, but only if all the data are included in the analysis. When 1944, an exceptional year fiscally, is dropped from the analysis, the only predictor is FISCAL. PRICES is displaced by FISCAL

TABLE 3
Regression Parameter Estimates of Presidential Elections, 1892–1988

	1944 Election Included (N = 25)		1944 Election Excluded (N = 24)	
	VOTE	ELECT	VOTE	ELECT
	Step-wise regression (* = significant at .10 level; ** = significant at .01 level)			
Step	1	1	2	1	1
FISCAL		−0.58**	−0.57**		−0.66**
PRICES	−1.28**			−1.28**	
GROWTH			0.05*		
Intercept	55.30	0.13	0.08	55.25	−0.06
R²	0.28	0.35	0.43	0.28	0.43
	Complete Regression (t-statistics in parentheses; * = significant at .10 level or better)			
FISCAL	−1.28 (−0.71)	−0.49* (−2.59)	−1.36 (−0.69)	−0.59* (−3.01)
PRICES	−1.07* (−2.07)	−0.03 (−0.61)	−1.06* (−1.94)	−0.01 (−0.27)
GROWTH	0.21 (0.71)	0.03 (1.07)	0.21 (0.68)	0.03 (1.06)
PRESIDENT	2.55 (0.67)	0.29 (0.73)	2.44 (0.61)	0.15 (0.38)
Intercept	52.32	0.05	52.28	0.004
R²	0.36	0.45	0.36	0.49

NOTE: In a step-wise regression, only those variables that meet a significance test are included; in a complete regression, all variables are taken into account regardless of statistical significance.

as a predictor of ELECT whether or not 1944 data are included in the analysis. In other words, whereas the only predictor of VOTE is the rate of inflation/deflation, this variable has no effect on ELECT, the best predictor of which is FISCAL, with economic GROWTH having a secondary influence.

Surprisingly, the variable PRESIDENT is not statistically significant. Fiscal and economic variables are much better predictors of election outcome than whether the incumbent president is running for another term. The word "surprisingly" is used because Fair (1988: 170) found that "[w]hen the president himself . . . is running, he has an advantage of 4.49 percentage points" in the popular vote. It should be noted, however, that Fair's analysis only covers elections between 1916 and 1984 — hence it omits three elections in which a sitting president lost his bid for reelection (those of 1892, 1896, and 1912), as well as one (1988) in which the incumbent party retained the White House even though the president himself was not running, the first time this has happened since 1928. Thus, when a longer time period including more elections is analyzed, it appears that having the president himself at the top of the ticket has no effect on whether his party retains control of the White House.

Also shown in Table 3 is a complete regression for ELECT and VOTE. It includes all variables, whether found significant in the step-wise regression or not. Notice that when all the predictors are included, only PRICES has a significant effect on VOTE, and only FISCAL has a significant effect on ELECT. Neither PRESIDENT nor economic GROWTH has a statistically significant effect on election outcome.

Summary and Conclusion

This paper set out to test whether, when economic factors such as inflation, deflation, and economic growth are taken into account, fiscal policy still has a statistically significant effect on election outcome and, if so, how much of an effect. The results of the analyses are mixed. Fiscal policy is the single best predictor of incumbent reelection or defeat: If fiscal policy is expansionary, incumbents tend to lose the election, and to win if fiscal policy is cut-back. However, when election outcome is measured more precisely as the percent of popular vote won by the incumbent, fiscal policy is displaced by a variable measuring absolute change in the level of prices during the election year. When it comes to predicting not whether the incumbent party wins or loses but its actual share of the vote, the best predictor is the rate of inflation/deflation in the year of the election. As for economic growth, it is of secondary importance: it has a statistically significant effect in the step-wise regression, but only on whether the incumbent party wins or loses, not on the popular vote. Even that effect disappears in the complete regression.

In answer to the initial question, does fiscal policy matter in presidential elections, and if so, how much, the answer is an ambiguous "it depends." It depends on whether one is interested in predicting whether the incumbent party meets victory or defeat, or whether one wants to know its share of the popular vote. If the former, then fiscal policy matters, and it is more important than any other variable. But if one wants to predict the incumbent's share of the vote, fiscal policy is not that important — what counts is the rate of inflation/deflation.

The practical implications of these findings would seem to be straightforward. Incumbents are interested first of all in being reelected. But they are not indifferent to the margin of victory or defeat — a large victory margin gains them greater respect from the opposition party, the Congress, the bureaucracy, the media, interest groups, and foreign governments, while a small share of the vote is a humiliation few politicians can take with equanimity. Thus, incumbents are well advised to keep their eye on fiscal policy *and* on the rate of inflation/deflation. Although the two variables are positively related, both need to be monitored separately, since the correlation is not that strong (Pearson's r is approximately 0.40).

Theoretically, these findings call into question the emphasis which some authors, such as Tufte (1978), have placed on economic growth as a predictor of presidential elections. In fact, fiscal policy and inflation/deflation are much more important than economic growth over the 1892–1988 period. There is a certain rationality in this: fiscal policy and inflation/deflation seem to be more directly or at least more immediately affected by governmental decisions on spending and the money supply, respectively, than economic growth, which is driven largely by the choices of producers, consumers, and investors, including many from abroad. This is not to say that economic growth does not matter — only that its importance as a predictor seems to have been overrated, at least when elections prior to 1916 are included in the data set.

* An earlier draft of this paper was presented at the 1989 meeting of the Southern Political Science Association, Memphis, TN. Thanks to anonymous reviewers of this journal for their valuable suggestions. Thanks also to Cecily Fruchey for typing this manuscript.

APPENDIX
Fiscal, Economic, and Political Data, United States: 1892–1988

Year	F	F'	F"	FISCAL	GROWTH	PRICES	PRESIDENT	VOTE	ELECT
1892	2.7	8	1	1	7.48	4.07	1	43	– 1
1896	2.9	7	– 1	1	– 3.89	2.69	0	47	– 1
1900	2.9	0	– 6	– 1	1.10	4.74	1	52	1
1904	2.7	– 7	– 7	– 1	– 3.02	1.19	1	56	1
1908	2.6	– 4	3	– 1	– 9.96	0.72	0	52	1
1912	2.0	– 23	– 19	– 1	4.04	4.12	1	25	– 1
1916	2.8	40	63	1	6.38	12.15	1	49	1
1920	6.7	139	99	1	– 6.14	13.94	0	34	– 1
1924	3.5	– 48	– 187	– 1	– 2.16	0.19	1	54	1
1928	3.0	– 11	37	– 1	– 0.63	1.60	0	58	1
1932	9.2	197	208	1	– 15.39	10.27	1	40	– 1
1936	11.0	20	– 177	– 1	13.15	0.23	1	61	1
1940	11.6	5	– 15	– 1	7.60	1.62	1	55	1
1944	44.3	281	276	1	5.92	2.46	1	53	1
1948	14.9	– 66	– 347	– 1	2.69	6.70	1	50	1
1952	20.7	39	105	1	1.29	2.22	0	44	– 1
1956	17.1	– 17	– 56	– 1	0.08	3.41	1	57	1
1960	18.4	8	25	1	0.41	1.67	0	50	– 1
1964	18.6	1	– 7	– 1	3.98	1.49	1	61	1
1968	20.8	12	11	1	3.62	3.99	0	43	– 1
1972	20.9	0	– 12	– 1	3.86	4.70	1	61	1
1976	22.6	8	8	1	1.97	6.40	1	48	– 1
1980	21.6	– 4	– 12	– 1	– 5.50	9.00	1	41	– 1
1984	22.6	5	9	1	5.79	3.70	1	59	1
1988	21.7	– 3	– 8	– 1	3.10	3.40	0	53	1

Sources: Calculated from the following sources. U.S. Department of Commerce publications: *Statistical Abstract of the United States* (Washington, D.C.: 1989); *Survey of Current Business*, July 1987; *Historical Statistics of the United States. Colonial Times to 1970*, (Washington, D.C.; 1975); *The National Income and Product Accounts of the United States, 1929–1982*, (Washington, D.C.: 1986). Also, Joint Economic Committee, *Economic Indicators* (various issues); and A. G. Cuzán and R. J. Heggen, "A Fiscal Model of Presidential Elections in the United States: 1800–1980," *Presidential Studies Quarterly*, Winter 1984, p. 108.

Notes

Cuzán, Alfred G. and Heggen, Richard J. 1984. A fiscal model of presidential elections in the United States: 1880–1980. *Presidential Studies Quarterly* XIV (1): 98–108.

———. 1985. Expenditures and votes: In search of downward-sloping curves in the United States and Great Britain. *Public Choice* 45: 19–34.

Fair, Ray C. 1988. The effect of economic events on votes for president: 1984 update. *Political Behavior* 10 (2): 168–179.

Lichtman, A. J. and Killis-Borok, V. I. 1981. Pattern recognition applied to presidential elections in the United States, 1860–1980: Role of integral social, economic, and political traits. *Proceedings of the National Academy of Sciences* 78 (11): 7230–7234.

Peacock, A. R. and Wiseman, Jack. 1961. The Growth of Public Expenditures in the United Kingdom. Princeton: Princeton University Press.

Tufte, Edward. 1978. *Political Control of the Economy*. Princeton: Princeton University Press.

The Democrats' "Southern Problem" in Presidential Politics

NICOL C. RAE
Assistant Professor of Political Science
Florida International University

Abstract

Since 1964, the Democratic party has been persistently weak in presidential elections in the South, while continuing to dominate most elections for lower level offices. This paper explains the party's failures in presidential politics in terms of structural changes in the Democrats' presidential nominating process which have undermined the position of the South within the national party. The process as it now operates is almost guaranteed to produce Democratic presidential nominees who are unacceptable to the overwhelming majority of White Southerners. While Jimmy Carter in 1976 seemed to have restored Democratic dominance, this proved to be illusory, and in the 1980s the party became weaker than ever in southern presidential politics. The attempt to reassert southern influence by re-structuring the primary calender in 1988's "Super Tuesday" primaries also failed. Only a severe national recession can probably revive the presidential Democratic party in the region.

> *No southerner ever dreams of heaven, or pictures his Utopia on earth,*
> *without providing room for the Democratic party.*   John Crowe Ransome[1]

In presidential politics, at least, this is no longer the case. The South ceased to be solidly Democratic at this level during the 1950s, and in recent years it has been the party's weakest region in presidential elections. Their consistently poor electoral performance in the southern states has, moreover, doomed the Democrats' efforts to win nationally. The sole Democratic presidential triumph of recent years (in the South and nationwide) in 1976, is the exception that proves the rule. It has proved impossible for the Democratic party to win presidential elections without winning at least some of the electoral votes of the southern states, yet with each presidential election since 1976, this has appeared as an increasingly remote possibility.

While losing presidential elections in the South, the Democrats nevertheless remain the region's dominant party beneath the presidential level. Although Republicans are now competitive in senatorial and gubernatorial elections in the South, they still hold only about a third of the region's House seats, and the Democrats enjoy overwhelming and secure majorities in almost all southern state legislatures.

This paper will try to explain one side of this paradox, the persistent weakness of the Democratic party in presidential politics in the South since 1964. The main emphasis will fall on the party's revised nominating process, which is structurally biased in favor of candidates with little appeal to most southern white voters, and in which the South appears unable to exercise any real leverage—in contrast to the situation half-a-century ago. Finally, various southern attempts to increase their leverage over the party's presidential nominating process, and the Democrats' future prospects in southern presidential politics will also be discussed.

The Solid South in Presidential Politics

In the period from 1876 to 1948 the South was the heart of the Democratic party's presidential coalition. No region was as Democratic as the South in presidential elections, although due to the national stigma which attached to the South after the Civil War, it was all-but-impossible for a southerner to win the party's nomination.[2] The "solidity" of the South was achieved by various means in presidential nominating politics, all of which were designed to prevent the national party from ever seriously addressing the race question.

Southern delegations were selected in closed caucuses or by state committees, and consisted largely of representatives of the white power structure that had been erected in the southern states in the final decades of the 19th century.[3] Their essential task at the national convention was to preclude the selection of a nominee "unacceptable to the South" (that is, unsound on the race question). To maximize the bargaining power of their states and of the region as a whole, southern convention delegations generally adhered to the so-called "unit rule"—casting the delegation's total convention vote as a bloc on the floor of the convention.[4]

The combined voting power of the southern delegations was thus a formidable barrier for any candidate regarded as unfavorable to the South to overcome. Yet in case such a candidate did appear, the South had an additional device which essentially guaranteed that no Democratic nominee would be selected who might offend southern sensibilities. This was the "two-thirds rule" which prevailed at Democratic conventions up to 1936. Nomination required two-thirds of the total convention vote, and this more or less gave a veto over the nominee to the southern delegations voting in unison. The two-thirds rule also increased the possibility of deadlocked conventions which embittered Democrats and damaged their prospects in the general election—the 103-ballot marathon of 1924 is a case in point.[5]

The southern influence over the national Democratic party persisted into the New Deal era. While FDR's administration posed no threat to the southern system of segregation, his measures to relieve the depression actually reinforced Democratic strength in the White South during the 1930s (after the significant Republican "bolt" of 1928).[6] The economically-backward South benefited more than any other region from the New Deal's social and agricultural relief programs, and public works projects such as the TVA.

The collapse of the Democratic presidential party in the South during the post-New Deal period was due to two interrelated factors: 1) social and demographic changes within the Democratic party's national coalition and within the South itself, which destroyed the social and economic environment that had sustained the Solid South; and 2) procedural changes in the means by which the Democratic party selected presidential candidates, most specifically, the move to a primary system as opposed to a convention system of presidential nomination. These factors will now be discussed in turn.

The Disintegration of the New Deal Electoral Coalition and the Emergence of a New South

Despite FDR's success in avoiding the issue, it was clear that the Democrats as a national party would soon have to address the problem of the southern race system. During the 1930s blacks in the northern urban centers—where they could vote—had realigned in favor of the Democrats due to support for FDR's relief programs.[7] As the GOP began to recover its electoral strength in areas such as the Midwest in the mid-1940s, the black vote, concentrated in urban areas in states rich with electoral college votes, became increasingly crucial to Democratic presidential success. The inclusion of a mild civil rights plank in the 1948 Democratic platform was the first real challenge to southern segregation from the national party, and a gamble that the Democrats could consolidate their new electoral strength in the North, while retaining enough of their hitherto-solid southern support to win in November.

The gamble succeeded, for despite the defection of four southern states to Strom Thurmond's States' Rights ticket, Harry Truman was able to defeat Republican Thomas E. Dewey. After 1948 the southern veto on presidential nominees who were prepared to challenge segregation, was no longer operative (FDR had persuaded the party to abandon the two-thirds rule in 1936), and the White South became increasingly uncomfortable with the Democratic party.

Rapid social changes inside the South were also gradually undermining Democratic presidential strength there, and it was those changes that laid the foundations for a viable southern Republican party. The South's economic and industrial development created a larger southern business class, which was clearly to the Republicans' advantage. Indeed the growth in the Republican presidential vote in the South's new urban centers was noticeable as early as the 1940s.[8] These areas continued to grow apace in the decades which followed, and the urban middle-class vote in the South became the basis of Republican electoral strength.[9]

The GOP also benefited from the net effect of migrations in and out of the South. Groups leaving the region in the post-war period tended to be loyally-Democratic, lower-status, whites and blacks, while those attracted into the South by the postwar business expansion tended to be Republican-leaning business types.[10] This again weakened Democratic support in the urban and suburban areas of the South—particularly in the expanding 'rim South' states of Texas, Florida and North Carolina.

As it became apparent that the Democratic party nationally, had become the more committed of the parties regarding civil rights for blacks, the Republicans were able to add rural, lower-status, whites to their middle-class, business, base and present a serious challenge to the Democrats in presidential elections in most southern states. Eisenhower carried Virginia, Texas, Florida, and Tennessee in 1952, and four years later he added Louisiana while becoming the first Republican presidential candidate

TABLE 1
Presidential Republicanism in the South Since 1964

State	No. of Elections 1964–1988	No of Republican Victories	Percent
Alabama	7	5	71
Arkansas	7	4	57
Florida	7	5	71
Georgia	7	4	57
Louisiana	7	5	71
Mississippi	7	5	71
North Carolina	7	5	71
South Carolina	7	6	86
Tennessee	7	5	71
Texas	7	5	71
Virginia	7	6	86

to win a plurality of the southern popular vote. In 1960 Nixon held Florida, Virginia and Tennessee for the Republicans and was competitive in most of the region. Four years later Republican Barry Goldwater turned American post-civil war electoral geography on its head by sweeping the five states of the Deep South — Mississippi, Alabama, Georgia, Louisiana and South Carolina, and losing almost everywhere else. By 1964 it had become clear that white southerners, the traditional mainstay of the Democratic party, were increasingly prepared to vote for Republican candidates in presidential elections.[11]

The presence of southern populist George Wallace on the presidential ballot in 1968, with an appeal pitched explicitly at the lower-status white constituency which had been attracted to Goldwater in 1964, restricted the Republican presidential advance somewhat, but Nixon was still able to win Florida, Virginia, Tennessee, North Carolina and South Carolina. In 1972 Nixon united his 1968 vote with Wallace's and swept the entire region, and apart from the 1976 aberration the South has been solidly in the Republican column since.

The declining identification with the Democratic party among white southerners has been the key to the southern presidential realignment.[12] And while the Democrats have been partly compensated by the overwhelming support of southern blacks since they were admitted to the electorate in significant numbers after the 1965 Voting Rights Act, this has been insufficient to make-up for the loss of droves of southern whites to the GOP.[13] Even in 1976, Gerald Ford still carried a majority of the southern white vote, although Carter got enough when added to his formidable performance among blacks to carry every southern state but Virginia.[14] This dire performance among white southerners remains the Democratic party's gravest problem in presidential politics, since without winning more of their votes, the Democrats cannot win the southern states they require to envisage presidential success on a national scale.

In place of their old lily-white coalition, the Democrats need to construct a biracial "class" coalition of blacks and lower-status whites to defeat the white, middle-class, GOP. While they have only succeeded in accomplishing this once in

TABLE 2
Democratic Strength at Different Electoral Levels in the South in 1988

State	Democratic Percent for President	Democratic Percent for U.S. Senate[1]	Democratic Percent of Legislature[2]
Alabama	40	—	85
Arkansas	43	64[1]	88
Florida	39	50	60
Georgia	40	—	80
Louisiana	45	—	84
Mississippi	40	47	91
North Carolina	42	44[1]	65
South Carolina	38	—	72
Tennessee	42	66	61
Texas	44	60	64
Virginia	40	71	68

[1] For Arkansas and North Carolina the figure is the Democratic percentage in the Governor's race.
[2] The Democratic percentage of the total membership of the state legislature after the 1988 elections.
Source: *National Journal*, 12 November 1988

presidential politics since 1968, it has nevertheless been the persistence of such a bi-racial coalition which has accounted for their remarkably consistent success in southern elections beneath the presidential level.[15]

There has thus been no overall realignment in the South in favor of the Republican party, which has conspicuously failed to replicate its dominance at the presidential level at the other levels of government. Indeed in the state legislatures Democratic dominance — with one or two exceptions — remains overwhelming. The South evidences the split-level realignment which has characterized national politics since 1968, but in an exaggerated form: the Republican presidential dominance is greater, while the Democrats retain an apparently impregnable advantage at the lower electoral levels.

This curious state of affairs is largely due to the electoral behaviour of the swing group in contemporary southern politics — lower-status whites. The latter habitually abandon the Democrats in presidential politics these days, but in lower-level contests sufficient of them "come home" to enable a bi-racial Democratic coalition to prevail. This coalition was the key to the successful election of the "New South" generation of governors during the 1970s, as their populist "new politics" appeal often succeeded in winning over alienated poorer whites who had inclined towards Goldwater and Wallace during the 1960s.[16] Just as Carter triumphed in the 1976 presidential race with such a strategy, so many southern Democratic politicians of a similar stamp were able to triumph in state politics.

The swing constituency of poorer whites remains highly responsive to populistic Democratic appeals on economic issues, despite their distaste for the Democrats' post-1968 foreign policy stances and social liberalism.[17] Moreover, the Democratic party's strength these days is its ability to deliver services to constituents using the advantages of incumbency at both the federal and state level. Replace these Democrats with economy-minded Republicans and precious services and programs might disappear. It is also generally still true that the Democrats speak the language of the lower-status white much more convincingly than most Republicans can.

The situation of the lower-status southern white is often described as one of "alienation" and "dealignment."[18] There is little doubt that this section of the electorate is the most cross-pressured in the South: pulled toward the Democrats on economic issues and towards the GOP on defense and social questions. These voters resolve their dilemma quite rationally by consistently splitting their votes. In presidential elections where defending the nation and setting an appropriate national tone is concerned, they tend to vote Republican, whereas in congressional and state races which deal mainly with services and programs with a direct impact on their personal economic situation, they continue to favor Democrats. By thus avoiding ideological consistency they get the best of both worlds.[19]

Of course, this presents real problems to the Democrats in trying to win presidential elections in the South. However as most of the lower-status whites have not firmly realigned themselves as Republicans, there is ostensibly no reason why, if the Democrats produced presidential candidates similar to those they produce in congressional and state elections in the South, they could not also do better in presidential elections there.

This brings us to the second set of factors involved in the Democrats' presidential weakness in the region—the inability of their nominating process to generate candidates with real appeal to white southerners: candidates who could perhaps convince a sufficient number of lower-status southern whites that they would not leave the nation defenseless or deliver it into the hands of Jesse Jackson, Gloria Steinem and Norman Lear. Unfortunately for southern Democrats, the party's nominating process as presently constituted operates against such a candidate's emerging as the party's nominee.

The South & the Democrats' Presidential Nominating Process

The first factor which undermined southern influence over the Democratic party's presidential nominating process, was, of course, the abolition of the two-thirds rule in 1936. This was done to prevent another deadlocked marathon which reflected badly on the entire party as in 1924, but the effect on the South's ability to veto candidates of whom it disapproved was profound, although the implications did not become fully clear until 1948. The surprising thing was that the southerners did not apparently perceive the threat to their power involved in the abolition of the rule, and it expired with surprisingly little resistance at the 1936 convention.[20]

The process of reform of the nominating process over the next half-century would continue to undermine the power of the white South within the party. Abolition of the whites-only primary after the Supreme Court's 1944 *Smith* v. *Allwright* decision, and the gradual enfranchisement of blacks in delegate-selection processes were a direct assault on the old white power structure. In 1964 the presence of lily-white national convention delegations from the South at the Democratic national convention had become a grave embarrassment to the party, and the struggle for black representation climaxed with the momentous decision to seat the integrated Mississippi Freedom Democratic delegation in place of the lily-white regular delegation at the 1968 convention.[21] National rules were now beginning to undermine the solidity of the southern delegations.

TABLE 3
Processes for Selecting the Democratic National
Convention Delegation in the Southern States,
1968 and 1988

State	Process Used in 1968	Process Used in 1988
Alabama	Delegate Primary[1]	Presidential Primary
Arkansas	State Party Committee	Presidential Primary
Florida	Presidential Primary	Presidential Primary
Georgia	State Party Committee	Presidential Primary
Louisiana	State Party Committee	Presidential Primary
Mississippi	Caucuses	Presidential Primary
North Carolina	Caucuses	Presidential Primary
South Carolina	Caucuses	Caucuses
Tennessee	Caucuses	Presidential Primary
Texas	Caucuses	Presidential Primary
Virginia	Caucuses	Presidential Primary

[1] Primary used to elect delegates only, with no presidential preference poll.
Source: Austin Ranney, The American Elections of 1980 (Washington, D.C.: AEI, 1981), Appendix D, pp. 366–368; and Rhodes Cook, "The Nominating Process" in The Elections of 1988, ed. Michael Nelson (Washington, D.C.: CQ Press, 1989), p. 30.

These changes were confirmed by the further reforms of the nominating process introduced by the McGovern-Fraser Commission between the 1968 and 1972 conventions. These changes mandated state parties to make their delegate-selection procedures as "open" and "representative" as possible, and also required "Women, Minorities and Youth" to be represented in a state's convention delegation in accordance with their presence in the state's general population. Finally, the Commission prohibited the use of the unit rule.[22]

Rather than risk handing over the state party apparatus entirely to proponents of the "new politics", most state party leaders both inside and outside the South preferred to respond to the Commission's guidelines by establishing a presidential primary election.[23] Between the 1968 and 1988 the number of presidential primaries inside the South increased considerably.

The net effect of all these changes was to finally shatter southern solidity by fragmenting the South in Democratic presidential nominating politics. Southern convention delegations were now divided between blacks and whites, liberal and conservatives, men and women, and between the devotees of different presidential candidates (due in large part to the McGovern-Fraser Commission's requirements of proportional representation).[24] While blacks and liberal white southerners gained as a result of the changes, representatives of the more traditional white southerners lost out. Indeed, the South almost ceased to be a distinctive factor in the Democratic presidential nominating process.

Southern candidates and candidates with potential appeal to the white South have also suffered from the structure of the new primary-based nominating process. To mount a serious challenge for the nomination it is necessary for presidential aspirants to perform creditably in the crucial early contests in Iowa and New Hampshire.[25] Democrats in these states, however, do not tend to favor the kinds of Democratic candidates who might appeal to the White South. Iowa's political culture is isolationist, pacifistic, and progressive, while New Hampshire Democrats have tended to favor maverick candidates — Eugene McCarthy, George McGovern, Gary Hart — as opposed to those associated with the traditional Democratic coalition of ethnics, Labor and the white South.

Because of the effects of media momentum on candidates' visibility and fundraising, candidacies that fail to register at least a top-two finish in Iowa, and particularly, New Hampshire, tend to be stillborn.[26] By the time that the primary season reaches the South the also-rans in New Hampshire are generally no longer regarded as being serious contenders. The southern or southern-oriented candidacies of John Glenn, Fritz Hollings and Reuben Askew all died in New Hampshire in 1984. In 1988 a similar fate befell Richard Gephardt, although he had won in Iowa a few weeks previously. As we shall see below, the South concentrated its 1988 primaries on one day to try and distract media attention from Iowa and New Hampshire and increase its regional clout. Moreover, one southern champion in 1988, Tennessee Senator Albert Gore, pointedly ignored Iowa and New Hampshire, to concentrate on gaining a delegate windfall in the southern states.

We can therefore see that the early primaries in unfavorable terrain for southern contenders usually act to create Democratic frontrunners with very limited appeal in the South, a factor that militates heavily against the party's prospects in the region in November. Of course, up to this point I have studiously ignored the exceptional case which contradicts everything discussed above. In 1976 Jimmy Carter won in Iowa and New Hampshire, swept the South in the primaries, got nominated, and won the presidency largely due to an almost solidly Democratic South in November. The Carter triumph, however, was based on a peculiar configuration of circumstances that are unlikely to recur again in Democratic presidential nominating politics.

Jimmy Carter: the Exceptional Case

Jimmy Carter's long-shot campaign for the presidency in 1976 succeeded due to good planning, good fortune, and the context of the election.

Carter's managers appreciated the implications of the move to a primary-centered nominating campaign better than those of his opponents. Thus Carter was off and running early and everywhere, after leaving the Georgia statehouse in 1974. The Carter campaign further understood the critical nature of the Iowa caucuses and the New Hampshire primary and invested a great deal of time in both states.[27] Carter also had the moderate-to-conservative side of the Democratic party all to himself in those early contests while liberal opponents divided-up the liberal vote. Having established himself as the early frontrunner after New Hampshire, Carter united blacks, liberal whites and a sufficient number of lower-status white Democrats attracted by his populist, "anti-politics" themes, to defeat George Wallace in the Florida primary. From then on he was virtually unbeatable.

Yet even given the Carter campaign's excellent strategic sense, they could still not have succeeded outside the unique context of the 1976 election. For a country traumatized by the effects of Vietnam and Watergate, Carter's "government of love" had a particularly significant resonance. By capitalizing on the general revulsion with politicians, Carter was able to avoid taking the more explicit issue-positions that might have doomed his campaign in the early primaries. To conservative Democrats he sounded like a conservative, and while liberals might have preferred Morris Udall to Carter, they far preferred Carter to George Wallace, or Cold War veterans like Scoop Jackson or Hubert Humphrey.

Another unique attribute of the Carter campaign was Carter's strong appeal to black voters in both North and South. Carter's southern Baptist background, ironically was probably his greatest asset in cultivating black voters. The presence of key black political spokesmen from Georgia such as the Rev. Andrew Young, Coretta King and the Rev. Martin Luther King Sr., in the Carter entourage also enhanced Carter's appeal to black Americans.[28]

In the general election, Carter became the first Democratic presidential contender in recent years to obtain a respectable southern white vote, sufficiently respectable, indeed, when added to his formidable black voting base, to carry him to victory in November over Gerald Ford in every southern state save Virginia, although the Republican still secured a majority of the southern white vote.[29]

Carter's coalition in both the nominating and general election campaigns definitely showed a clear route by which a White Democrat from the Deep South could win the presidency. Yet it was a coalition that only the post-Vietnam and Watergate mood of 1976 probably could have produced, and it was fundamentally unstable. For instance, Carter won despite his southern background not because of it, and he certainly did not run in the early primaries as Dixie's candidate—had he done so he would probably not have fared as well as he did in Iowa and New Hampshire. It is also hard to envisage another white southern candidate with such a powerful appeal as Carter had to both blacks and lower-status whites in the South, particularly as black candidates are likely to be a regular feature in future Democratic presidential contests. Lower-status whites were attracted to Carter because they saw him as a more physically vigorous version of their ailing hero George Wallace, and it should be noted that after defeating Wallace in Florida, Carter took pains to give no offence to the Alabama Governor or his supporters over the remainder of the 1976 nominating campaign.[30] By straddling or evading the policy issues which divided the races in the South, Carter was able to put together a coalition of blacks, and lower-status whites alienated from Washington politics since the mid-1950s.

Once in office, President Carter could no longer avoid taking clear positions on these issues as he had done in the 1976 campaign, and given the nature of his administration and of the national Democratic party it was inevitable that he would fall on the side of social liberalism on most questions, while neglecting the economic populism that had won him the South in 1976. By doing so he alienated the southern white component of his coalition sufficiently to ensure his defeat in the region and in the nation in 1980. Whatever their merits, the Panama Canal Treaty, the Energy policy, the emphasis on promoting the rights of women and minorities—achievements in which Carter took special pride—were not particularly well-received in the White South. By the late 1970s, evangelical white southerners who had supported Carter as one of their own in 1976, had largely deserted the administration and the Democratic party.[31]

Ronald Reagan by emphasizing issues such as the "sell-out" of the Panama Canal, abortion, school prayer, busing, and the restoration of national pride, evoked a powerful response in the white South. In the 1980 election he restored the post-1968 Republican presidential advantage in the region and the Republican grip was reinforced in 1984.[32] Carter was an aberration in the pattern of Democratic nominees, and 1976 was an aberrant election. In office, when the white South saw Carter as being just another liberal Democrat, albeit with a southern accent, the brief Democratic revival in southern presidential politics was quickly extinguished.

The Super Tuesday Debacle

In 1984 the compression of the primary election season demanded by the Democratic National Committee, led to the states of Florida, Georgia and Alabama holding their primaries on the same day (11 March). Theoretically this should have been an advantage to the three southern favorites for the presidential nomination — John Glenn, Fritz Hollings and Rueben Askew — who might reasonably have hoped for a windfall of delegates and favorable publicity from a series of triumphs in the southern region. In reality, however, the first 'Super Tuesday' was a victim of the media momentum generated by the Iowa caucuses and the New Hampshire primary. Those two states had produced a tight contest between Walter Mondale — representing the Labor wing of the Democratic party — and Gary Hart — representing the 'new politics' tradition of McCarthy, McGovern, and, to some extent, Carter. Neither was very attractive to the white South, but after the New Hampshire primary, they were being treated by the news media as the only two viable contenders. Indeed the Hollings and Askew campaigns were terminated before Super Tuesday! The short space of time between New Hampshire and the three southern primary states, together with the fact that some important northern states — principally Massachusetts — were holding their primary on the same day — led to a whirlwind Dixie campaign, with Hart, Mondale, Glenn and the Rev. Jesse Jackson hopping madly from airport to airport to create 'soundbites' for local news in the various southern media markets.[33]

After Mondale was routed by Reagan in the November election, southern state party leaders and Democratic elected officials gave serious thought as to how the South could increase its leverage over the nominating process and in the national counsels of the party. They worried that continuing electoral obliteration at the presidential level would eventually filter down to the lower electoral levels, and that many conservative white Democratic officeholders might defect to the GOP in order to save their electoral skins.[34] Prominent southern and border state politicians such as Senator Sam Nunn, Senator Charles Robb and Congressman Richard Gephardt formed the Democratic Leadership Council (DLC), in an effort to steer the Democrats' policy and image away from close identification with liberal interest groups — Feminists, Minorities, Labor, Teachers, Gays — and "weakness" on defence issues.[35] A 1985 special election, in which a Democrat held-off a strong Republican challenge in a rural, white, Texas congressional district by using the issue of protectionism, seemed to indicate that by combining a more resolute image on foreign and defence policy with economic populism, the Democrats might be able to break the Republican hold on the white South and reconstruct their bi-racial coalition on a national level.[36]

TABLE 4
The Overall Result of the "Super Tuesday" Primaries in 1988

Candidate	Primaries Won[1]	Percent of Total Vote	Delegates Won	Percent of Delegates
Dukakis	5	26	356	32
Jackson	5	27	353	32
Gore	5	26	318	28
Gephardt	1	13	94	8
Others	0	9	0	0
Total	16	100	1121	100

[1] On March 8, 1988 primaries were held in 10 of the 11 southern states (South Carolina held a caucus on another date) plus Kentucky, Maryland, Massachusetts, Missouri, Oklahoma, and Rhode Island. The figures in the table do not include the returns from the states that held caucuses on "Super Tuesday."
Source: Adapted from tables in *Congressional Quarterly Weekly Report*, 12 March 1988, 636–638.

Optimism about Democratic prospects in the South increased after the 1986 midterm elections, when the Democrats regained Senate seats in Georgia, Alabama, North Carolina and Florida, which they had lost in 1980, and held on to what initially seemed like a very vulnerable seat in Louisiana. Campaigning on economic populist themes even Democrats with a liberal political profile, such as new Georgia Senator Wyche Fowler, were able to build black-white coalitions and get elected.[37] (Of course, it might be added that the crop of defeated incumbent Republican Senators elected in the 1980 Reagan sweep, were not particularly impressive.)

As the centerpiece of their strategy to enhance southern leverage over the 1988 Democratic presidential nominating process, the DLC and southern state and local party leaders devised the idea of a truly "Super" Tuesday—concentrating *all* of the South's primaries and caucuses on one date in March. By rigging the primary schedule in such a fashion, the devisers of Super Tuesday reckoned that they would finally dilute the influence of Iowa and New Hampshire and give an opportunity for a candidate more representative of southern opinion to emerge at the end of the process.[38] On paper the idea seemed very good. In practice the authors of 'Super Tuesday' might have learned from the more limited concentration of contests in 1984, that the outcome of their scheme might be quite different from what they had intended.[39]

For the southern leaders had failed to appreciate that the more primaries are concentrated on one date just after Iowa and New Hampshire, the more important Iowa and New Hampshire become. This is simply because it is Iowa and New Hampshire which still determine which candidacies are adjudged viable heading into the southern regional primary. Thus in 1988 the clear Democratic frontrunner heading into Super Tuesday with the full benefit of media momentum, was the New Hampshire victor Massachusetts Governor Michael Dukakis, who hardly seemed to be the kind of southern favorite the authors of Super Tuesday had envisaged.[40] The most explicitly southern contender, Senator Albert Gore, avoided Iowa and New Hampshire entirely so as to concentrate on Super Tuesday, but by doing so he inevitably suffered in terms of momentum and viability which in turn affected his Super Tuesday performance.[41] Another candidate with potential appeal to the South,

TABLE 5
The 1988 Democratic Primary Vote by Time Periods

Candidate	Pre Super Tuesday	Super Tuesday	Post Super Tuesday	Final Outcome
Dukakis	39%	26%	54%	42%
Jackson	11%	27%	31%	29%
Gore	6%	26%	5%	14%
Gephardt	24%	13%	1%	6%

Source: Adapted from figures in Rhodes Cook, "The Nominating Process" in *The Elections of 1988*, ed. Michael Nelson (Washington, D.C.: CQ Press, 1989), p. 53.

Congressman Richard Gephardt, succeeded in narrowly winning the Iowa caucuses, but he had to devote so much of his money to campaigning in Iowa and New Hampshire, that did not have sufficient funds remaining to mount the necessary TV advertising campaign in the southern media markets required for Super Tuesday. In a different way he was another victim of 'Big Mo' or the search for it.[42]

Another factor from 1984 which was repeated in 1988, was that several significant northern states—most particularly Massachusetts and Maryland—insisted on scheduling their primary on the same day as Super Tuesday (8 March). This reduced somewhat the attention that candidates could give to the South, and also gave an additional boost to Dukakis, the clear frontrunner in both states, since he could claim some substantial victories even if he won nothing in the South, and thus maintain his momentum. Moreover, the holding of so many primaries and caucuses on the same day only served to dilute the attention received by individual southern states.

The next difficulty was that the two most obviously southern contenders, Gore and Gephardt, were not perhaps the most effective champions that Dixie could have put forward. Both had fairly liberal voting records in Congress, and neither really aroused a great deal of enthusiasm among activists in the region. Gephardt had some appeal to white lower-status southerners with his populistic protectionism, and Gore tried to depict himself as the only real defence "hawk" in the Democratic field—not a particularly difficult task in 1988 it should be added—but neither really struck a profound chord in the South in the way that Wallace, Carter or Ronald Reagan had done. Despite having helped in the creation of the DLC and Super Tuesday, more authentic southern Democrats such as Governor Charles Robb of Virginia or Senator Sam Nunn of Georgia refused to enter the race, showing a certain lack of faith in their own creation.[43] The final problem with the Gore and Gephardt candidacies was that they tended to undercut each other—both being aimed at the more conservative white vote. In the absence of one of them, the other might have made much more out of the opportunity of Super Tuesday than either of them did individually.[44]

Another factor that the framers of the southern regional primary appeared to have overlooked, was that the southern Democratic primary electorate was no longer so socially and ethnically homogeneous as to be readily "delivered" for a regional champion of a moderate-to-conservative stamp. Conservative white southern voters largely stayed away from the polls on Super Tuesday, and exit poll data showed that the Democratic primary electorate in 1988 was disproportionately "liberal" in orientation, compared to the general electorate in the southern states.[45] In these circumstances the Super Tuesday victories of Jackson and Dukakis appear less surprising.

In 1988 Jesse Jackson did even better among southern blacks than in 1984, so well, in fact, that thanks to the splintering of the white vote between various candidates, Jackson was able to win 5 Deep South states and a harvest of delegates (see Tables 4 and 5 above).[46] Indeed, Jackson was the real winner of Super Tuesday, since these successes enhanced greatly the viability of his candidacy in subsequent northern primaries.

Aside from the black vote, there were also substantial numbers of liberal Democratic enclaves within the south — particularly in the large metropolitan areas and academic communities of Florida, Texas, Georgia and North Carolina — which responded very warmly to the Dukakis candidacy.[47] With his southern opponents undercutting each other and Jackson getting virtually all of the black vote, Dukakis, the northeastern liberal, was able to carry the two largest southern states, Florida and Texas (in the latter he also got a lot of support from Mexican-American voters). This further increased Dukakis's momentum and created a false impression of national strength. Gore was able to carry Arkansas, Kentucky, North Carolina, Tennessee and Oklahoma, but these successes were obscured by the strength of Jackson and Dukakis in other parts of the South. Gephardt won only his home state of Missouri, although it should be re-emphasized that had he and Gore not been competing for the same voters, one of them might have achieved a much more convincing southern sweep.

The other question that arises, of course, is whether a southern favorite could win the nomination even if he did emerge with a solid bloc of delegates and frontrunner status after Super Tuesday. To win in the South might compel a candidate to have become too closely identified with that region for the comfort of liberal Democratic primary voters in the North and West. A southern candidate might also adopt issue-positions so incongruent with those of Democratic activists nationally, that they would be unable to convert Super Tuesday success into a successful nomination. The experience of Albert Gore in 1988 is instructive in this regard. Gore had positioned himself so far to right (relatively speaking) on defence issues, and identified himself so closely with the South, in his effort to gain some momentum from Super Tuesday, that he alienated potential support in the Midwestern and Northern primary states that immediately followed.[48]

The final problem with a regional primary to enhance southern leverage over the Democratic nominating process, is that if the ploy did succeed, other regions would quickly follow suit with their own regional primary to enhance their own influence in the process *vis a vis* the South. (There were hints of this in 1988, when the New England states and some Midwestern states also considered coordinating the dates of their primaries.) From four or five regional primaries it might be but a short distance to a national primary (as the logical culmination of the rationalization of the presidential nominating process). After one successful Super Tuesday there might not be too many more, and then where would the South be?

Conclusion: Waiting for Recession?

The Democrats' presidential problem in the South is not very easily soluble in the short term. The southerners know what they have to do; build a black-white coalition around economic issues as they have done at the congressional and state and local level in the South. But the problem they face is that the issues of presidential politics are far more divisive of that coalition than state issues, or the service issues which predominate in congressional elections. On the major issues of presidential politics in recent years, white southerners have tended to be interventionist in foreign policy, more conservative on moral and law and order questions (which a president can influence through the Justice Department and federal court appointments), and they tend to identify strongly with national symbols closely associated with the presidency (such as the flag). Outside black areas and liberal enclaves, southern voters in presidential elections have felt very uncomfortable with recent Democratic presidential candidates including one of their own, Jimmy Carter, when they discovered that he was not quite what they had expected.

As we have seen the structure of the Democratic nominating process now discriminates against the South's interests, and this problem becomes even more acute with the likely movement of the date of California's presidential primary in 1992 to the week following New Hampshire and preceding Super Tuesday. This will further reinforce both the influence of New Hampshire, and that of liberal Democrats (who dominate the California Democratic party) over the nominating process, at the expense of the more moderate Democrats in the South.[49] In the primary system liberals, single-issue and advocacy groups, and the news media, have much more influence than they did in the era of brokered conventions and the unit rule. In the old system of brokerage the South exerted considerably more leverage over the national party in candidate selection, while in the new system, the South has found it much more difficult to exert influence, primarily because in the new politics the outcome is determined more by interest groups, candidate organizations, and media expectations, than by mobilizing local, state, or regional party leaders. Super Tuesday was an attempt to reassert southern leverage within the reformed nominating system, but its failure shows how the whole logic of that system and the logic of regarding the South as a separate entity with particular interests, are in conflict. The new system operates according to national criteria through national media, and usually suppresses regional effects, even in the most culturally distinct region of the country. In this sense southern politics and society have become like the rest of the US, and it is too late to go back to the old Solid South model.

On the other hand, Democrats do need to win some southern states to have any chance of reaching the White House. To achieve this end they probably need a downturn in the economy — which certainly helped in 1976 — to attract lower-status white voters on bread-and-butter economic issues. Economic populism still has considerable electoral potential in the South, particularly when much of the region remains largely unaffected by the southern economic boom. In congressional and state elections which focus on how effectively incumbents have serviced their state or district, Democrats retain a clear advantage over the more parsimonious Republicans throughout the South. Given a national recession, the prospects of a renewal of the presidential Democratic party in the South are therefore quite good. In such circumstances the themes of the 1988 Gephardt primary campaign — economic populism with a protectionist flavour, which neutralizes Republican attacks on Democrats' patriotism — might well be very electorally effective in the southern states.

Failing an economic downturn, however, the recreation of a presidentially-Democratic South will likely prove to be a hopeless task for the Democrats.

Notes

1. John Crowe Ransome, "Reconstructed but Unregenerate" in *I'll Take My Stand: the South and the Agrarian Tradition*, by 'Twelve Southerners' (Baton Rouge, LA: Louisiana State University Press, 1977), pp. 26–7.

2. On Democratic dominance in presidential elections in the South see V. O. Key, Jr., *Southern Politics in State and Nation* (New York: Knopf, 1950), pp. 315–344, 385–405; Dewey W. Grantham, *The Life and Death of the Solid South* (Lexington, KY: University Press of Kentucky, 1988), pp. 58–77; and Everett Carll Ladd, Jr. (with Charles D. Hadley), *Transformations of the Party System: Political Coalitions from the New Deal to the 1970s*, 2nd ed. (New York: Norton, 1978), pp. 42–46.

3. On black disfranchisement and the creation of the one-party 'Solid South' see Key, *Southern Politics*, pp. 531–643; Grantham, *The Life and Death of the Solid South*, pp. 1–57; and C. Vann Woodward, *The Strange Career of Jim Crow*, 3rd ed., (New York: Oxford University Press, 1974), pp. 67–109.

4. On the history of the unit rule see Howard L. Reiter, *Selecting the President: the Nominating Process in Transition* (Philadelphia: University of Pennsylvania Press, 1985), pp. 133–6.

5. On the two thirds rule see *Ibid.*, pp. 133–4.

6. On the South and New Deal see Nancy J. Weiss, *Farewell to the Party of Lincoln: Black Politics in the Age of FDR* (Princeton, NJ: Princeton University Press, 1983), pp. 157–179; and Ladd & Hadley, *Transformations of the American Party System*, pp. 42–46.

7. On black realignment during the 1930s see Weiss, *Farewell to the Party of Lincoln*, pp. 180–235.

8. On the 'presidential Republicans' of the 1940s see Key, *Southern Politics*, pp. 278–280, 292–297.

9. Earl Black and Merle Black, *Politics and Society in the South* (Cambridge, MA: Harvard University Press, 1987), pp. 259–275; and Jack Bass and Walter DeVries, *The Transformation of Southern Politics: Social Change and Political Consequence Since 1945* (New York: New American Library, 1977), pp. 274–275.

10. Paul Allen Beck, "Partisan Dealignment in the Post-War South", *American Political Science Review* 71 (1977), 477–496; and Black and Black, *Politics and Society in the South*, pp. 313–314.

11. Alexander P. Lamis, *The Two-Party South* (New York: Oxford University Press, 1984), pp. 24–30.

12. Black and Black, *Politics and Society in the South*, pp. 237–245, 264–275; Lamis, *The Two-Party South*, 20–43; Harold W. Stanley, "Southern Partisan Changes: Dealignment, Realignment or Both?", *Journal of Politics* 50 (1988), 64–88; and Norman H. Nie, Sidney Verba, and John R. Petrocik, *The Changing American Voter*, enlarged ed., (Cambridge, MA: Harvard University Press, 1979), pp. 217–223.

13. Black and Black, *Politics and Society in the South*, pp. 269–271; and Nie *et al. The Changing American Voter*, pp. 226–229.

14. On the 1976 election result see Bass and DeVries, *The Transformation of Southern Politics*, pp. 409–412.

15. Lamis, *The Two-Party South*, pp. 31–42; and Black and Black, *Politics and Society in the South*, p. 11.

16. Lamis, *The Two-Party South*, pp. 31–39.

17. Lamis, *The Two-Party South*, pp. 218–232.
18. Beck, *American Political Science Review* 71 (1977), 477–496; Stanley, *Journal of Politics* 50 (1988), 64–88.
19. On 'split level realignment' see Everett Ladd, "The 1988 Elections: Continuation of the Post-New Deal System", *Political Science Quarterly* 104 (1989), 1–18; and Michael Nelson, "Constitutional Aspects of the Elections" in *The Elections of 1988*, ed. Michael Nelson (Washington, DC: Congressional Quarterly Press, 1989), pp. 181–209.
20. On the abolition of the two-thirds rule see Reiter. *Selecting the President*, p. 135; and Weiss, *Farewell to the Party of Lincoln*, p. 184.
21. Bass and DeVries, *The Transformation of Southern Politics*, pp. 203–207.
22. On the McGovern Fraser reforms see Byron E. Shafer, *Quiet Revolution: the Struggle for the Democratic Party and the Shaping of Post-Reform Politics* (New York: Russell Sage Foundation, 1983); Nelson W. Polsby, *Consequences of Party Reform* (New York: Oxford University Press, 1983); and Austin Ranney, "The Political Parties: Reform and Decline" in *The New American Political System*, ed. Anthony King, pp. 214–247.
23. Polsby, *Consequences of Party Reform*, pp. 53–64.
24. Polsby, *Consequences of Party Reform*, pp. 72–78; and Reiter, *Selecting the President*, pp. 73–77. See also Byron Shafer, *Bifurcated Politics* (Cambridge, MA: Harvard University Press, 1978).
25. William G. Mayer, "The New Hampshire Primary: A Historical Overview" in *Media and Momentum: the New Hampshire Primary and Nomination Politics*, eds. Gary R. Orren and Nelson W. Polsby, (Chatham, NJ: Chatham House, 1987), pp. 9–41.
26. On "momentum" and the New Hampshire primary see William C. Adams, "As New Hampshire Goes . . ." in *Media and Momentum*, eds. Orren and Polsby, pp. 42–59.
27. On the strategy of the Carter campaign see Jules Witcover, *Marathon: the Pursuit of the Presidency 1972–1976* (New York: Viking, 1977), pp. 105–138.
28. On Carter and blacks see Witcover, *Marathon*, p. 337; and Lamis, *The Two-Party South*, pp. 37–39.
29. Bass & DeVries, *The Transformation of Southern Politics*, pp. 409–412; and Lamis, *The Two-Party South*, pp. 37–39.
30. On Wallace and Carter in 1976 see Witcover, *Marathon*, pp. 253–273.
31. On the surge in Republican support among white southerners, and particularly evangelical Christians, in the late 1970s see Kevin P. Phillips, *Post-Conservative America: People, Politics & Ideology in a Time of Crisis* (New York: Vintage Books, 1983), pp. 90–91, 188–192.
32. On the collapse of Carter's white southern support in 1980 see William Schneider, "The November 4 Vote for President: What Did It Mean?" in *The American Elections of 1980*, ed. Austin Ranney, (Washington, DC: American Enterprise Institute, 1981), pp. 212–262.
33. On the 1984 primaries in the South see Gerald Pomper, "The Nominations" in *The Election of 1984: Reports and Interpretations*, ed. Gerald Pomper, (Chatham, NJ: Chatham House, 1985), pp. 1–34 (esp. 11–23); and Nelson Polsby, "The Democratic Nomination and the Evolution of the Party System" in *The American Elections of 1984*, ed. Austin Ranney, (Washington, DC: American Enterprise Institute, 1985), pp. 36–65.
34. 'Democrats Losing South, Kirk is told', *International Herald Tribune*, 18 February 1985.
35. On the formation of the DLC see Germond and Witcover, *Whose Broad Stripes and Bright Stars?*, pp. 39–41; and Dan Butz and David S. Broder, "The Rift in the Democratic Party Grows Wider", *Washington Post National Weekly Edition*, 11 March 1985.
36. Michael Barone, "How Democrats, the Free-Trade Party, Got to be Protectionists", *Washington Post National Weekly Edition*, 14 October 1985
37. On the 1986 Senate elections in the South see Germond and Witcover, *Whose Broad Stripes and Bright Stars?*, pp. 45–48.
38. On the genesis of Super Tuesday, 1988 see Germond and Witcover, *Whose Broad Stripes and Bright Stars*, pp. 41–42; Harold W. Stanley and Charles D. Hadley, "The Southern Presidential Primary: Regional Intentions With National Implications", *Publius* 17 (1987), 83–100; David S. Broder,

"In Presidential Elections, as the South Goes, So Goes the Nation", *International Herald Tribune*, 28 May 1986; Ronald Brownstein, "Moving Up", *National Journal*, 1 March 1986.

39. Several observers noted the flaws in the Super Tuesday strategy: Jack Germond and Jules Witcover, "South's Regional Primary May Not Be Decisive", *National Journal*, 8 March 1986; Alan Ehrenhalt, "Democrats Wooing Dixie Face Catch-22", *Congressional Quarterly Weekly Report*, 2 August 1986; William Schneider, "South's Primaries: A Hollow Shell?", *National Journal*, 22 February 1986; and David S. Broder, "A 'Told You So' in Advance of Not-So-Super Tuesday", *International Herald Tribune*, 2 March 1988.

40. On the effects of New Hampshire momentum on the Super Tuesday result see Charles D. Hadley and Harold W. Stanley, "Super Tuesday 1988: Regional Results and National Implications", *Publius* 19 (1989), 19–37.

41. On Gore's strategy see Thomas B. Edsall, "Gore's Southern Star Fading", *International Herald Tribune*, 6–7 February 1988.

42. On the Gephardt campaign see Germond and Witcover, *Whose Broad Stripes and Bright Stars?*, pp. 244–266 and 282–286.

43. James R. Dickerson, "Nunn Decides Not to Seek White House", *International Herald Tribune*, 28 August 1987.

44. For data on the 1988 Super Tuesday Voting see Rhodes Cook, "One Side is Clearer, the Other Murky", *Congressional Quarterly Weekly Report*, 12 March 1988.

45. On the absence of conservative Democrats from the polls on Super Tuesday see Hadley and Stanley, *Publius* 19 (1989), 19–37; and Craig Allen Smith and Kathy B. Smith, "Myths about Presidential Campaigning in the South: Dramatic Myths vs. Empirical Hypotheses in 1988" (Paper presented at the "Citadel Symposium on Southern Politics, Charleston, SC: March 9, 1990).

46. Cook, *Congressional Quarterly Weekly Report*, 12 March 1988.

47. Cook, *Congressional Quarterly Weekly Report*, 12 March 1988. On the false expectations created by Dukakis southern showing on Super Tuesday see Germond and Witcover, *Whose Broad Stripes and Bright Stars?*, pp. 289–290.

48. On Gore's disastrous New York and Wisconsin campaigns, see Witcover and Germond, *Whose Broad Stripes and Bright Stars?*, pp. 311–318.

49. On the effects of shifting the date of the California primary see Michael Oreskes, "Big State, Big Change, Big Risk for Democrats, *New York Times*, 19 February 1990.

Book Reviews

RONALD REAGAN, *An American Life: The Autobiography.* (New York: Simon & Schuster, 1990), 726 pp. $24.95 hardcover (ISBN 0-671-691-98-8).

Ronald Reagan's autobiography — *An American Life* — tells the remarkable story of how he made his way from Dixon, Illinois (a boyhood of odd jobs, lifeguarding, baseball, and football; the discovery that there was a thrill in acting and that he was good at it) to nearby, church-oriented Eureka College; after graduation, into radio broadcasting (sports announcing) and thence to Hollywood and instant screen success; into movie-lot union activity that brought him in only a few years to presidency of the Screen Actors Guild and to frequent public speaking for the Guild, mainly on labor/management relations in the movie industry (including accounts of an effort by local leftists to gain control of the union). These talks led to weekly appearances before a nation-wide radio/TV audience as host of the General Electric Theatre, plus talks to workers at GE plants throughout the country (for the speaker, "a postgraduate course in political science") and speeches to major audiences (e.g., San Francisco Commonwealth Club, Detroit Economics Club) dealing with issues of national import (tax rates were too high; government was spending too much and was too intrusive; the real problem was big government not big business; communism was a threat to democracy everywhere).

Established now as a super-effective public speaker, with a widely-attractive, enterprise-oriented message, and having determined for himself that he was a Republican not a Democrat, the move from podium to politics came easily and naturally: co-chairman for Goldwater in 1964 (a greatly admired speech for the candidate was "one of the most important milestones in my life"); California Governor in 1966; at the 1968 Republican presidential nominating convention, a few votes he did not seek; 1970, a second term as California governor; 1976, a narrow loss to Gerald Ford for the Republican presidential nomination ("It was a big disappointment because I hate to lose"); 1980, defeating George Bush for the Republican presidential nomination and Jimmy Carter for the office.

Telling this story absorbs about a third of the book, the remainder is on his presidency: a rather skimpy treatment of domestic policy (a lot about taxes and the budget; not much about money policy) but a full and perceptive account of his uninterrupted involvement in foreign affairs: intervening in Lebanon ("sending the marines to Beirut was . . . my greatest sorrow as president"); the "rescue mission" to Marxist-led, coup-affected Grenada (concerned for the safety of several hundred Americans attending medical school there, and urged to intervene by the Organization of Eastern Caribbean States, "we didn't ask anybody . . . we just did it"); the mainly fruitless effort to reduce tensions in the Middle East and gain the release of Americans and others held hostage there; the Iran/Contra affair (on which more below); and negotiations with a succession of Soviet leaders on arms reduction.

What comes through is a picture of a warm, compassionate man, thoroughly sincere, highly mission-oriented, and patriotic to the core; a raconteur from the beginning (it made him the Great Communicator), always something of an actor (had a love for it all his life), straightforward in personal relations ("I have always placed a lot of faith in the simple power of human contact"), fluent in popular speech (changing "bureaucratese into people talk"), goodnatured in manner (perhaps to a fault; it could invite underestimation of his grasp of major issues), and (outside of acting and public speaking) sufficiently unburdened by professional expertise to be innovative on sticky technical problems (proposing Star Wars the prime example). On finishing the book one asks: To what extent will it answer criticisms of his performance as president?

It should go a long way to that end. More important than anything else it may accomplish, it should refute the frequent charge — reflected in the title of a recent book, *Sleepwalking Through History* — that he was inadequately attentive to presidential duties. Whatever the facts may be regarding his day-to-day involvement in domestic policy (he set goals and "general ground rules," otherwise limited himself to being available to discuss problems and if necessary to "fine-tune the policies"), excerpts from his personal diary (reproduced *in extenso*) show beyond any reasonable doubt that he was deeply and continuously involved as the central figure in foreign policy. This president may have *seemed* languorous, but his diary tells a different story. In any case, a president should be judged by the program he proposes, and by the results obtained, not by what was, or appears to have been, his "management style."

To begin with, Mr. Reagan must be credited with having come to the White House with a bold, clearly articulated program. What it proposed to do would raise hackles in the liberal community, as it did. On the domestic side it would curb the increase of government spending, reduce government's intrusions into private affairs ("eliminate needless boards, agencies and programs"), and cut the top tax rates from 70 to 50 percent, phased in over three years. The proposal to cut taxes (ultimately agreed to by Congress, in slightly modified form) was the centerpiece of his "economic recovery plan." It was inspired (he reveals) not by supply-side economics, which he bluntly disowns, but by having worked as an actor under a 94 percent top rate, and was expected to give the economy (it was in recession at the time) a stimulus that would bring down inflation, unemployment and interest rates and (miracle of miracles) help produce a balanced budget ("by 1984 at the latest"). At the same time he would strive for a Supreme Court that would "interpret the Constitution, not try to rewrite it," with a woman to be his first nominee.

The fundamental goal on the foreign affairs side was to "reverse the effects of years of neglect of our armed services." This would provide a basis on which to seek agreement with the Soviets on arms reduction; beyond that, it would strengthen America's hand in confronting the international spread of communism, most importantly in Central America. Finally, there would be an urgent effort to reduce tensions in the Middle East and gain the release of Americans held hostage there.

As with all presidencies, there were both minuses and pluses in the results, and while the book is not written as a point-by-point defense of what was done, and of course is not an unbiased account, it provides much of what is relevant to an even-handed appraisal, in a laudably candid manner.

Going first to the domestic record, this reader's conclusion is that while there were big pluses in it the outcome was more minus than plus. It began with a miscalculation of the cyclical risk. White House staff have said they saw recession coming in 1981, but there is no evidence in this book, nor was there any at the time, that policy was being shaped with that risk in mind. In any case, before the first year was over the economy was in a deep recession, brought about largely by a severely disinflationary money policy, designed and executed by the Federal Reserve. It had GNP plunging nearly 3.5 percent between fall-1981 and fall-1982, ultimately lifting the unemployment rate to 11 percent. The economic recovery plan surely did not contemplate achieving its goals in this way, but it was mainly recession, and the monetary restraint that precipitated it, that cut the inflation rate (consumer price index) from 13.5 percent in 1981 to 3.2 percent in 1983 (it rose a bit thereafter — to 4.4 percent in 1988) and brought interest rates down from 17 percent (on high-grade corporate bonds) to about 12 percent (10 percent in 1988). However, on a schedule that is about par for the course, a brisk recovery began in the fall of 1982: in six months the ground lost in recession had been regained, and by 1988, as the administration ended, the economy was at new high levels of production, employment and income. For the Reagan period as a whole, the economy grew 2.9 percent a year, a remarkably good average for a period in which the inflation rate was being sharply reduced.

The most serious minus in the domestic record is that recovery and growth were achieved in 1982–88 in large part by an expansion of credit that left every part of American society, public and private, awash in debt. The president was not blameless in this, but neither was Congress, neither was the Federal Reserve, and neither was the financial community. It was the era of junk-bonds (Mr. Reagan did not invent them) and was followed (inevitably) by a collapse of financial institutions that compares closely with the 1930s. As the economic program hoped for, and despite an increase in defense spending, there was a sharp slowdown in the increase of overall budget outlays (from nearly 16 percent in Fiscal 1981 to 6.4 percent in Fiscal 1989), but tax reductions in 1982–83 and 1986 (the first, ill-timed and excessive; the second, a praiseworthy overhaul of the code that tax experts and presidents had been wanting for years to launch), plus the 1981–82 recession's effect on the tax base, allowed a gap to form between Treasury income and outgo that caused enormous budget deficits and boosted the public debt in eight years from $900 billion to $2.125 trillion. In part as a consequence of these fiscal developments, a deficit emerged in our international transactions that is still in course and has turned the U.S. from a creditor nation into a debtor nation.

Contrasting with the negative balance of these domestic results, the net on the side of foreign policy was clearly positive, indeed strikingly so. There was no reduction of Middle East tensions, and there were repeated disappointments on the release of hostages, but in East/West relations, in particular in arms reduction, the progress was historic. Thanks mainly to the unraveling of the Soviet economy (Reagan was early to sense this), but also to his pushing of four successive Soviet chiefs, to his launching of the Star Wars project (it may have come from science fiction, but he seems actually to have invented the idea), and to the rebuilding of U.S. military strength (it made Desert Storm possible), an end came suddenly to Soviet mischief-making around the world.

The blemish on this record (and the pity is that it didn't have to happen) is of course the ill-advised and badly-botched Iran/Contra affair. Many will read the book specifically for what it says about that incident: they will find that the memoirist has written about it at great length and, so far as this reader can judge, candidly. How an opportunity arose for gaining influence with certain anti-Khomeini "Iranian moderates" who might soon accede to power there, and who had "offered to persuade the Hizballah terrorists to release our seven hostages" is told in some detail: "Israel . . . had a large stock of TOW missiles in its military stockpile. (It) requested our permission to ship some . . . to the Iranian moderates; . . . the Iranians would pay for (them) and the United States would replenish Israel's stock . . . and be paid for them. . . . We would have to waive for Israel our policy prohibiting any transfer of American-made weapons to Iran."

Obviously, it was an undertaking on which the president would have opposition from Congress—indeed, he had opposition from the top ranks of his official family: Shultz, Weinberger and Regan were opposed—but it is not the law of the land that the president must accede to every limitation proposed for him by Congress: he "wanted to explore any avenue that offered the possibility of getting the hostages out of Lebanon" and he was assured that "everything about (the Iran initiative) was within the law and within the president's powers."

Understandably, the diversion to the Contras of funds generated in this transfer of weapons created a whole new set of questions. White House staff officers knew that helping the Contras had a high priority with the president ("I told the staff: We can't break the law, but, within the law, we have to do whatever we can to help the Contras survive") but evidence that funds had been diverted came to Reagan as "a bombshell." Describing the disclosure, he writes: after "an initial reaction of surprise, shock and disbelief . . . I told the cabinet and the White House staff that we were going to do everything we could to get to the bottom of the matter, immediately make public the discovery, and hide nothing."

It was of course an unfortunate and regrettable affair. As for Mr. Reagan's role in it, he deserves to be taken at his word: "North didn't tell me about this. Worst of all, John P(oindexter) found out about it and didn't tell me." And it is surely relevant to a reader's conclusions regarding the incident that, as Mr. Reagan recalls, both the Tower Commission and congressional investigating committees "agreed . . . with what I had been saying from the beginning: that I had had no knowledge of any diversion of monies to the Contras."

The book ends with a few pages on the leading features of the record, somewhat extravagant in their reporting of economic successes but not so in what they say about the immensely improved state of East/West relations and the greatly brightened outlook for democracy and freedom in the world. It should have a good effect on future studies of the Reagan presidency, specifically because it will require that, henceforth, commentary on it will have to be directed more to substance, less to style.

RAYMOND J. SAULNIER

Professor Emeritus of Economics
Barnard College, Columbia University

HELENE VON DAMM, *At Reagan's Side: Twenty Years in the Political Mainstream*. (New York: Doubleday, 1989), 341 pp. $18.95 hardcover (ISBN 038-524-4452).

This book provides some valuable perspectives on the Reagan Presidency. Helene von Damm worked for Ronald Reagan as his personal secretary during his governorship; as the northeast finance director of his 1980 campaign; as secretary, deputy director and director of presidential personnel in the Reagan White House; and finally as ambassador to her native Austria (until Nancy Reagan eased her out of the post). Despite Mrs. von Damm's emphasis on the importance of loyalty in evaluating those who served Reagan, she is not above making a few candid comments of her own on his strengths and weaknesses as president.

Like Reagan's current biographer, she finds Ronald Reagan to be an illusive figure. He liked people and was a positive person who could disarm his bitterest opponents with self-deprecating wit. He inspired "fierce loyalty" to those around him and was kind to but aloof from his staff. "In all the years I knew him I never once saw him lose his temper with an aide." Yet "getting to know Ronald Reagan proved to be an elusive goal." He appeared to have no close friends. Mrs. von Damm asserts that he may be a "much more complex individual than he would have us believe" and she suggests that there's an "inner Ronald Reagan which no one ever gets to see, with the possible exception of Nancy, but even then, I wonder" (p. 60).

The most interesting chapter in the book is her detailed account of the attempt of Reagan's California advisers to pick his Cabinet for him in 1980. It shows the president interacting with his "Kitchen Cabinet" to choose a Cabinet and White House staff reasonably well balanced in Republican party terms while being loyal to his objectives.

The Ronald Reagan who emerges from these pages is a man seemingly detached from his job and more interested in themes and ideas than in policy and administration. According to Mrs. Von Damm, the President's attention waned quickly when it came to policy issues. He "hated bureaucratic writing and would quickly get bored and pick up a copy of *National Review* or *Time* instead" (p. 52).

She correctly describes Reagan's view of government as "conservative, slightly libertarian" and asserts that Reagan's views on government were "much more philosophically based that that of other politicians" (p. 66, citing Reagan's opposition to compulsory motorcycle helmet laws). The President liked to kick around ideas with

Ed Meese, but he was easily bored by the details of policy making. On policy issues his attention span was very short:

"Those who knew him for over twenty years knew all of his little habits. . . . Bill Clark and Ed Meese both cultivated very direct styles of speaking. No circumlocution. They got straight to the point and they'd maintain eye contact with him as he spoke. As soon as his eyes wandered, they'd try another approach" (p. 320).

But Reagan was so passive a decision-maker on day to day matters that Mrs. von Damm found her job as personal secretary to the President of the United States rather unfulfilling:

"My job continued to dispirit me. Though I was serving a man I loved and admired, his style of management wasn't conducive to keeping a personal secretary stimulated and involved. He was never the initiator. . . . *He would make decisions as they were presented to him*" (p. 188; emphasis added).

According to Mrs. von Damm, only excellent staffing arrangements could compensate for Reagan's passivity and lack of interest in issues. Although a staunch Reaganite, she confesses that under the 1981–1984 "troika" of Baker, Deaver and Meese, which emerged after Reagan's attempted assassination, "there was a certain balance of power and competition" with Meese ensuring that "the policies and issues reflected Ronald Reagan's philosophy," Deaver protecting "the body and image" of the President, and Baker making "sure the apparatus worked and moved" (p. 255).

Yet, although heavily dependent upon good staffing arrangements, President Reagan did not take an active interest in ensuring that his staffing arrangements served his needs. A proposed job switch in which Baker would have become National Security Adviser and Deaver Chief of Staff was aborted only because Bill Clark, Bill Casey, Ed Meese and Cap Weinberger heard about it and suggested that they could not continue to serve the President under that arrangement. Like the famous job switch between Baker and Regan which did occur in 1985, this switch was arranged by the two individuals involved to serve their own careers but was not carefully considered by the President for the implications for his own staffing needs.

Mrs. von Damm thinks the Reagan Revolution was aborted in Reagan's second term because the President was no longer surrounded by loyal Californians like Meese, Weinberger and Bill Clark who were invaluable to Reagan because they knew his instincts and could contradict him if he thought he was on the wrong track.

"In fact, as I look back at the entire Administration, I'd have to say that where Ronald Reagan erred was in failing to appreciate what the people around him did. If he had stuck with the original band of Californians. . . . I think he and the goals of the Reagan Revolution would have been protected. For unlike many others who joined the Reagan team later, they did not have their own agenda. . . . I'm not saying that [his non-California advisers] didn't want to serve him well. I'm just saying that they lacked time and memory with him. They didn't know his strengths and weaknesses. . . . They didn't feel comfortable with his political instincts, and were always trying to move him to positions they thought would be more politically acceptable" (p. 318–319).

In my view, this conclusion gives far too little weight to the essential role which moderates such as James Baker and Howard Baker (to say nothing of Nancy Reagan) played in keeping the Reagan Revolution within politically acceptable grounds and in helping the President manage his remarkable political comebacks after the recession of 1982–83 and the Irangate affair in 1986–87. It is naive for Mrs. von Damm to think that Reagan might have enacted a far more conservative program than he did. In fact, one of the chief causes of Reagan's political ingenuity was his ability to judge the mood and even the inner feelings of the American public. As numerous polls have indicated, the American public's attachment was more to Ronald Reagan the person and to the values he espoused than it was to his programs.

Although Mrs. von Damm often does not do justice to Reagan the politician, she does cast considerable light on Reagan the conservative ideologue. So long as one bears in mind the perspective from which she writes, there are a number of valuable insights about Ronald Reagan in this book.

JEFFRY M. BURNAM

Professional Staff Member
United States Senate

DILYS M. HILL, RAYMOND A. MOORE and PHIL WILLIAMS, (Eds.), *The Reagan Presidency: An Incomplete Revolution?* (New York: St. Martin's Press, 1990) 284 pp. $24.95 hardcover (ISBN 312-03646-9).

The content of this book is readily summed up in the title; it is an early attempt to assess the Reagan Presidency in retrospect.

One of the most significant essays is perhaps that on "Managing and Organizing the Reagan White House" by Marcia Lynn Whicker. It summarizes both successes and failures of the Reagan administration, focusing on the "White House Troika of the first Administration," James Baker, Michael Deaver and Edwin Meese (it praises their leadership), Reagan's success in reawakening national pride, the appointment of David Stockman to OMB, and the early cabinet council system. Failures are listed as the Baker-Regan job swap, the Iran-Contra scandal, the Reykjavik summit, the Bork/Ginsburg rejections, the Defense Department procurement scandal, and ethics scandals. Most of these are associated with the second administration. The author says "Reagan's dramatic management style . . . worked better in the first term, when he had a well-functioning administrative team in the White House. . . . To reformers of the presidency who wish constantly to reshape the organizational structure of the White House, the Reagan lesson seems to be that actual organizational arrangements are less important than the quality of people close to the President, making key decisions and providing crucial advice . . ." (p. 65).

Dilys M. Hill and Phil Williams stress the influence of the "new right" in policy terms under President Reagan. They state that his policy successes "depended crucially on his choice of personnel." They note that the Cabinet process enabled the President to manage issues directly. They add that "the Reagan Presidency was marked by the skill, from the administration's point of view, with the Senior Executive Service (SES) of the bureaucracy used to increase the number of appointees who did not fall within the career civil service rules" (p. 17). The analysis points to the "effectiveness of James Baker at Treasury and the continued adroitness of George Shultz's approach to the summit with the Soviet Union . . ." (p. 20). Problems and vulnerabilities, including those examined in the Tower Report, are also analyzed.

Gillian Peele in "The Agenda of the new Right" concludes that "Conservatives had the excitement of access to power" (p. 44) and that: "The conservative movement has over the last eight years lost much of its momentum. . . . Some . . . leaders have lost their ideological bite as a result of absorption into the mainstream of Congress . . ." (p. 45).

Tinsley E. Yarbrough in "Reagan and the Courts" cites the conservative impact of Reagan appointees on not just the Supreme Court, but also the entire federal court structure. He adds that ". . . President Reagan may already have had a significant impact on the courts and civil liberties policy. To a much greater degree than any president since Roosevelt, he lent attacks on the courts the enormous prestige of his office . . ." (p. 91).

Of "Reagan's Relations With Congress," Louis Fisher concludes that Reagan ". . . came to office with important experience from a major state. His ability to communicate to the people was vastly superior to any president in the television age. . . . The tragedy of Ronald Reagan is that these ample gifts came to so little . . ." (p. 112).

Charles W. Dunn and J. David Woodard state in an excellent analysis, "Ideological Images for a Television Age: Ronald Reagan as a Party Leader" that: "In the minds of most Americans Ronald Reagan made the Republican Party, not vice versa. Their loyalty to the party is based on Reagan's success. Unlike his predecessors, Reagan was able to maintain his popularity after his election, and re-election. . . . Ronald Reagan was an effective leader because he tugged at the grass-root heartstrings of America. The Republican Party benefited—but only incidentally—from this popularity . . ." (p. 130).

Joseph J. Hogan says of "Reaganomics and Economic Policy" that budget and trade deficits are the primary legacies of the Reagan administration. He states: "In sum, the process of making a necessary transition from the economic legacy of the Reagan administration is likely to be a complex, difficult and protracted adjustment" (p. 158).

In "Domestic Policy in an Era of 'Negative' Government," Dilys M. Hill states: "The impact of the Reagan era on domestic policy was a vigorous assertion of a new policy perspective which rejected the 1960s and 1970s belief in social intervention and problem solving. What is striking is that, while Congress struggled to safeguard programs, there was little concerted resistance to this changed perspective; social engineering appeared dead . . ." (p. 176).

Raymond A. Moore writes in "The Reagan Presidency and Foreign Policy" that "Reagan's first term was a time when the old 'cold warrior' engaged in ideological warfare with the Soviets, prepared a buildup of U.S. forces and set the stage for a second term of performance in negotiation by the administration's pragmatists . . ." (p. 197).

Phil Williams comments in "The Reagan Administration and Defense Policy" as follows: "On the one hand, it is possible to argue that it was eminently successful. Not only did the President restore American pride and prestige, but the defense policy provided the necessary support for a foreign policy towards the Soviet Union which was initially somewhat bellicose but which gradually became more conciliatory. . . . An alternative view of the defense policy is that it fell far short of the rhetoric. The gap between organization and achievement was a large one, even if it was covered by the President's plans not only as a great illuminator but also as a great eliminator. If the 1970s was a decade of neglect — and this is an over-simplistic characterization — the 1980s was a decade of profligacy and waste in defense spending. . . . [A]t one level, U.S. defense policy from 1981 to 1988 seemed to have been eminently successful. The rhetoric of the Reagan defense policy made the American public believe that the difficulties stemming from the decade of neglect had been overcome . . ." (pp. 226–228).

On "The Reagan Legacy," Dilys M. Hill and Phil Williams write: ". . . By revitalizing the Presidency Reagan avoided, or at least postponed" a feared result voiced by James David Barber that without the President's power 'the people may turn him into an entertainer.'

"The revitalized Presidency . . . did not bring the radical recasting of American politics that Reagan had sought — the hoped-for revolution was incomplete. . . . Grenada and Libya symbolized both a revitalized Presidency and a regenerated United States. . . .

"The restoration of American pride and the regeneration of American power were major achievements of the Reagan administration. Yet both achievements had a certain fragility about them . . . (pp. 233–234).

"The real legacy of the Reagan administration was mixed: an incomplete revolution in terms of policy given the failure of the new right to achieve its social agenda. . . . But the legacy in terms of American Confidence was very real . . ." (p. 239).

The analysis is balanced and this one study represents one of the better attempts to get to the underlying mood and achievements of the Reagan Administration.

WILLIAM C. SPRAGENS

Spragens Research/Analysis
Herndon, Virginia

TOM WICKER, *One of Us, Richard Nixon and the American Dream* (New York: Random House, 1991), 731 pp. $24.95 hardcover (ISBN 0-394-55066-80).

In recent years, several solid biographies of Richard Nixon have appeared. Tom Wicker's *One of Us*, while more of a journalistic account than the scholarly, exhaustively comprehensive volumes by Stephen Ambrose and Richard Morris, is a stimulating and useful addition to the lengthening historiographical literature on the thirty-seventh President.

One of Us is in some respects two skillfully interwoven works. Principally, Wicker offers a well-written overview of Nixon's years in public life, and the ways in which his complex, conflict-ridden personality both served and betrayed him during his extraordinary career. Along the way, Wicker—a veteran *New York Times* political reporter—engages in an honest reappraisal of his own highly critical judgments and commentary about Nixon. Wicker's willingness to subject his own views about the most controversial American of the past fifty years to self-evaluation is most laudable, and his book is much the better for it.

Wicker's central theme is that Nixon was "one of us" because, to a greater degree than most politicians, he understood *and shared* the resentments, fears, and aspirations of middle-class, "Silent Majority" Americans. In particular, Nixon had a longstanding preoccupation with the "haves" and "have nots" of American life; Nixon despised the former and concurred with the prejudices of the latter. As a student at Whittier College, Wicker reminds us, Nixon helped polarize the campus' two main social groups, the upper-crust "Franklins" and humbler-stock "Orthogonians," whose first president was Richard M. Nixon. This instinctive dislike for well-born, naturally urbane, Ivy League-patrician types explains Nixon's immediate and highly personal hostility to Alger Hiss, whose celebrated espionage case in the late 1940s made Nixon a household word.

Lacking charisma, personal charm, or polished social skills, Nixon persuaded millions of Americans to vote for him, over a span of several decades. What was the essence of his appeal? The post-war generation was ambitious to get ahead and not inclined to be apologetic about wanting to share in the "American Dream." Not surprisingly, a large segment of such people identified with the ambitious, hard-driving scrambler from California. Like them, Nixon had inherited no wealth; he owed his success to his own initiative and hard work. Like them, Nixon wanted to climb the ladder of success as high as he could. Like them, Nixon experienced setback and defeat in his life, but such experiences only made him more determined than ever to come back and prove his adversaries wrong. These factors explain the admiration, if not affection, which much of the American public had for Nixon; warts and all, he was "one of us."

Of course, a sizeable number of Americans, particularly those of liberal political inclination, despised Richard Nixon. Their detest began with his first Congressional campaign, in which he used hardball tactics to unseat a New Deal-era California Democrat, Jerry Voorhees. Opposition to Nixon grew immensely during the Hiss/HUAC investigations, and he became a permanent villain to liberals in 1950 when he defeated Helen Gahagan Douglas in a brutal contest for a U.S. Senate seat. Refreshingly, not only does Wicker avoid typical Nixon-bashing in his accounts of these episodes, he bends over backwards to explain events from Nixon's perspective. Many readers, including those familiar with Wicker's past writings, will not be accustomed to so balanced a portrayal of Nixon. While hardly a model politician, the Richard Nixon of *One of Us* comes off as a not unethical figure endowed with considerable ability and entitled to much credit, starting with his role in the HUAC hearings that exposed Alger Hiss as a Communist spy.

While the focus of *One of Us* remains firmly on the most newsworthy events in Nixon's career, Wicker is quite effective at revealing the sensitive and emotional side to his subject's character and behavior. This approach is most successful in the discussion of the 1952 Fund Crisis, which nearly forced Nixon — running as the Vice Presidential nominee with Dwight Eisenhower — off the Republican national ticket. Nixon saved himself with the famous "Checkers" speech, which liberals forever after have scorned as the epitome of slick, self-serving and insincere political gimmickry. But Wicker sympathizes with Nixon's predicament; having been abandoned by press, party, and Eisenhower, Nixon toughed it out on his own and survived. Wicker also contends that Nixon's political personality was permanently affected, indeed warped, by this episode, the most traumatic of his career until Watergate.

After eight years as Vice President, Nixon lost the 1960 Presidential race to John Kennedy by an agonizingly close and disputed margin. Resisting pressure from friends, Republican party officials, and others, Nixon refused to contest the outcome, despite reports of fraudulent returns in Illinois and elsewhere, which if overturned could have tipped the election Nixon's way. Such an exercise, Nixon felt, would have demeaned the Presidency, cast a shadow over the Kennedy Administration's legitimacy, and hurt the country. Nixon realized that the principled thing to do would be to accept the verdict as it stood, however painful to him personally. For this heroic decision, Wicker lavishes his highest praise on Nixon.

Clearly, the author's own interest in the Nixon era peaks with the 1968 campaign. Wicker knowledgeably recounts the Democratic primary contests of that year, highlighted by Bobby Kennedy's (late) entry into the race. But the author's obvious preference for Democrats does not lessen his determination to be fair. Gone, in 1968, was the "old Nixon" of 1946 and 1950; in his place was a super-cautious figure — especially on the most pressing issue of the time, the Vietnam War — who nearly followed in Tom Dewey's 1948 footsteps by blowing a sure victory. Most accounts of this campaign condemn Nixon for his cynical silence on the war. Wicker, however, defends Nixon's refusal to discuss the war's conduct and prospects for peace while on the campaign trail: had Nixon spoken out or offered detailed plans for ending the war, he would have been accused of undermining President Lyndon Johnson's frantic efforts to bring the boys home. Nixon's campaign posture on Vietnam was less a strategy than a given set of circumstances over which he had little control.

Wicker's assessments of the Nixon Presidency are strikingly revisionist. The conventional wisdom has it that Nixon was a total failure on the domestic front, yet he achieved great things in foreign policy. Wicker's interpretation is just the opposite. He gives his old nemesis high marks for a host of domestic accomplishments, including the de-segregation of Southern schools and various environmental advances. Probably Nixon did not have "liberal" goals as such in these areas, yet he was a born political pragmatist, and his conservative credentials permitted him to meet Congressional Democrats more than halfway in fashioning a responsible domestic agenda. From Wicker's liberal vantage point, Nixon's record looks all the more impressive when compared to those of his successors, especially Ronald Reagan. Wicker concedes that, at the time, the press generally overlooked Nixon's positive domestic achievements;

interestingly, the author even concludes that pundits and other Nixon-haters were wrong when they mounted the campaign that defeated Nixon's nomination of Clement Haynesworth to the Supreme Court.

On the other hand, Wicker is sharply critical of Nixon's Vietnam policy. Wicker thinks America's role in that tragic conflict should have been ended much sooner. At a cost of many thousands of additional lives, Nixon chose to stay the course his entire first term; what, in the end, did the nation gain from this additional sacrifice?

In sum, Wicker's *One of Us* appreciably advances our understanding of the man who enjoyed and endured one of the most remarkable careers in U.S. political history. Wicker's own assessments are the result of mature reflection on controversies now well in the past; this book simply could not have been written without the emotional distance which comes with the passage of time. *One of Us* is by no means the definitive account of Richard Milhous Nixon; indeed, the 1962 gubernatorial race and the exhaustively-mined subject of Watergate received scant attention. Still, his subject's many flaws, as well as his claim to greatness, are on full display in Tom Wicker's engrossing work.

GEORGE SHORE

Temple University

LOUIS FILLER, ed. *The President in the 20th Century.* Vol. 2, *The Presidency in Crisis: From Lyndon B. Johnson to Ronald Reagan.* (Englewood, NJ: Jerome S. Ozer, Publisher, 1990), 341+ pp. $33.95 hardcover. (ISBN 0-89198-140-3).

The responsibilities that accompany the presidential office have always been daunting, but our recent experience suggests that perhaps the burdens placed on this office are simply too immense to be handled effectively. At least, that is one impression gained from Louis Filler's collection of presidential speeches, inaugural addresses, State of the Union messages, interviews, and press conferences covering five presidential administrations, from Lyndon Johnson to Ronald Reagan.

To illustrate the difficult path presidents have trod over the past two decades, the author has taken from the public record presidential communications in various forms — primarily speeches — to the most significant problems they faced. The five chapters, each devoted to a president, contain from eight to twelve selections. Filler has interspersed these selections with his own commentary and analysis, to reacquaint the reader with the context and to provide a transition from one presidential pronouncement to the next.

To read this collection is to revisit our recent political upheavals. A brief survey of some of the contents will convey a sense of this theme. The first chapter, devoted to Lyndon Johnson, has the new president accepting the reins of power in a speech to Congress after the Kennedy assassination and promising the nation an active reform agenda. Thereafter, there are instances of Johnson addressing the need to eliminate poverty, guarantee civil rights, and win the war in Vietnam.

The Vietnam burden continued to plague the Nixon administration. Nixon is revealed presenting his "Vietnamization" program, a plan to extract the United States from the embattled country, while protecting the capacity of the South Vietnamese to defend themselves. Several selections on the Nixon presidency are also devoted to Watergate and Nixon's unsuccessful attempt to minimize the gravity of the scandal. As congressional impeachment proceedings progress, he tenders an unprecedented presidential resignation, declaring that the "fight through the months ahead for my personal vindication" would not serve the national interests.

Assuming office at a critical juncture in national politics, Gerald Ford attempted to lay the Watergate scandal to rest. Ford is presented explaining his controversial decision to issue a presidential pardon to President Nixon. The rest of Ford's brief tenure in office is represented by his attempts to address the nation's economic troubles and by a last desperate appeal to Congress to salvage the collapse of the South Vietnamese government.

The arrival of Jimmy Carter as president was due in part to the electorate's dissatisfaction with the Washington political establishment and Carter's promise of a restoration of integrity in government. This theme is echoed in the Carter selections, along with the president's emphasis on the promotion of human rights in American foreign policy. Other major Carter addresses included here are his call for support of the Panama Canal Treaties and his announcement of progress in steps toward peace between Israel and Egypt.

Filler's coverage of the Reagan presidency extends only to 1981, hence the selections offered are not representative of his entire two terms of office. On the other hand, the Reagan entries do convey a sense of his major domestic concerns, including a reduction in federal government activities, lower taxes, and a recommitment to invigorate the private sector of the economy. Unfortunately, the major crisis of the Reagan presidency, the Iran-Contra Affair, is not addressed.

Filler's commentary does not attempt a detailed evaluation of each of the presidents covered, yet the author does occasionally indicate his assessment of presidential performance during this tumultuous period. Johnson is treated sympathetically. Though not denying the scandalous nature of the Watergate affair, Filler is disturbed by the capacity of that incident to overshadow the achievements of the Nixon presidency. President Ford is given credit for the Nixon pardon. The Carter presidency is faulted, however, for having neither a coherent vision of where it wanted to take the nation nor the political skills to make the gears of government turn smoothly. Conversely, Reagan is credited for possessing an ideology that provided a sense of direction for his administration.

One recurrent theme in Filler's commentary is the tendency of the media, in its adversarial role, to undermine the credibility of the occupants of the office. This effect was particularly pronounced in the presidencies of Nixon, Ford, and Reagan, in the author's view. Thus the long-standing hostility of the national media to Nixon and his presidency made it unlikely that the Watergate scandal would be kept in perspective alongside Nixon's achievements. Similarly, the author believes both Ford and Reagan were hampered by a lingering suspicion among media elites, despite evidence to the contrary, that they were too simple-minded and intellectually deficient to handle the demands of the office.

Though the presidential record presented here is largely a picture of crisis, and ultimately failure, it is simplistic to identify the media as the main culprit. To his credit, Filler locates the source of the failure in a broader context, specifically the bitter discord that emerged in a nation confronted with divisive social issues, a faltering economy, and a threatening international environment. Amid such circumstances, it is no wonder the office and the men who occupied it were subject to extraordinary pressure.

D. BRUCE HICKS

Assistant Professor of Political Science
Cumberland College

MICHAEL BARONE, *Our Country: The Shaping of America from Roosevelt to Reagan.* (New York: The Free Press, 1990), 670 + pp. $29.95 hardcover (ISBN 0-02-901861-7).

This large book is journalistic in style (the author is a Senior Writer for *U.S. News and World Report* and was formerly an editorial page writer at *The Washington Post*), but it contains ninety-three pages of scholarly and journalistic references. Barone focuses on the electoral and political strategies and fortunes of Presidents and presidential hopefuls, members of Congress, and the Democratic and Republic parties. He discusses the leadership styles of officials, the ways they understood and utilized issues, and major electoral outcomes. He offers excellent characterizations of individuals, and he encapsulates important demographic and social changes which have had significant political effects. For example, he examines the legitimation and growth of trade unions during the 1930's and 1940's, and he traces the dramatic growth of government during and since World War II.

Three basic themes guide Barone's work. He argues, first, that in spite of the obvious importance of economic issues, particularly in the twenty years after the New Deal, Americans are more often divided politically along cultural than along economic lines. One important aspect to this division concerns what it means to be an American. Second, he argues that in wartime Americans want larger government and cultural uniformity, while in peacetime we want smaller government and cultural diversity. Third, he emphasizes that individuals matter, that particular political leaders had important effects on political events that were not determined by social forces, effects quite different from those that other leaders would have had. In particular, Barone insists that Franklin Roosevelt's personality and actions had enormous consequences for American political life.

While Barone does not provide a great deal of original material in this book, every reader will learn new information from it. Moreover, Barone relates events and political decisions very coherently. Above all, the book is highly enjoyable to read.

ROBERT B. THIGPEN

Professor of Political Science
University of New Orleans

RICHARD E. NEUSTADT, *Presidential Power and the Modern Presidents: The Politics of Leadership from Roosevelt to Reagan.* (New York: Free Press, 1990), $22.95 hardcover, 371 pp., including Index (ISBN 0-02-922795-X) and James P. Pfiffner (ed.), *The Managerial Presidency.* (Pacific Grove, CA:Brooks/Cole, 1991), $18.25 papercover, 264 pp. (ISBN 0-534-13194-8).

The two books under review are testimony to the evolution of presidential studies over the past three decades. On the one hand we have an expanded version of Neustadt's enduring study of *leadership* in the modern presidency; and on the other we have a collection of short essays on *management* in the modern presidency.

Even three decades ago, in its earliest incarnation, *Presidential Power* looked at issues of power, authority and influence through a wide angle lens. Now, with the addition over the years of five substantial chapters that constitute almost half of the volume in its current form, the book has the breadth and weight that befits an authentic classic. Pfiffner's collection, in contrast, hones in on one aspect of the executive's job and, in keeping with the fashion of the times, gives it close inspection.

To return to Neustadt is to be reminded of a political science that was, perhaps, kinder and gentler than that of the thirty intervening years. For while Neustadt's original volume may have been many things, it was not, in what are now considered conventional terms, methodologically rigorous. It was, rather, a more personal document that grew frankly out of the author's own experience in Washington. In fact, one can reasonably speculate that it was accessible to practitioners—the most famous of whom was, of course, John Kennedy—precisely because it eschewed the jargon of political science in favor of plain English. Pfiffner's volume, in turn, is almost entirely objective in tone; moreover it contains just enough tables, figures and typologies to qualify for what has come in the intervening years to be considered serious social science.

To appreciate Neustadt's seminal contribution one must go back in time, to when presidential power was thought of primarily in terms of constitutional rights and constraints, institutional arrangements and functions, and systemic patterns and proclivities. The actual *dynamic* of presidential power, the human dimension if you will, had been left out of the equation. Thus it was left to Neustadt—whose strength has always been his intuitive and practical understanding of what makes men and, very occasionally, women, tick—to draw to our collective attention that which now seems self evident: that presidential power depends on the capacities of presidents to persuade others to follow where they lead.

It is good to be able to report that the two chapters that constitute the latest additions to what has turned out to be a work in progress are among the best in the book. Testifying again to the idiosyncratic way in which Neustadt works, they are focused primarily on the Iran-Contra story—which is, after all, a tale not of "presidential leadership," but rather one of—shades of James Pfiffner—presidential management. Consider this lesson learned from the damaging affair, delicious and sage at the same time. The voice is Neustadt's, political scientist, psychologist and, most endearingly, *mensch*: "Never let your Nancy be immobilized. . . . The moment your arrangements make 'her' isolation possible, you'd better dig into details yourself. . . . Such simple rules may not apply to everyone, or all the time. A President experienced enough might do without a Nancy. (Though why should he? A second pair of eyes, if truly trustworthy, never hurt.)"

The essays in Pfiffner's volume constitute a timely and useful discussion of the managerial aspects of the executive's task. While seven of the eighteen pieces are not new, having these multiple variations on the same theme bound between two covers provides a service to those among us who believe that so far as the American presidency is concerned, bad management virtually precludes good leadership (shades of Richard Neustadt).

The central concern of this book is the "extent to which presidents can exercise control over the executive branch bureaucracies and the question of whether they should try to exert that control." The essays are divided among three sections whose names evoke their contents: Organizing the White House, Presidentializing the Bureaucracy, and Presidential Control of Policy. Given the roster of contributors— among them Hugh Heclo, Samuel Kernell, Bruce Buchanan, Richard Rose, Francis Rourke, Terry Moe, Charles O. Jones, George C. Edwards III and Louis Fisher— it is not surprising that the overall level of the contributions is high. With the additional help of Pfiffner's skilled editorial hand (he also contributed two chapters), the collected essays constitute a carefully constructed overview of a domain of executive responsibility that is increasingly recognized as being of paramount importance.

In tandem, the two volumes under review confirm the interdependence of leadership and management. There can be little doubt that at least so far as the late twentieth century American presidency is concerned, these two capacities necessarily go hand in hand.

BARBARA KELLERMAN

Professor of Political Science
The George Washington University

PETER G. BOYLE, ed. *The Churchill-Eisenhower Correspondence, 1953–1955.* (Chapel Hill: University of North Carolina Press, 1990), 250+ pp. $24.95 hardcover. (ISBN 0-8078-1910-7).

The letters in this book cover the period from Dwight D. Eisenhower's inauguration as president in 1953 until Prime Minister Winston Churchill's retirement in

1955. This personal correspondence that is mostly concerned with governmental affairs illustrates the interests, views of world affairs, and personalities of the two leaders.

The association between the two men dated back to World War II, and the correspondence reflects the mutual respect that developed. It also reveals the concerns each had about the other and the foreign policies of the country he represented. Churchill distrusted the extreme right wing of the Republican Party, and he saw his role as a restraining influence. On the issue of Formosa, for example, Eisenhower wrote of American "self-respect" and its weariness at "being dupes" in response to Churchill's concern that removing the Seventh Fleet restraints on the Nationalist Chinese might widen the war in the Far East (pp. 18–19). Eisenhower thought that the Anglo-American partnership Churchill wanted would not solve all the problems on the international scene, and he wanted to broaden America's contacts in the world. Churchill balked at widening discussions over the Suez Canal zone when a joint British-American initiative "might by itself settle a dispute peaceably to the general advantage of the free world" (p. 35). When both men resumed making plans for a meeting in Bermuda after Churchill recovered from a stroke, Churchill wrote that they "should have a much better talk together alone" without the French, although Eisenhower thought there might "be considerable value in a good talk between us and the French" over problems with the European Defense Community (EDC), Indochina, and the North Atlantic Treaty Organization (NATO) (pp. 89, 94).

For readers unfamiliar with the background of Anglo-American relations and the Churchill-Eisenhower relationship up to 1953, Peter G. Boyle, a lecturer in American history at the University of Nottingham, provides a valuable twelve page introduction. Each topic is also preceded by a useful summary of the historical context, and references in letters are annotated for clarity. Each topic that is covered in the wide-ranging correspondence — the EDC, Formosa, atomic energy, relations with the Soviet Union following Marshal Josef Stalin's death, Iran, the armistice in Korea, Far-West trade, Egypt, Indochina, West German entry into NATO, and the Quemoy and Matsu incident — is introduced with helpful background information that puts the issues in a broader context. Boyle also raises a number of questions that go to the core of his subject: how did the Anglo-American relationship fare between 1953 and 1955, which nation's approach to the Soviet Union was more realistic, to what degree did Churchill restrain what he viewed as the extremes of a volatile American foreign policy, what assessment can be made of Churchill's effectiveness in his last years in power, and what conclusions can be drawn about Eisenhower as a statesman. The book also contains a thorough index as well of photographs of the two leaders.

Based on the correspondence, Boyle argues in a short concluding chapter that the two nations grew apart between 1953 and 1955. The United States surpassed England in economic and military power, divisive issues that are scarcely covered in the letters. Britain's declining power severely limited Churchill's leverage, especially in the Far East and with the Soviet Union. Eisenhower wrote Churchill acknowledging the fundamental disagreement between the two nations over United States policy in the Quemoy and Matsu incident and Churchill's difficulty in backing the United States position in Britain. This was not a request for advice, but a call for solidarity for a course already taken, lest their "political enemies exploit every sign of weakness" (p. 192). Colonialism remained an equally sensitive subject as well as one in which England was on the losing side. Eisenhower had little influence over Churchill, who remained determined not to preside over the disintegration of the British empire. To Eisenhower's counsel that "a fierce and growing spirit of nationalism" was forcing the end of colonialism "as a relationship among people," Churchill pointed with pride the British policy of "bringing forward backward races and opening up the jungle" (pp. 165, 167).

Regarding Eisenhower's unfriendly attitude toward the Soviet Union, Boyle argues that Churchill was one of those who eventually influenced Eisenhower to meet Premier Nikita Khrushchev in 1959. Although Churchill was unsuccessful in getting Eisenhower to seize upon Stalin's death as an opportunity for an earlier summit meeting, he felt "old age notwithstanding, a responsibility and resolve to use any remaining influence I may have to seek, if not for a solution at any rate for an easement" of tensions, especially since "appalling preparations are being made for measureless mutual destruction" (p. 167). These fears of a nuclear world war haunted both leaders.

Boyle argues that the correspondence support the reassessment of Eisenhower's reputation of an intelligent man with a sound grasp of the issues. Many of the long letters, concerning such matters as Egypt, the communist threat, his concept of a domino theory, colonialism, the EDC, or China, provide conclusive evidence that Eisenhower did not abrogate responsibility to Secretary of State John Foster Dulles. Eisenhower referred to information Dulles had provided him or discussions they had, but the conclusions are Eisenhower's. The subjects Churchill wrote about reveal themes that had dominated his political career as well as his continuing hopes for the world, although old age and failing health prevented him from doing much more than write.

ARLENE LAZAROWITZ

Lecturer, History
California State University, Long Beach

WALDO HEINRICHS, *Threshold of War: Franklin D. Roosevelt and American Entry into World War II.* (New York: Oxford University Press, 1988), 220+ pp. $21.95 hardcover (ISBN 0-19-504424-X). $8.95 papercover (ISBN 0-19-506168-3).

Waldo Heinrichs argues persuasively that full understanding of American entry into World War II requires "a modern synthesis combining the story of deepening participation in the war against Hitler with the related story of the road to Pearl Harbor and placing American policy in its global context" (p. viii). In *Threshold of War: Franklin D. Roosevelt and American Entry into World War II*, he examines the nine months from the passage of Lend-Lease to America's declaration of war, as the conflict moved from "interconnected regional crises toward a unitary global balance of forces" (p. vii). The events are well known, but Heinrichs's juxtaposition of war news, intelligence information, strategic plans, limitations on resources and public support, and speculations about options and consequences give the story new dimension.

Heinrichs begins in March 1941 as the United States reached a "new foreign policy consensus," still opposed to a declaration of war but willing to "aid Britain short of war even at the risk of war" (pp. 11–12). Simultaneously, "Germany and Japan were reaching the limits of regional expansion. Any further aggression would have global reverberations" (p. 12). Uncertainty and speculation impeded policy-making. Ineffective coordination and evaluation of information diluted abundant intelligence data. But President Roosevelt was evolving a "War Council," and "Anglo-American collaboration was becoming an unprecedented transnational enterprise" (p. 19).

In April, the U.S. and Japan extended their security boundaries. Roosevelt moved the Atlantic defense zone to the 26th meridian but rejected convoy escort because neither the Atlantic Fleet nor American public opinion were ready. Japan concluded a neutrality pact with the Soviet Union. With the Hull-Nomura talks, the Roosevelt Administration tried to ease relations with Japan and perhaps "dissociate Japan from Germany" (p. 49).

May resembled March in unanswered questions. Would Germany attack in the Middle East? Russia? through Spain to northwest Africa and the Atlantic islands within flying distance of Brazil? American resources remained thin. FDR's advisers debated moving ships to the Atlantic to relieve the British or leaving a strong fleet at Pearl Harbor to discourage the Japanese.

Hitler attacked the Soviet Union on 21 June 1941, which bought time for the free world. FDR cautiously opened a supply line to Russia and moved ahead with Atlantic patrols, U.S. defense of Iceland, and convoy escort in the Western Atlantic, while continuing to resist Navy arguments to get into the war.

July was "a wonderful clarifying month for Roosevelt and his advisers" (p. 144). Contrary to expectations of quick capitulation, Russia resisted the German advance. Japan now became "the incalculable component of this global scheme of ordered force" (p. 145). Was its move into Indochina a step toward Singapore? FDR's Administration considered economic deterrents and air reinforcement of the Philippines. But "Roosevelt could see the whole picture now" and "knew what direction he wanted to take" (p. 145).

Heinrichs sees the Atlantic Conference in early August as "a critical juncture in the evolution of Roosevelt's world policies." FDR worked "to establish the political basis for waging and winning the war" (p. 151). More important, "maintaining a Russian front against Hitler became the centerpiece of his world strategy." He would "enter the Battle of the Atlantic at the risk of war" to supply the Soviet Union "no less than Britain" (p. 159). Similarly, "severe containment" of Japan might tempt a Japanese move southward but that would be preferable to Japan attacking Russia; and "draining of Japan's oil supplies would progressively reduce its capacity for war" while American military power increased (pp. 159–60). The Administration elected a "deviously managed" (p. 177) *de facto* oil embargo wrapped in red tape of export licenses and use of frozen funds.

Heinrichs says that "no single decision or day marked the point when Roosevelt crossed over from benevolent neutrality to belligerency and risk of war," but Friday, 5 September 1941, "seems to epitomize the transition" (p. 179) with convoy escort, promise of aid to Stalin, the undercover embargo, and departure of the first B-17s for Manila. Ironically, that same day, a Japanese Imperial Conference determined to try diplomacy until October, and then "decide to go to war with the United States, Great Britain, and the Netherlands" (pp. 184–85). Japan's demands had increased, but delay served American interests. Therefore, negotiations continued while Germany drove on Moscow, Tojo replaced Konoe, American analysts speculated whether Japan might move north or south, and air reinforcement of the Philippines accelerated.

But by 26 November, the die had been cast. Washington expected Japan to attack soon. Response depended on the location of the attack. At the beginning of December, FDR assured the British of support but might need time to make political and Constitutional arrangements. Japan attacked Pearl Harbor on 7 December, and the United States declared war the following day. By 11 December, "nine months to the day since the passage of Lend-Lease" (p. 220), the United States was at war with all three partners of the Axis.

Heinrichs tells his story well. Although initially referring to FDR as "this most elusive and dissembling of presidents" (p. vii), he takes pains to examine rather than merely castigate the President's actions and motives. *Threshold of War* suffers slightly from its artificial scheme of months-as-chapters which sometimes interferes with analysis of problems or breaks down as the author moves backward or forward in time to provide context. Murky reproduction, particularly in the paperback edition, reduces the value of a series of potentially enlightening maps from the *New York Times*. Heinrichs neglects Latin America and rarely ventures below the highest levels of federal bureaucracy in examining the creation of policy. Nevertheless, his step-by-step approach teaches the valuable historical lesson that FDR, his advisers, his would-be allies, and his enemies-to-be were compelled to respond to evolving current events and never had the advantage of knowing how their actions would turn out. Since lively debate continues about American entry into World War II, some readers will welcome *Threshold of War* and others will want to argue with it; but friends and foes alike may read it with profit.

SUSAN ESTABROOK KENNEDY

Professor of History
Virginia Commonwealth University

JOHN MILTON COOPER JR. and CHARLES E. NEU, eds. *The Wilson Era: Essays in Honor of Arthur S. Link.* (Arlington Heights, Ill.: Harlan Davidson, 1991), 356+ pp. $26.95 hardcover (ISBN 0-88295-877-1). $18.95 paper (ISBN 0-88295-872-0).

Arthur S. Link is the most distinguished and productive historian of his age. The author of a five-volume biography of President Woodrow Wilson (still definitive although unfinished), editor of the monumental *The Papers of Woodrow Wilson* (72 + vols., Princeton: Princeton University Press, 1966), director of thirty-one doctoral dissertations, a history professor of distinction at Northwestern and Princeton universities, Link dominates his field and perhaps his historical era. John Milton Cooper, Jr. and Charles E. Neu have tried to define Link's significance in the historical profession as well as the current state of Woodrow Wilson scholarship. They have handsomely succeeded. In the process they (and Link as the subject and catalyst) have produced a volume of collected essays that will remain essential reading for Woodrow Wilson and his era, for historians, graduate students, and academics, who need to know how the historical profession worked in the post World War II era. The book is equally useful for the ongoing history of the Wilson papers project, which along with the *Library of America,* is the most monumental scholarly and documentary publishing undertaking of our time.

The volume's main topics include Link's biography and his development as an historian; Progressive era studies; the League of Nations dispute; Wilson's relations with Edward House; the influence of religion on Wilson's politics; assessments of the Wilson Papers project; and a reexamination of Wilsonian idealism versus George Kennan's realism in foreign policy. A full bibliography of Link's writings, a list of the doctoral dissertations he directed, and brief introductory comments by the editors and George McGovern fill out the volume. What makes the collection so extraordinarily useful is the consistent quality of the individual essays, the way in which many of them relate to each other, and the successful integration of Link's historical career into the current, very much alive historiography of Woodrow Wilson's presidency.

George B. Tindall's "The Formative Years" gracefully describes Link's growing up in rural North Carolina and his education at the University of North Carolina at Chapel Hill. Tindall's essay serves the dual function of illuminating the early education of a potential scholar and the academic development of a major Southern university and its history department before the enormous growth that followed World War II. Richard Leopold's essay is both a touching personal memoir of his close friendship with Link and an intimate view of the historical profession in the late 1940s. Leopold traces Link's happy and productive years at Northwestern, his early development as an academic superstar, and Northwestern's rivalry with Princeton and the East when Link won the editorship of the Wilson papers in 1954.

William A. Link's essay on the "Social Context of Southern Progressivism," Steven J. Ross's work on "Cinema and Class Conflict," and William H. Harbaugh's on "The Conservation Movement," are useful examples of progressive era social history. Harbaugh's piece on the limits of voluntarism in American agricultural policy is particularly impressive in its breadth and use of new sources. Ross's work should be read in conjunction with his recent *American Historical Review* article (April, 1991) which gives his subject the broader context it requires. Ralph B. Levering's examination of the domestic political effect of the League of Nations controversy in Democratic North Carolina and Republican New Jersey is a splendid example of the specificity of history, one that may well define how different historical research is from the models of political science. John Milton Cooper addresses one of the key issues in Wilson historiography, the political motivation of Wilson's final national train campaign and the effect of his impending illness on the League fight in the Senate. The questions remain open, but the discussion is rewarding. Charles Neu's new research on the strange relationship between Edward House, Wilson, and Wilson's two first ladies, Ellen and Edith, underlines the bizarre nature of House's limited contribution to Wilsonian foreign policy. John M. Mulder's relating of Wilson's religious beliefs to his political decisions is heavy going and is only partly persuasive.

Dewey Grantham's assessment of the Wilson papers project is balanced and useful. He traces the changes in editorial policy as the project matured, and surveys the critical historical commentary. Thomas J. Knock's comparison of Wilson's and George Kennan's apparently opposing views of the basis of U.S. foreign policy—idealist versus realist, internationalist versus balance of power—shows that the two men were not as far apart as is commonly believed. Kennan's own comments confirm Knock's view and add a welcome coda to the debate.

The principal usefulness of this volume lies in the breadth of the undertaking. Wilson was a rare American intellectual who became president. As an academic and an historian he preserved many of his papers in an age when the typewriter, not the computer, the telephone, or broadcast media—radio or television—dominated. Link's five volumes remain monumental political biographies of a complex time that historians still have not finished with. His further work in superintending the publication of the enormous body of Wilson's papers is ongoing archival history that is just beginning to make its mark. Eventually the historians who direct graduate students will realize and exploit the treasures that Wilson and Link together have left. It is precisely this unique collaboration between an historical figure and his biographer that Cooper and Neu have captured so well in this rich volume. This is history—the finished product, and the process as well. The book could well serve as a text for any introductory graduate history course and as a book historians might consider giving to social science colleagues as a demonstration of what historians ideally do. The publisher for the most part has produced a book as handsome as its conception and writing, although one would always prefer the footnotes at the bottom of the page and not at the end of chapters.

RICHARD H. COLLIN

Professor of History
University of New Orleans

RICHARD H. COLLIN, *Theodore Roosevelt's Caribbean: The Panama Canal, the Monroe Doctrine, and the Latin American Context.* (Baton Rouge and London: Louisiana State University Press, 1990), 598 + pp. (ISBN 0-8071-1507-X).

In this impressively researched and masterfully crafted volume, diplomatic historian Richard H. Collin presents a generally compelling case for three intricately interwoven theses. 1. that Theodore Roosevelt was the first truly "modern president", both in terms of his willingness to maximize executive power and of his elevation of foreign policy concerns to a parity with domestic issues, 2. that a full understanding of the multifaceted economic, cultural, ideological and political context of Latin America, the United States, and Europe in which Roosevelt had to operate makes it intellectually impossible to reduce the president's Caribbean policy to any simple model of imperialism, 3. that T.R.'s actions and policies can only be fairly judged when they are placed within the context of time and place and judged on their own merits, rather than as the beginning phase of a century-long pattern of U.S. domination of Latin America. Viewed from these perspectives, Collin argues strongly that Roosevelt's Caribbean policy was exceeding "moral", i.e., based upon the President's considered judgment regarding the long-term best interests of the western hemisphere and productive of the best outcomes realistically possible. To illustrate his contentions, Collin painstakingly leads the reader through the complex intricacies of people, events, and ideas that shaped the building of the Panama Canal, the issuance of the Roosevelt Corollary to the Monroe Doctrine, and the establishment of "Cuba Libre, Cuba Triste."

It is difficult to dispute the contention that Roosevelt was the first modern president. "In any nation which amounts to anything," Collin quotes the Rough Rider, "those in the end must govern who are willing actually to do the work of governing; and in so far as the Senate becomes a merely obstructionist body it will run the risk of seeing its power pass into other hands" (p. 445). Even more straightforward was Roosevelt's assertion that "while President I have *been* president, emphatically. I have used every ounce of power there was in the office and I have not cared a rap for the criticism of those who spoke of my 'usurpation of power'." Believing that "the efficiency of this Government depends upon its possessing a strong central executive," T.R. did his best to "establish a precedent for strength in the executive." While apologizing to no one for his belief in the efficacy of power, Roosevelt was careful to state his conviction that "responsibility should go with power and that it is not well that the strong executive should be a perpetual executive" (p. 458). At bottom, Collin concludes, Roosevelt's actions in the Dominican Republic, and elsewhere in the region, were "part of a long and complex period of adjustment between the Congress and the executive that included a more active American Caribbean presence with a stronger emphasis on responsibility after limited strategic goals had been achieved" (p. 458).

Much more controversial are Collin's other two theses which could easily be marshalled into an *apologia* for imperialism. In meticulously reconstructing the context in which Roosevelt operated, Collin places much of the responsibility on European and Latin American governments, and on the U.S. Senate, while portraying T.R. as a leader of vision, compassion, integrity, and realism. Roosevelt's chief goal, he insists, was to prevent the European powers from turning the Caribbean into "Latin America's Balkans" and to establish once and for all the independence of the western hemisphere. Moreover, many European leaders were only too happy to allow the United States to build and operate an isthmian coral, to broker their financial disputes with Latin American governments, and to serve as the policeman of the Caribbean. If anything, his judgment on the leaders of Colombia, the Dominican Republic, and Cuba is even harsher. Much of the impetus for Roosevelt's actions in Panama, Collin asserts, should be attributed to the intransigence and duplicity of Colombian president Jose Marroquin, "Dominican leaders manipulated the various European interests as well as the United States fear of European domination in the Caribbean" (p. 349). Latin America leaders proved unwilling or unable to address their region's fundamental socioeconomic and political problems, while the president's freedom of movement was severely curtailed by a Senate jealous of its prerogatives, suspicious of Roosevelt's motives, and determined to exercise its hegemony. The energies that might have been expended in designing more imaginative solutions to Latin America's massive problems were spent trying to get the smallest arrangement past a hostile Senate.

Overall, Collin concludes, Roosevelt's biggest accomplishment was to disengage both the U.S. and Latin America "from European domination through diplomacy, not belligerence" (p. 548). While acknowledging that Roosevelt made mistakes—his inordinate grant of power to French canal official Phillipe Bunau-Varilla in Panama or his trust in the fiscally irresponsible Santo Domingo Improvement Company, for example, Collin still insists that the Rough Rider "moved the United States closer to Europe, won European assent to the Monroe Doctrine, made peace and a realistic diplomatic understanding with Japan, and tried to temper American power in the Caribbean with a genuine understanding of Latin American sensitivities, political disappointment, and suspicions" (p. 561). What Latin America really needed, Collin argues, was a genuine Latin American nationalism independent from both Europe and North America, a solution that had some hope of success before the untimely death of Cuba's Jose Marti in 1895.

Equally controversial is Collin's assertion that Roosevelt's Caribbean policies, if viewed within their complete context, were not the beginning of America's sorry record of intervention in Latin American affairs. Roosevelt's main purpose, he insists, was the exclusion of Europe, not the subjugation of Latin America, and his main weapons were diplomacy and moral suasion, not economic penetration, military force, or covert subversion. The proper context for understanding Roosevelt's Caribbean policy, lies "in the world of Marti, Marroquin, and U.S. Senator [John Taylor] Morgan and in the president's struggle to prevent Germany from replacing Spain in the region," not in trying to make the era part of "Fidel Castro's Cuba, Daniel Ortega's Nicaragua, or Manuel Antonia Noreiga's or Omar Torrijos' Panama" (p. xiv).

While the author constructs a powerful case for all three of his major propositions, it is unlikely that those historians who have been critical of T.R.'s Caribbean policy will heed the injunction to reserve judgment until they understand the complete context in which Roosevelt operated. In stressing the importance of context, Collin sometimes underestimates the importance of continuity in attitudes and actions that have characterized United States Latin American relations for nearly a century and a half. For all of his commendable concern with establishing the context, the author apparently consulted few sources that might have conveyed a more critical analysis of Roosevelt's policies and who surely would have agreed with Collin's observation that "both North and South America might have been better served if Jose Marti, not Theodore Roosevelt, had freed Cuba and become the intellectual and political leader of a new and independent Caribbean nationalism" (p. 558).

JOHN D. BUENKER

Professor of History
University of Wisconsin-Parkside

MARK E. NEELEY, JR. *The Fate of Liberty: Abraham Lincoln and Civil Liberties.* (New York: Oxford University Press, 1991), xvii + 278 pp. $24.95 hardcover (ISBN 0-19-506496-8).

At the initial meeting of the first graduate seminar I ever attended, the professor declared that Abraham Lincoln was a dictator and then proceeded to prove the point by giving facts and figures on arbitrary arrests during his administration. One wonders if Mark Neeley had a similar experience, for he begins with a comparable assertion but then spends the remainder of the book disproving it.

Neeley's research indicates that there were between 13,500 and 14,000 individuals imprisoned by military authorities during the war—the exact figure will never be known because of unreliable nineteenth-century record keeping—but Lincoln's role in bringing about these arrests was minimal. Indeed, Neeley admits that Lincoln was probably unaware of most trials by military commissions unless they involved prominent individuals or friends or relatives of important people. Following the Whig conception of the president's role—that the chief executive should function something like a chairman of the board—Lincoln appointed others to oversee the imprisonment of the war's opponents and seldom interfered with their activities. Until February 1862 the State Department was charged with enforcing martial law, and 864 individuals were arrested. Not only was the number of individuals apprehended small when compared to those seized later in the war, but also military authorities were responsible for the majority of them, not the State Department. This was possibly the case because the State Department had little means to carry out the policy. Arrests became more numerous once the process was transferred to the war Department; it had the means of enforcement, and unlike Secretary of State William Seward, whose talk was sometimes stronger than his actions, Secretary of War Edwin Stanton proved to be firmer at stamping out opposition.

While Neeley's calculation of the number arrested is large, he points that it would be a mistake to conclude that all these individuals were apprehended for political reasons or because they openly opposed the war. In this respect, historians have made too much of Clement Vallandigham's arrest and banishment to the Confederacy. Neeley points out that even Lincoln was embarrassed by General Ambrose

Burnside's enforcement of his own infamous Order #1, which threatened the imprisonment for anyone who spoke out against the war. Contrary to accepted ideas, arrests were made for various other reasons and few of these focused solely on political considerations. More numerous cases involved fraud and corruption in dealing with the government, fraud in recruiting practices, selling contraband and other supplies to the Confederates, desertion, and engaging in guerilla warfare. Moreover, most arrests occurred in the slaveholding border states rather than the free states of the North. During his extensive research in War Department records, Neeley could identify only 624 of the 5,442 civilians arrested as coming from north of the border states and Washington, D.C.

In addition to the Vallandigham case, historians have stressed the Supreme Court decision in *Ex parte Milligan* while discussing the repression of civil liberties during the war. An Indiana copperhead, L. P. Milligan was tried by a military commission and sentenced to hang. The Supreme Court in 1866 declared the trial illegal, stating that civilians could not be hauled before military courts in areas where civil courts remained open and operating. Neeley disputes the claim that the case had a great deal of impact in its own time and in the future. While radical Republicans in the postwar era had qualms about the decision's effect on Reconstruction in the South, they did not let it stand in their way. Despite the Supreme Court's opinion, there were 1,435 trials by military commission between April 1865 and January 1869, and such trials continued even after that date.

The subtitle, "Abraham Lincoln and Civil Liberties," implies that Lincoln's role will be discussed much more that it actually is. Lincoln is on the periphery of the discussion rather than at the center. Although one chapter does focus on "Lincoln and the Constitution," the book delineates the roles of administrative departments and individuals other than Lincoln himself. Still, this does not diminish the importance of the topic. If scholars are to have a full understanding of policy and practice during the Lincoln administration, they must investigate more fully the part played by less prominent individuals. Lincoln assumed the power to declare martial law, but it fell to others to enforce that policy. Neeley has skillfully shown just how effective they were.

EUGENE H. BERWANGER

Professor of History
Colorado State University

JAMES M. MCPHERSON. *Abraham Lincoln and the Second American Revolution.* (New York: Oxford University Press, 1990), 152 + pp. $17.95 hardcover (ISBN 0-19-505542-X).

Abraham Lincoln a great revolutionary leader? The thought is likely to strike the reader as perverse, and yet, James M. McPherson's graceful prose and elegant argument in support of this thesis are compelling. Lincoln, we learn was that rarest of all revolutionaries—one who radically remodeled in order to renew. Change in the *right direction* is progress, and Lincoln, who understood more clearly than any man before or since that in 1776 this nation set out in the right direction, determined to keep it on that path even if it required revolutionary change in social and political institutions.

Although the book is composed of seven essays, each worthy of standing on its own, it has an internal logic and sequence. The first essay lays the foundation for the argument that the Civil War was indeed a revolution. It begins with a survey of American and European commentators of the era and also of historians all of whom considered the war to be a true revolution. McPherson then turns to describe the challenge to this thesis by the revisionists of the 1960s and 1970s who maintained that the Civil War was a bogus revolution that produced little real change in the nation or the lives of the slaves. In rebuttal McPherson points out that the revisionists are reading history backwards. The war ended the South's political domination of the national government, destroyed its economy and social order and led to an astonishingly swift increase in black literacy, land ownership and political power that was only partially arrested by the 1870s counter-revolution. The war assured the victory of "competitive democratic free-labor capitalism" and the Republican party's policy of economic development.

Lincoln's role as "conservative revolutionary" is the subject of the second essay where the focus is on Lincoln's war aims of restoring the Union and the Declaration of Independence—the great "charter of freedom"—against an unjust counter-revolution with a hypocritical definition of liberty. He gives a clear and convincing account of Lincoln's position on emancipation, its relationship to his military strategy and the revolutionary impact of the Emancipation Proclamation.

The third essay analyzes Lincoln's concept of liberty comparing it to the founders' concept of freedom from governmental oppression. Here McPherson draws on the distinction between negative and positive liberty to clarify Lincoln's definition and reveal it as containing a significant "shift of emphasis" in the direction of positive liberty, a shift that arose from Lincoln's pragmatism and courage on the uses of power.

The pivotal essay is the fourth and the heart of the book, in which McPherson, drawing on Carl von Clausewitz's distinctions between national strategy and military strategy and between limited war and total war, makes the case for Lincoln as a master strategist who shaped a national policy appropriate to the military goal of unconditional surrender. Here we see Lincoln as the paradigm of the Commander in Chief and appreciate more fully the fact that only the president can fill this role.

This leads directly to the essay on Lincoln as a master rhetorician whose skillful use of figurative language and vivid image account for his success in defining and communicating the national policy and energizing and inspiring the people. Though there are many illustrations of Lincoln's eloquence provided for our delight, none is more irresistible than McPherson's analysis of the Gettysburg Address.

And why was this master strategist, this master rhetorician the hero of the

Second American Revolution? In a metaphor that Lincoln would have appreciated, McPherson answers, in the sixth essay, using Archilochus' distinction between the "hedgehog who knows one big thing and the fox who knows many little things." It was the depth of Lincoln's understanding of the original central aspiration of the nation and his steadfast refusal to be diverted from the course. The vacillating foxes, men like Greeley and Seward, provide a fascinating contrast to Lincoln's constancy — or as Lincoln stated in his last public address, "Important principles may and must be inflexible."

In the peroration, McPherson analyzes the relationship between liberty and power with specific attention to the Civil War amendments, and concludes that the fruit of the Second American Revolution was "positive liberty achieved by overwhelming power."

McPherson has given us a sparkling insightful book about a conservative revolutionary hero who, because he knew the difference between change and progress, led the revolution to *restore* "the last best hope of the earth." This book is a small but brilliant jewel that everyone will want in his collection.

JUDITH A. BEST

Distinguished Teaching Professor of Political Science
State University of New York at Cortland

ROBERT V. REMINI. *The Jacksonian Era.* Arlington Heights, Ill.: Harlan Davidson, Inc. Pp. ix, 140. Paper, $8.95 (ISBN 0-88295-864-X).

The Jacksonian Era, a new title in the *American History Series* edited by John Hope Franklin and Abraham Eisenstadt, comes from the pen of Robert V. Remini. The book is primarily intended for class room use. Accordingly, it represents a succinct summation of Remini's larger biographical studies of the seventh president and his time.

Andrew Jackson was a controversial man while he lived, and so he remains for his interpreters. The question for them has always been, did age spawn Jacksonian democracy or did "the Hero" sire the age? Remini answers it as both.

Jacksonian scholars, and those of the presidency generally, will find little that is new in this slim volume. Whether they buy into his assessment of Jackson is largely a matter of their interpretative orientations. For example, those who discount the significance of personality will discount the Remini approach, as will those who cleave to the assumptions of social history. All may however admire the author's skill in crafting an entertaining, instructive reading of a complex man and an equally intricate era within the confines of one hundred and twelve pages of text. No small feat that. Scholars also ought to esteem the volume for its bibliographical essay, an up-to-date compilation of Jacksonian scholarship that makes a handy finding aid, especially for the non-specialist.

Undergraduate and graduate students alike should warm to Remini's prose style. It is vigorous and pungent, even compelling. Beyond that, Remini knows the value of good story telling. His tale of "Old Hickory" is well told, and it reminds us how fetching narratives can be seductive introductions to the pleasures of historical inquiry.

WARREN M. BILLINGS

Research Professor of History
University of New Orleans

GEORGE C. EDWARDS III. 1989. *At the Margins: Presidential Leadership of Congress.* New Haven, CT: Yale University Press, pp. 233. Cloth, $27.50 (ISBN 0-300-04404-6); Paper, $12.95 (ISBN 0-300-04899-8).

Presidential scholars have long relied upon case studies and insider accounts to study their subject: The institution of the White House and the person occupying it. Methods typically are verbal, anectodal, impressionistic, and frequently biased. By limiting the scope of inquiry to a single institution at a single point in time often with the examination of a single individual in it, presidential scholars have virtually precluded the use of more rigorous scientific techniques. Comparisons of national leaders are not possible they argue, due to differences in cultures, government structures (particularly in comparison to parliamentary leaders), and political climates. Not even comparisons across presidencies are often attempted since personalities, congressional margins, and institutional factors have all changed. In short, the method of science, which requires that measurement of relevant concepts be replicable and alternative possible explanations be shown to be inconsistent with the data are rejected by students of the presidency, in favor of the method of history, which focuses on contexts rather than concept measurement and requires only that the chosen explanation be consistent with known facts. In such a field, this book by George Edwards stands out.

Edwards, long a pioneer in the application of science to the study of executive leadership, has turned his considerable analytic and research skills to the subject of presidential leadership in Congress. Not content to rely on aggregated presidential success box scores used by other scholars, he painstakingly develops an extensive data base of presidential support of all individual members of Congress between 1953 and 1986. This data base allows him to examine issues and subtleties that aggregate analysis obscures.

Recognizing that there is a considerable controversy and disagreement surrounding the question of how to measure presidential support, Edwards develops four different indices each for the House and the Senate for each of the years in his study. The most inclusive measure is the overall support index, which includes all votes on which the president has taken a stand.

A second measure, the nonunanimous support index, excludes issues on which the president takes a stand but that are not controversial. He defines controversial issues as those on which the winning side numbered less than 80 percent of those who voted. The single-vote index is even more exclusionary. It recognizes that multiple votes may occur on a single bill, so that the president's support score if this is not accounted for reflects in part the proportion of votes a single bill has as much as overall congressional action. Thus, the single-vote index includes only the most important vote per bill, so that each bill receives the same weighting.

The fourth index focuses on key votes. A key vote must be a matter of major controversy, a test of presidential or political power, and a decision with potentially great impact on the nation and citizens.

Each of the above indices is calculated for each single representative and senator by calculating the percentage of support each member of Congress gives the president on the votes represented in each measure in each year. Votes for each index were also disaggregated further into separate indices for foreign and domestic issues. Armed with this new data and new measures of presidential support, Edwards is thus able to test hypotheses concerning the conditions under which support is greater, and the sources from which it comes. He arrives at numerous conclusions, including the following.

While substantial differences in support occur across the indexes in different years, the aggregate results reveal a strong consistency, especially among the three more exclusive measures. The index of nonunanimous support is the most representative and has the highest correlations with the other indexes. He concludes that the index of nonunanimous support and key vote support are the best measures of presidential influence in Congress.

Generally, presidents can rely on their own party support no more than two-thirds of the time, even on key votes. Support varies across house and across party. Democratic presidents receive their strongest support from House Democrats, but House Republicans are typically not supportive of Democratic presidents. House Democrats are more supportive of Republican presidents than House Republicans are of Democratic presidents, so that Democratic presidents suffer more from House Republicans than Republican presidents do from House Democrats.

By contrast, senators of each party, especially Republicans, give the opposition party moderate support. Senators of each party, especially Republicans, are also quite supportive of presidents of their own party. Partisanship, then is stronger in the House than in the Senate, with Republican senators, perhaps because they represent broader, more heterogeneous constituencies, being more moderate than their House counterparts.

When support scores are examined for individual presidencies, substantial variation occurs across the study period. The partisan gap for Republican presidencies has grown in the House, especially on key votes. Democratic presidents, however, have experienced a decline in the partisan gap, perhaps due to increased Republican acceptance of Democratic policies, or to the fact that the only recent Democratic president, Carter, had relatively moderate policies. The greatest shifts in response to presidential party occur on foreign policy issues, likely due to the greater relative role presidents play in foreign policy, and to the impact of stronger constituency preferences and demands on domestic policy votes.

Edwards further analyzes the different foreign and domestic policy support indexes to examine the long standing thesis in presidential literature that the institution is really two presidencies — one foreign and one domestic. He finds that while there is evidence supporting the two presidency thesis in the Eisenhower period, corroboration diminishes across time as the two presidencies decline in distinction. Contrary to conventional wisdom, the source of the two presidencies is not congressional bipartisanship or deference in foreign affairs, nor the relative advantages of the president in foreign policy making. Rather, the two presidencies were a natural result of the president proposing foreign policies but not domestic ones. With a decline in the appeal of presidential foreign policies to the opposition, the two presidencies have similarly diminished.

In three interesting chapters on public opinion, Edwards uses regression analysis to examine the linkage between presidential approval with the general public and presidential support within Congress. He finds that the two concepts are closely related but conceptually distinct. When controlling for party so that only relationships between presidents and members of the same party are examined, the linkage between the two is strongest for House Democrats, and positive. The linkage for Senate Democrats is more moderate but still positive. The linkage for House Republicans is much weaker than for House Democrats and actually negative. Senate results are quite mixed. Additional analyses are presented for each individual presidency included in the study scope.

Edwards closes by examining the role of presidential legislative skill in obtaining presidential support within Congress. He determines that presidential legislative skill is not closely linked to presidential support. Rather, partisan balances within Congress; presidential resources, organization, and willingness to provide amenities, services to members of his party, and presidential approval in public opinion polls are a far more important factors in presidential legislative success.

This book, in conclusion, represents a fine piece of social science: It analyzes a new data base competently and cogently to make conclusions about important questions and to shed additional light on long standing controversies in the presidential literature. It is well written and draws on the author's immense knowledge of the institution as well as scientificially rigorous analyses. In short, it is well worth reading and emulating.

MARCIA LYNN WHICKER

Virginia Commonwealth University

JOHN R. BOND AND RICHARD FLEISHER. *The President in the Legislative Arena*. (Chicago and London: The University of Chicago Press, 1990), 259 pp. $47.00 cloth (ISBN 0-226-06409-3). $16.95 paper (ISBN 0-226-06410-7).

Presidents face institutional challenges in passing their legislative agenda in Congress. *In the President in the Legislative Arena*, Bond and Fleisher provide a far-reaching analysis of presidential-congressional relationships which influence presidential legislative success in Congress. They compare competing presidency-centered and

Congressional-centered explanations of presidential legislative success. Their study considers presidential success on roll calls among groupings of congressmen from 1953 to 1984. This analysis permits explanations of presidential-Congressional relations under a variety of circumstances and conditions; e.g., majority and minority president's success with domestic and foreign policy issues. This book extends their analysis from several journal articles during the 1980s. Bond is a professor of political science at Texas A&M University; and Fleisher is an associate professor of political science at Fordham University.

Bond and Fleisher directly address the factors which forge cooperation within the built-in institutional conflicts of presidential-congressional relations. They develop a four-party faction model in Congress (i.e., liberal Democrats, conservative Democrats, liberal Republicans, conservative Republicans) to analyze congressional behavior in support of and in opposition to the President. An earlier version of this model was developed by James MacGregor Burns (*The Deadlock of Democracy* (1963)). The authors focus on conflictual roll call votes and indicate the unifying factors and trade-offs among factions. They argue that presidents face great difficulty to generate "unified" (75 percent voting together) support from more than two of the party factions.

The authors analyze the extent of how "unified" voting among congressional leaders and between congressional leaders and followers contributes to presidential success in Congress. Agreement among leaders and followers involves several different casual processes which are not mutually exclusive. Their empirical measures of leaders and followers are good indicators of different levels of agreement within and among congressional leaders and followers. These measures offer insight into the effectiveness of congressional leaders and allow judgments about the effects of presidential negotiations with these leaders. The authors combination of variables; e.g., the four-party factions, and important and unimportant votes, often leads to suggestive hypotheses for future research.

The authors' main thesis is "the distribution of partisan and ideological forces among Congressmen sets the basic parameters of presidential success or failure in Congress" (p. 117). They argue congressional-centered variables (partisanship and ideology) provide a stronger linkage to presidential legislative success than presidential centered variables (presidential leadership skills and presidential public popularity). Bond and Fleisher find greater stability in presidential success when considering these congressional variables. They find that in almost two-thirds of the "important legislative votes" both the president's party base and opposition base provide "unified" support for and against the president. This analysis also indicates there is considerable variation in the behavior of party factions. In many instances these partisan/ideological factions may fail to unify for or against the president's position.

Bond and Fleisher find the presidency-centered variables are less likely to have a direct effect on large numbers of Congressmen. They carefully examine the theoretical idea "that variation in the president's popularity with the public influences congressional support for his policy preferences" (p. 25) and suggest the effects of presidential popularity are marginal at best. Bond and Fleisher find weak and inconsistent correlations between presidential popularity and presidential legislative success.

Their findings are contrary to several other authors, especially Edwards, who found that the president has greater levels of legislative success when he is more popular than unpopular. Presidential popularity can have longterm rather than immediate effects. Bond and Fleisher find that presidential popularity can alter the partisan and ideological composition of Congress through midterm and presidential elections.

Presidential legislative skills are difficult to assess. Bond and Fleisher use perceived levels of presidential legislative skill as their indicator. They find that for both majority and minority presidents the perceived level of presidential legislative success had little effect on the president's chances of victory. They draw these relationships based upon roll call votes and find only low correlations concerning the influence of presidential legislative skills. Both presidency centered variables are less susceptible to direct measurement and may not be adequately reflected by correlational analysis. Throughout their analysis Bond and Fleisher argue the presidency-centered variables have only a marginal impact on the president's probability of legislative success or failure. This finding implies that presidential-congressional legislative relations are relatively fixed or bounded between elections.

Bond and Fleisher's study is a major step toward a sophisticated framework of presidential-congressional relations. Their theoretical analysis permits an assessment of presidential legislative successes both across presidents and within a single administration. They alter the scholarly focus on presidential legislative success to congressionally-centered linkages (partisanship and ideology) and away from president-centered linkages (leadership skills and public popularity). This excellent scholarly analysis provides new avenues to study presidential-congressional legislative relationships.

STEVEN PURO

Associate Professor of Political Science
St. Louis University

STUART BRUCHEY, *Enterprise: The Dynamic Economy of a Free People* (Harvard University Press, Cambridge, Massachusetts, 1990), 623 pp. and index, $49.50 Cloth (alk. paper) (ISBN 0-674-25745-6); $24.95 paper (alk. paper) (ISBN 0-674-25746-4-11).

Professor Bruchey's book should command a prominent place in the literature on American economic history. It is outstanding both for its scope (tracing the development of the American economy from colonial times to the present) and for the thorough and thoughtful use it makes of monographic and journal literature pertaining to its subject. It is also one of the book's merits that it connects the economy's development with what was occurring simultaneously in the nation's social and political life without being, as I read it, a rigorously economic interpretation of the whole American scene. Finally, it is written in a fast-moving and spirited style.

I was impressed anew on reading it at how different the forces shaping the development process get to be after 1920 from what they were prior to that, and how different the problems of analysis confronted by the historian become at around that time. In the pre-1920 world the story could be told well enough, as Bruchey tells it, in terms of demographics, the character of the people and their "values," the opportunities open to them to exploit an exceptionally rich endowment of land and mineral resources, and the availability of a rapidly improving infrastructure and an increasingly efficient technology. And there was the security and convenience of being free to pursue private economic interests in a supportive, even permissive, social, legal and governmental context. In this world, economic development was moved mainly by the dynamics inherent in the system, directed by market forces for the most part strongly competitive.

Beginning around 1920, however, and without any of the earlier forces being displaced, development began to be impacted increasingly by impulses emanating from government. These took many different forms, as Professor Bruchey shows very well, but a good case can be made for the proposition that the seminal event was the discovery by the then newly-established Federal Reserve System that it could have a farreaching effect on the economy through a more conscious management of something it was already doing—buying and selling federal securities in the open market. By expanding or contracting the reserves of the banking system it could enhance or constrain the ability of the banks to extend credit, and thus influence the condition of the economy. In this way, "open market operations" were born, and the USA and economic policy have not been the same since. Economic development begins to be moved (sometimes for the better; sometimes for the worse) by forces that have an *ex machina* quality to them, and the task of explaining the development process calls new analytical disciplines into play.

Professor Bruchey handles very well this shift into what, analytically speaking, is a new era. There is a good account of the 1920s and of the speculative excesses that made that decade the excitingly prosperous period that it was. There is a good account also of what brought the 1920s to a crashing end, including the contributions to that debacle of some inept Federal Reserve and other governmental actions. There is a similarly good account of the 1930s, with more credit for Herbert Hoover than he usually gets, and more realism about FDR's record than is typically applied to it. And there is a fair and balanced account of the economy under Mr. Truman. At that point, however, this reader's questions about the book's interpretations of events, and its evaluations of government policies, began to multiply, which brings me to the second main point I would make about the book.

Briefly, the point is that, so far as I can tell, it carries the story only through 1986, certainly not beyond 1987, and because it does not encompass what happened in the closing years of the 1980s and is continuing into the 1990s it misses the collapse of the "junk bond" era, the related collapse of the savings and loan industry and its federally-administered deposit guarantee system, the only slightly less lurid and costly problems of the commercial banking system, the unprecedented wave of personal and corporate bankruptcies, and the explosive increase in federal debt, much of it owed to investors overseas. And because these misadventures are to such a large extent traceable to things that happened two to three decades earlier, it would seem to me that if Professor Bruchey had been concluding his book with them in the background (no fault of his that he wasn't) he would have evaluated government policy in the 1950s, and 1960s and the 1970s differently than he did. I must ask to be indulged in this, having had some hand in the shaping of policy in the 1950s, but he might want, for example, to reconsider his view that Eisenhower as president was unduly concerned about inflation and overly impressed by the virtues of a balanced budget.

Moreover, it is not only the evaluation of Eisenhower's policies that is involved here: Mr. C. Douglas Dillon, who served with great distinction in both the Eisenhower and Kennedy administrations (in the former as Under Secretary of State; in the latter as Secretary of the Treasury), noted recently (in *The Eisenhower Centennial: Across the Nation, Around the World*, a brochure published by The Dwight D. Eisenhower Centennial Commission) that it was Eisenhower's success in overcoming inflation that ". . . made it possible for the Kennedy administration to pursue policies of noninflationary growth that gave our country one of its most prosperous and healthy periods of economic growth during the years 1961–1965. . . ." It could be added that inheriting a federal budget that was in structural balance, with what that meant for the monetary policy options open to the Federal Reserve, was a further assist to the Kennedy administration.

Obviously, Professor Bruchey cannot be faulted for not covering events that took place in large part after his writing was completed, but what is involved in missing the traumatic events of 1988–90 illustrates how important it is in appraising policy in any particular historical period, in this case the years 1950–85, without being able to take account of what happened subsequently as a result of developments during the period in question.

R. J. SAULNIER

Barnard College
Columbia University
New York City

DAVID SCHMIDTZ, *The Limits of Government: An Essay on the Public Goods Argument*. (Boulder, CO: Westview Press, 1990), 160 + pp. $38.50 hardcover (ISBN 0-8133-0870-4). $12.95 paperback (ISBN 0-8133-0871-2).

The author, an assistant professor of philosophy at Yale University, explores the idea of public goods and claims that although a public goods argument can justify the state, a state very much larger than a minimal state could be justified only by some other argument. Schmidtz criticizes the view that only the state could create public goods (goods that must be produced collectively but which benefit persons who do not join the collective effort to produce them); he thinks such goods may be produced without coercion, that is, without the state, in many cases. However, after delineating the differences between the teleological justification of institutions (justification that posits *goals* and shows which institutions are necessary to achieve these goals) and emergent justification (justification on the basis of the *process* by which institutions arose), Schmidtz argues that a public goods perspective can teleologically justify property rights that are enforced by the state.

Schmidtz provides a helpful analysis of "assurance contracts" and shows how they could help generate public goods without coercion. An assurance problem arises because a person may feel that it would be fruitless to contribute to a public good unless she could be assured that others will contribute enough so that her own contribution will not be wasted. An assurance contract specifies that if others do not contribute enough so that the good is provided, one's own contribution can be reclaimed. Schmidtz states that some assurance contracts may leave unsolved the familiar free rider problem, a problem which can be solved only by means of a coercive governmental apparatus. Nonetheless, he insists that assurance contracts can often be enforced by market actions unsupported by state coercion. Schmidtz believes that we should use such contracts wherever possible to provide public goods because governmental institutions can obviously be misused. Moreover, he thinks his position is supported by an analysis of the morality of a cooperative society. He discusses egoism, altruism, and reciprocity as modes of voluntary interaction among rational agents and argues that reciprocity is superior not only to egoism but also to "nonstrategic" altruism (altruism that does not mask egoism), because reciprocators give one another mutual incentives to reciprocate. Forcing people to cooperate through governmental coercion, while sometimes necessary to solve free rider problems, tends to undermine the reciprocity essential to social cooperation.

Schmidtz offers other stimulating analysis of the public goods argument. For example, he shows how an investigation of the prisoner's dilemma, that difficult form of conflict between the individual and collective interest, can clarify aspects of the public goods approach. He also provides a helpful summary of experimental data on choices concerning public goods (experiments under "laboratory" conditions in which subjects sought to maximize various holdings). This book will be of considerable interest to those concerned about the concept of public goods and about the extent to which public goods should be provided by the state rather than by markets.

ROBERT B. THIGPEN

Professor of Political Science
University of New Orleans

L. SANDY MAISEL, ed., *The Parties Respond: Changes in the American Party System* (Boulder, CO: Westview Press, 1990), xviii, 363 pp. including index. $50.00 hard (ISBN 0-8133-0881-X).

It's the old problem of premature obituaries. For the past two decades, scholars have been announcing the demise of the party system of the United States. The editor and contributors to *The Parties Respond* demonstrate that it just isn't so. Changing, yes; dying, no. This excellent collection of original essays documents that the parties are still very much alive and remarkably adaptive. After a brief look at the past, the papers describe trends that forecast how the parties are likely to evolve in the coming years. *The Parties Respond* also contributes to our understanding and expectations regarding that other rapidly changing institution, the presidency.

The collection includes fifteen essays and research reports that examine U.S. party history, recent trends in state and national party organization, interactions between voters and parties, and parties' nominating and campaign functions, and patterns of congressional and presidential party behavior and development. The authors assess the probable future of current trends. The volume has a superb seventeen-page reference bibliography. The three distinguished textbook authors who are among the contributors will undoubtedly assign this volume as a supplementary text. Professional activists and consultants should be sure to add it to their libraries.

American political parties have always been suspect, thanks to President Washington's warnings, the rise of corrupt urban and county machines, the rampant patronage grabs of the nineteenth century, and the name-calling din that party politicians incessantly level at each other in their contests for office. Parties process such unpleasantries as competing ambitions, allocation of society's resources, policy demands, and conflict in innumerable forms. But, argues editor Sandy Maisel, parties per se are not inherently good or evil. "Rather, they are functional. They are extra-constitutional institutions that bridge gaps in the constitutional structure of American democracy" (Page 308).

By the 1960s, according to historian Joel Silbey, other institutions—the media, organized interest groups, political consultants, and even individual candidates for office—were actively building bridges of their own over those gaps. The electorate's attachment to party symbols and party leaders *qua* party leaders was on the decline. Campaigns were increasingly candidate-centered rather than party-managed. The peer assessments and brokered coalitions of the past were being displaced by opinion polls, media commentary, and single-issue movements. Wrote columnist David Broder, *The Party's Over* (1971). Deeply concerned and hoping to halt the trend, a tiny bipartisan group of political scientists and party leaders came together as a Committee for Party *Renewal*. After all, can there be democracy without a vibrant and competitive party system? Can there be a powerful presidency without partisanship in a presidential electorate?

The contributors come up with a good many well-researched surprises and reassurances. Previously weak or non-existent state party organizations are now being increasingly professionalized, adequately financed, permanently maintained, rendering substantial service to candidates, and becoming more tightly integrated into the national party, according to John Bibby's findings. The national, congressional, and senatorial committees have continued their long-term institutionalization, "becoming fiscally solvent, organizationally stable, . . . more diversified in their staffing" and have adopted more "professional-bureaucratic decision making procedures" (Paul Herrnson, p. 50). The national committees have also become more influential in their relations with state and local party committees, in their recruitment of candidates for office, and even in their dealings with the much-feared PACs (political action committees). These are hardly pictures of a disintegrating party system.

As for the presidency and the presidential electorate, there is further positive news. During the Reagan years, the national parties moved further apart on the liberal-conservative continuum, presumably sharpening the policy choices available to the voters (William Stone et al. in Chapter 4). This tendency notwithstanding, both Democrats and Republicans have difficult balancing acts to perform in reconciling their respective, often divergent constituencies (E. J. Dionne in Chapter 14), which is quite a different formulation from the earlier view that both parties anxiously seek to situate themselves at some mythical political center. Calvin Mackenzie describes how presidential patronage has become a bureaucratic White House system rather than a party-oriented resource.

Warren Miller re-analyzes data about the decline in party identification and the rise in the proportion of independent voters since the later 1960s. His conclusion is newsworthy. "It was the refusal and delay of the young in accepting partisan ties, not the lasting rejection of loyalties once held by their elders, that produced the indicators of dealignment in the mid-1970s." The 1980s, however, saw the youth cohort committing itself to parties, that is, becoming aligned rather than unaligned. This latter tendency has been increasingly in the direction of conservatism and the Republican party, particularly among the more educated youth.

Other chapters describe how divided government (Republican president and Democratic Congress) has become the normal condition (Morris Fiorina), how, despite the great advantage of incumbency, both inter-party and intra-party competition have increased, the latter becoming an entirely open process at the state and local levels (Sandy Maisel et al.), how the prevalence of primaries and open caucuses has altered nomination and election campaign strategies (Elaine Kamarck), how the parties have been constricted in their role as financial donor, but have been able to retain the role of financial broker (Frank Sorauf and Scott Wilson), and the several ways in which congressional parties have become stronger, particularly on the House side (Barbara Sinclair). Gary Orren and William Mayer discuss the institutional tug-of-war between party and press, reminding us of those things that only parties can do. David Brady shows in what ways electoral and congressional coalitions differ.

The Parties Respond covers a great deal of ground, contributes new data to the body of knowledge about parties, draws important connections between party system and presidency, and can justifiably be considered a guidebook into the party politics of the 1990s.

RALPH M. GOLDMAN

Adjunct Professor
American University;
Professor Emeritus of Political Science
San Francisco State University

JAMES A. SMITH, *The Idea Brokers: Think Tanks and the Rise of the New Policy Elite* (New York: Free Press/Macmillan, 1991) xxi, 313 pp., including Index, Acknowledgments and Prologue. $24.95 cloth (ISBN 0-02-929551-3).

This excellent study deals with the impact of public policy "think tanks" on the Presidency and the White House, and it traces the development of this essentially modern trend.

The author, who was formerly a program officer at the Twentieth Century Fund, has taught American history at Brown University, Smith College, and the New School for Social Research.

In his prologue, the author states: "The first generation of policy research institutions was founded around 1910, an outgrowth of Progressive Era reform and the 'scientific management' movement. Established and maintained by private philanthropy, they operated in an era when the government had few intellectual resources at its command, and they were a welcome adjunct to the then much smaller public sector, often prodding the government to assume new social responsibilities. A second generation — the first to bear the label *think tank* — was created in the twenty years or so after World War II, when the government sought to marshal sophisticated technical expertise for both the Cold War national security enterprise and the short-lived domestic war against poverty. Their services were provided to the government on a contractual basis. A third generation, more numerous but generally with smaller budgets and staffs, was founded in the 1970s and 1980s; these think tanks were outgrowths of the ideological combat and policy confusion of the past two decades. Many of them are geared toward political activism and propaganda, rather than toward scholarship.

"Think tanks are largely twentieth-century inventions, but the expert adviser and the intellectual working in the shadows of power have had a role in political life for more than two millenia. . . .

"Contemporary advisory relationships suggest not only a different kind of adviser, proffering more specialized advice, but a different kind of political leader, one who is considerably more dependent on specialists. The experts set policy goals, chart directions, monitor results and (having first measured public sentiments) craft the words that will move the electorate. Even though modern presidents are literate . . . they still depend on experts to draft the words they speak and to study and outline the policy choices they confront. Medieval kings who were dependent on their counselors were sometimes dismissed as 'feeble creatures.' But modern presidents — and other political officials — are arguably feebler still, since government has grown vastly more complex, with leaders becoming far more dependent not only on their immediate counselors but on experts who are scattered throughout the bureaucracy. . . ." (pp. xv–xix).

Dealing with the early stages of the development of "think tanks", the author notes that "as a serious student of government, [Woodrow] Wilson saw the growing prominence of experts as a long-term threat to democratic institutions and a potential impediment to full and open political debate. . . . Although we have learned to be more skeptical about the possible extent of expert influence, Wilson's warnings serve to remind us how often our elected representatives have handed over difficult or contentious issues to expert commissions and task forces. . ." (p. 3).

The author notes that Herbert Hoover, less suspicious of experts than was Wilson, "tapped hundreds of experts for service on ad hoc commissions" (p. 11). He also notes that Franklin D. Roosevelt relied on his "Brain Trust" during the New Deal era. This helped lead to the reorganization of the Executive Branch in the late 1930s. Congress has also come to rely considerably on expert advice.

Some of the organizations examined in this study include the Carnegie Corporation (founded in 1911), the Rockefeller Foundation (1913) and the Russell Sage Foundation (1907), the New York Bureau of Municipal Research (1907), President Taft's Commission on Economy and Efficiency (1910), the Institute for Government Research (founded in 1916 and in 1927 renamed the Brookings Institution), the National Bureau of Economic Research (1921), the Twentieth Century Fund (1919), National Defense Advisory Commission (1940), Committee for Economic Development (1943), Ford Foundation (1944), RAND Corporation (1948) [associated with systems analysis], the Urban Institute (1967), Herman Kahn's Hudson Institute (1961), Marcus Raskin and Richard Barnet's Institute for Policy Studies (1961), American Enterprise Institute for Public Policy Research (AEI), identified with William J. Baroody and established in 1960, Institute for Educational Affairs (1978), the Hoover Institution on War, Revolution and Peace at Stanford (1959), Heritage Foundation (1973), Center for Strategic and International Studies (1962, independent in 1987 after earlier ties with Georgetown University), the Ethics and Public Policy Center (1976), Cato Institute (1977), and others which are listed in an appendix.

The author concludes: "Woodrow Wilson feared the notion of a 'government of experts.' . . . The relationship between knowledge and politics is one that demands constant scrutiny and deflection. It summons us to ask, again and again, what we really need to know to govern ourselves well. It demands that we test our theoretical knowledge by confronting real choices and their consequences. It requires us to use knowledge not as an intimidating bludgeon, but as a tool of education and persuasion. . . . Above all, it compels us to admit that political wisdom is different from knowledge of the physical world and that social science can neither replace politics nor relieve us of the responsibility for making value-laden choices. Finally, it calls for a healthy egalitarian skepticism of the authority of experts" (pp. 238, 239).

The value of this volume lies in its author's ability to tie together the various strands of history of the development of American "think tanks" and their influence on American presidents and the executive establishment. The main weakness of the work lies in the fact that so broad a subject is difficult to encompass in a single book. But the book is recommended for all students of the White House advisory process.

WILLIAM C. SPRAGENS

Spragens Research/Analysis
Herndon, Virginia
Professor Emeritus
Bowling Green State University

BRIAN R. FRY, *Mastering Public Administration: From Max Weber to Dwight Waldo.* (Chatham, N.J.: Chatham House Publishers, Inc., 1989), 264 pp. $16.95 paperback (ISBN 0-934540-56-X).

Brian R. Fry in *Mastering Public Administration: From Max Weber to Dwight Waldo* provides a vivid account of the lives and the works of eight major figures in the development of American public administration. From German sociologist Max Weber to Australian Elton Mayo, the accounts of these scholars' contributions to the discipline are clarified in a manner which unites history with social and occupational influence. This book introduces the reader to both the theory and the scholar.

Fry utilizes the historical approach and groups these scholars into the categories of the classical, behavioral, and administration-as-politics. Under the classical period, he addresses the works of Weber, Frederick Winslow Taylor, and Luther Gulick. The influence of Weber's formal training in economics and law is evident in his assertion that bureaucracy is a rational entity that is needed to bring order and rationale to an irrational society. His "ideal type" demonstrates how society can be controlled through predictability, calculability and impersonality. Criticisms include his formulating unattainable standards for an "ideal-type" bureaucracy which if cannot be attained, is neither rational nor efficient. Yet, Fry contends the criticisms pale in comparison to Weber's formulation of the concept of bureaucracy.

Social and occupational influences are also seen in the discussion of the remaining seven scholars. Taylor's Scientific Management was perceived as a way to promote greater efficiency in the management of the public business. Criticisms include a neglect of the human factor and the setting of arbitrary standards. Gulick, the departmentalist, is described as personifying public administration in the United States in theory and practice. His interest in the enhancement of executive power both within organizations and among the organizations in the executive branch helps in understanding the American presidency. He along with Herbert Simon of the behavioral period were both political scientists and among the first to question the validity of the politics/administration dichotomy. Fry contends that it is difficult to assess Gulick's ideas because they often changed and that Gulick was often led more by a passion for reform than by systematic research.

Mary Parker Follett, Elton Mayo, and Chester Barnard are also regarded as behavioralists. They are called precursors to the school while Simon's theories represent a radical departure from the Classical approach. A distinguishing feature of Follett's work is her treatment of the role of social conflict in group dynamics which she describes as neither good nor bad but simply inevitable. Follett asserts that "integration" is the best way to resolve conflict because it accommodates everyone. Beyond the charge of being too idealistic and not scientifically based, Fry's handling of Follett's contribution demonstrates her distinction as a forerunner of the behavioral period.

Elton Mayo's research led directly to the Human Relations discovery. He believed that monotonous and demanding routine machine work further complicates personal disorganization which leads to an inefficient worker. Criticisms are that his research was designed to empirically validate his own theories producing superficial and biased results in favor of management and neglecting the role of conflict in organizations.

Chester Barnard continued the belief of Follett that organizations were cumulative in nature and the work of Mayo that organizations must respond to the needs of the worker. Barnard believed that organizations are systems of cooperative management where participants make contributions in exchange for inducements. He believed that authority resides not in a position but in a relationship between a superior and a subordinate and is not exercised on issuance of a command but upon its acceptance. A criticism of Barnard is his allegation that managers cannot manage in an authoritarian manner.

Simon rejected the politics/administration dichotomy on the grounds that a science of administration must be based on decision making and suggested a fact/value dichotomy instead. Such a science, he believed, should use empirical analysis and inductive reasoning rather than casual observation and deductions. This decision making is affected by "bounded rationality" resulting in "satisficing" or only satisfactory decision making due to limited cognitive and analytical abilities. Unlike the other authors, Fry tends to personally critique Simon's works whereas he cites other critics in his reviews of the other theorists.

Dwight Waldo falls under the "Administration as Politics" approach. Waldo is not included for his substantive contribution to public administrative theory which Fry admits is very little, but rather for his critique of public administration in general. In critique of Waldo, Fry states that the work is "essential ambivalence." Waldo sees that public administration is necessarily involved in politics, but also sees some value in the politics/administration dichotomy. He states that public administration is both art and science, but fails to specify an area in which each might be applicable. Fry concludes by stating that Waldo has not so much resolved the problems of administrative theory as he has apparently learned to live with them.

JAMES D. WARD

Assistant Professor of Political Science
University of New Orleans

RICHARD WHELAN. *Drawing the Line: The Korean War, 1950–1953.* (Boston: Little, Brown & Co., 1990). 428 pp. $24.95 hardcover (ISBN 0-316-93403-8).

Since World War II, the United States has been involved in several conflicts, most of them small. Two of them, however, have significantly affected the course of American foreign policy in the post-war years: the Korean and Vietnam wars. In many ways our approach to Vietnam was dictated by the lessons the United States thought it learned from the Korean War, a war that Richard Whelan considers another world war.

Focusing primarily on the political and diplomatic aspects of the conflict, Whelan, who has also written a biography of the war photographer Robert Capa, tells well a story that most of us know as an unfortunate incident sandwiched between World War II and Vietnam. The North Korean invasion in June 1950 presented the United States with naked aggression, which, given the circumstances of war-ravaged Europe, a firmly established Communist China, and Russia with its newly acquired atomic bomb, the United States found impossible to ignore. Whelan points out that the American people have always reacted intensely to foreign acts of extremism. He also notes that in many instances America's vigorous response to such extremism is not the best route to take. America's ready desire to launch crusades pitting Good versus Evil has sometimes made things worse. Thus, for example, Truman's desire to unify Korea in the face of almost certain Chinese opposition, resulted in a prolonged war and a messy ending, which would color American perceptions of how to conduct the next war in the Far East with similar disastrous consequences.

Whelan provides a good historical survey of the Korean situation prior to 1950, helping the reader understand the relationships between Korea, China, Japan, and the Soviet Union. He makes clear the sometimes tortured path of diplomacy in the Far East during the first half of this century. Whelan's strength throughout his book is his ability synthesize the many complex issues involved in the war.

Using published memoirs, official documents, and secondary works, the author provides a solid account of the decisions and actions taken by Truman, MacArthur, Acheson, and their supporting cast of military and political officials. MacArthur does not fare well in this account. Whelan has little use for the general's ego or personality. But some of MacArthur's problems, Whelan believes, come from the deference shown him by the Pentagon and the Joint Chiefs. If those in Washington had taken a firmer hand in the beginning of the crisis, it is possible MacArthur would have not put himself in a position to ultimately be relieved of command. Of course, it is also possible, given MacArthur's level of self-confidence, that he would eventually conflict with any political authority.

Whelan believes Truman's decision to cross the 38th parallel was a fundamental mistake based on a faulty analysis of how the Soviets and Chinese would respond. The United States believed that to avoid another world war that Stalin would issue a warning to the United States not to cross the parallel. Ironically, as Whelan shows, it was perhaps from just such a fear of World War III that Stalin did not state any kind of ultimatum, but instead sanctioned the Chinese military response that ensued from the United States/United Nations invasion of North Korea. Until the Soviet and Chinese records relating to the war are opened to researchers, guessing their intentions will be the best we can do.

Once the Chinese actively join the fray, the war quickly stalemates and the slow trek toward a final truce. The U.S./UN diplomatic officials learn the frustrating lesson of negotiating from positions that change from week to week and month to month. During all this Truman decides not to seek another term, Eisenhower becomes president, the Republicans take over Congress and the attention of the country shifts to other concerns. Finally the armistice is signed in July 1953. 54,000 Americans died in the conflict, with another 103,000 wounded. No formal peace treaty has yet been signed officially ending the war.

In less than 400 pages Richard Whelan covers a lot of territory. Although his study does not reflect any research beyond published sources—and only monographs primarily—the author has provided a solid synthesis of the major events of the war. He describes the military situation enough to acquaint the reader with some of the exceedingly difficult fighting situations the U.S./UN forces faced, but his focus is political and diplomatic. For the specialist this book may not break new ground, although Whelan's analysis of the American decision-making is worth examining. For those unfamiliar with the war, this book is a good place to start.

EDWARD GOEDEKEN

Purdue University Libraries

MARTIN J. MEDHURST, ROBERT L. IVIE, PHILIP WANDER, and ROBERT L. SCOTT. *Cold War Rhetoric: Strategy, Metaphor, and Ideology.* (New York: Greenwood Press, 1990), 224 pp. $39.95 hardcover (ISBN 0-313-26766-9).

There is general agreement among scholars that the "Cold War" began shortly after the end of World War II, as the Soviet Union and the United States (and their allies) began to contend over the political future of Europe. There is less of a consensus concerning the struggle's end. Some mark a termination point in the 1970s, when Richard Nixon recognized the People's Republic of China and began a policy of detente toward the Soviet Union; others declared the contest over only a year or so ago, as the Berlin Wall came down and Communist governments across Eastern Europe followed suit; still others claim that the Cold War goes on, and cite Mikail Gorbachev's repression of the Baltic States as proof. Regardless of how its duration is defined, there can be little disagreement that the Cold War lasted for decades and produced profound effects on the participating nations, their allies, and even those countries who sought, mostly in vain, neutral corners.

Martin Medhurst and his colleagues have produced a work which is designed to focus on some of the ways in which important people, groups, and nations sought to persuade each other during this often tense, occasionally violent period. After an introductory chapter by Robert L. Scott, the book is divided into three sections, each containing three chapters by a single author (a final chapter, by Robert Ivie, concludes the volume). Each section follows the same pattern: the first chapter discusses theoretical issues, and the next two provide concrete examples of the functioning of those issues in Cold War speaking.

The concerns of the book's three sections reflect the subtitle: strategy, metaphor, and ideology. Medhurst, author of the "strategy" section, begins with an essay, "Rhetoric and the Cold War: A Strategic Approach." He examines the goals pursued by East and West during this period, and the ways in which rhetoric functioned to define and achieve those goals. This is followed by two chapters devoted to specific presidential speeches. Medhurst discusses an address given by Dwight Eisenhower to the United Nations in 1953 (known as the "Atoms for Peace" speech) and shows how it was designed to put the Soviets on the defensive, ready Americans for the trials of the nuclear age, and appeal to U.S. allies. His third chapter involves John F. Kennedy's speech announcing the resumption of U.S. nuclear testing in the atmosphere, and the argument here is that the oration allowed Kennedy to take a firm stance on the testing issue while preserving his options for later reversal of the policy.

Robert L. Ivie is the author of the "metaphor" section. His introductory chapter focuses on the use of metaphor in rhetoric generally and Cold War speaking particularly. The two chapters which follow look at metaphor in specific Cold War contexts: the rhetorical battle between broadcaster Edward R. Murrow and Senator Joseph McCarthy in 1954, and the speaking of three prominent opponents of the nuclear arms race (Henry Wallace, J. William Fulbright, and Helen Caldicott). Both pieces are carefully constructed and intelligently argued, but the third essay has been outdated by events. Ivie points out, accurately enough, that Wallace, Fulbright, and Caldicott were unable to influence significantly the build-up of the U.S. nuclear arsenal. He contends that their rhetoric suffered from poor choice of metaphors, especially in absence of metaphors which might have calmed American fears of the Soviet threat. Ivie argues that the only hope for significant disarmament in the future lies in rhetoric employing "symbiosis" metaphors, which contend that East and West need each other to survive. At the time of writing, he did not envision (as few of us did) Reagan's visit to Moscow, the signing of major new arms reduction treaties with the Soviets, or the apparent retreat of Communism from much of Europe. Thus, recent history has made some of Ivie's conclusions in his third piece almost irrelevant.

The third major section of the book is concerned with ideology, and Philip Wander follows the pattern of his colleagues by beginning with a theoretical chapter, this one concerned with ideological criticism. The two "application" chapters which come next represent something of a mixed bag. "The Rhetoric of American Foreign Policy," which originally appeared in *The Quarterly Journal of Speech* several years ago (one of three chapters in the book which are not original to the volume), has rightly come to be regarded as a classic study. In it, Wander argues that U.S. foreign relations in the modern age are reflective of two opposing philosophies: prophetic dualism (akin to the notion of Manifest Destiny) and technocratic realism (a more pragmatic view, which holds that negotiation with foes is possible and sometimes desirable). His third chapter, "Political Rhetoric and the Un-American Tradition," is less satisfactory. Here, Wander discusses the ways in which the accusation of being "un-American" has been used throughout U.S. history to stifle dissent, slow social reform, and win elections. The claim is not without its merits, but Wander's tone is so ideological as to interfere with scholarly judgment. Wander should consider whether ideological criticism requires blatantly ideological argument, and whether the latter is consistent with objectivity.

Cold War Rhetoric should be of considerable value to those interested in the study of presidential rhetoric, for at least two reasons. First, several of the chapters provide important critical insights into specific presidential addresses, while Wander's "Rhetoric of American Foreign Policy" should aid one's understanding of a whole genre of political rhetoric. Second, the book has value because it gives us a context for understanding modern presidential rhetoric, even that which is not specifically considered in this volume. The Cold War has been an important concern for every president from Truman to Bush, and our view of the rhetoric of those presidents can only be sharpened by the understanding this book gives of that "long twilight struggle."

J. JUSTIN GUSTAINIS

Associate Professor of Communication
State University of New York, Plattsburgh

JOHN LE BOUTILLIER, *Vietnam Now: A Case for Normalizing Relations with Hanoi.* Introduction by Richard M. Nixon. Foreword by Liz Trotta. (New York: Praeger/Greenwood Press, Inc., 1989), 115 pp. $18.95 hardcover (ISBN 0-275-93278-8).

Vietnam is the bad penny of American politics. Despite all the years of rhetoric and verbiage spilled out in books and articles, both scholarly and popular, it continues to bedevil the American system of constitutional polity. This current contribution to the debate on the aftermath of the Southeast-Asian War is no exception. *Vietnam Now* has serious flaws, both of logic and structure, despite the earnest zeal and obvious sincerity of its author.

John Le Boutillier earned his reputation as a dedicated member of the Reagan conservative "revolution" of the 1980s. He was a Republican congressman (at age 27!) from New York State, elected for the one term of 1981–83, and with a distinguished academic and writing background from his Harvard University studies. Active in many congressional committee posts relating to Southeast-Asia and missing-or-captured Americans from the war period (1964–73), he has since "evacuated" normal politics. His bitterness is very evident throughout this book.

After his congressional stint, Le Boutillier's great aim for the last eight years has been a moral crusade to bring the question of these American war prisoners of the Vietnam War era before the American public. His great hope was/is of pressuring our national Executive branch to *do* something effective in gaining the release of these secret captives. His links to private special-interest groups on the MIA/POW controversy echo to his almost fanatical faith in the existence of hundreds of living Americans as illegal war-captives still held and abused by the Communist regimes of Laos and Vietnam.

To get at the truth on these American captives, Le Boutillier has made many trips to Vietnam and Southeast-Asia as a whole during 1981–82, and most recently in 1988. (This last was the invitation of the Hanoi government, quite anxious to encourage every spark of sympathetic policy change in the U.S.) The author's partial successes in talks with Communist leaders has convinced him that the American presidents (right up to the present) have missed a golden opportunity in their dogmatic refusal to diplomatically recognize the Vietnamese Communist government as the sole legal authority in Vietnam as a whole. He insists indeed that ambassadors should be mutually exchanged without any concessions to the U.S. Lucrative trading concessions can then be offered to Hanoi, but only if the latter in turn will release its longsuffering American prisoners — and make a concrete schedule of steps to satisfy American objections on other issues (i.e. Vietnamese occupation of Cambodia; treatment of Amerasian children; political prisoners' treatment; American use of naval ports, etc.). The carrot of trade will tempt the current "reform"-leadership of Hanoi under Communist Party-Secretary Nguyen Van Linh. His Vietnamese economy is falling to pieces under its corrupt burden of state socialism. His pragmatism will lead him even to easing the Soviets out of their long-held (since 1978) military bases at Cam Ranh Bay and Danang — allowing the U.S. Navy to return and take over!

In short, Le Boutillier pictures a Communist Vietnam (indeed, all of Indo-China since Hanoi controls both Laos and Cambodia as satellites) ripe to throw off an unsatisfactory and ruthless Soviet influence, and then allow a free-market economy (and freer social structures?) to gradually flourish. But only if the Executive branch follows the common-sense proposals of the author. Why won't it? That is the problem Le Boutillier seeks to explain.

His book is a popular work, short in length and concise in its arguments. Written in a lively and easy style it makes its points in seven interconnected chapters, animated by personal conviction and seemingly very logical in the points raised. Its bibliography is fair-to-good in the scope of the books and articles cited, and the appendices have excellent material (especially the February 1973 letter of President Nixon to the North Vietnamese government). But its refusal to use footnotes makes it awkward for the ordinary reader to identify the sources used in any point made. The appearance of so many direct quotes from famous personalities *without* specific cited sources — or at least accurate dating and place of occurrence — is confusing to say the least. It is noteworthy that the preface by President Nixon refuses to explain the meaning of the famous secret letter of February 1973, and indirectly reproaches Le Boutillier for a naive optimism in interpreting Hanoi's motives so facilely ("horsetrading" in diplomacy is one very intricate business).

Le Boutillier paints the American presidential leadership from 1973 on in some very harsh colors *re* Vietnam: "This country's problem in Southeast Asia comes from a fundamental misunderstanding of U.S. power by national leaders. The United States has played the shrinking violet and has thus abdicated a leadership role in the region. Moscow has entered this vacuum, using both Vietnam and Kampuchea as cornerstones of its Pacific strategy . . . Washington has deliberately chosen to hide its head in the sand and relive the war, wrapped up in a combination of guilt, spite, and bitterness. . . . Meanwhile, Moscow has circled like a vulture and swooped down on Vietnam, picking it dry and using the remains for its own strategic design: to become the major player throughout the Pacific."

The moral bitterness of the book unsuccessfully combines with the theme of enlightened self-interest the author tries to urge on the Executive branch. The deceit and secretiveness of government policy are certainly factors in the apparent weakness and confusion of the State Department towards Southeast Asia, but these are not unique to Nixon, Carter and Reagan. The Vietnamese government has been Machiavellian enough in its own policies, and even the reform faction in Hanoi totally supported the brutal repression in China after June 1989 *and* opposed (futilely) the reforms, and then, collapse of Communism in Eastern Europe and its slow disintegration in the U.S.S.R. Hanoi's trustworthiness has not been evident in real policy reforms despite the author's claims. Le Boutillier seems more involved in wish-dreams than true concrete evidence here.

The most controversial of the author's views is his exposé of the secret cabal he insists ran the Reagan administration foreign policy. The president is seen as isolated by such subordinates as Robert McFarlane, William Casey, Richard Childress, Donald Gregg, and a number of others in the Defense Intelligence Agency and CIA. Reagan himself is not badly treated, but his overall policy of delegating authority to lesser officials is excoriated.

As a probe of foreign policy, *Vietnam Now* has too many weaknesses to convince the wary reader of the need to recognize formally Hanoi. Its inside view of the Reagan years and the Nixon '73 letter is useful, however. A book to be read with care, cross-checking with others.

THOMAS M. EGAN

Adjunct Professor
St. John's University

JOHN TAFT, *American Power: The Rise and Decline of U.S. Globalism* (New York: Harper & Row, 1989), 321 + pp. $22.50 hardcover (ISBN 0-06-016133-7).

American Power is an interesting and useful read for anyone interested in the evolution of twentieth-century American foreign policy. However, because the author assumes a good deal of knowledge about persons and events, and his concepts are not always clearly defined, it probably would work awkwardly in the classroom.

Taft is the producer of the television series "After the War" (to which this is the companion volume) and "America's Century". He argues that American foreign policy has been driven for most of this century by a small cadre of men, most of them Ivy Leaguers weaned during the Wilson era on Progressive ideals of positive government. Taft labels this movement "international liberalism". As the Progressives sought to spread democratic ideals at home, international liberals sought to spread them first to Europe, then to the entire world.

Thus the story of American foreign policy is the story of William Bullitt, Robert Murphy, George Kennan, Averill Harriman, David Bruce, Chester Bowles,

Henry Cabot Lodge Jr., and Ellsworth Bunker, and to a somewhat lesser extent people like Dean Acheson, Allen and John Foster Dulles, Christian Herter, Herbert Hoover, Henry Stimson, and Sumner Welles. Their core beliefs, which underlay foreign policies for both political parties through the Vietnam War, included free trade and investment, anti-imperialism, advancement of democracy, foreign aid, arms control, and multilateral institutions.

The "decline" referred to in the subtitle came after the Vietnam War, when this consensus collapsed, and no new consensus was able to replace it. The result has been incoherent policy making, and the lack of "broad, institutional, liberal commitments" by the U.S. on the international scene. This clearly frustrates the author, who regards the 1940–1970 period as a sort of "golden age."

The strength of this book is its delineation of how an idealistic strain in American foreign policy has developed. The roots of this year's debate over the Persian Gulf War and the "new world order" are clearly described here. Though the book was published before the late crisis, historical parallels in the debates are eery, viz. Chester Bowles in 1940: "We have already spent enough on the Second World War to clear away all our slums, build millions of homes, new schoolhouses, new parks and new buildings, dramatically raise our health standards and to send hundreds of thousands of our young people to college" (p. 172). Moreover, however it plays out, President Bush's proclamation of a new world order is Wilsonian idealism redivivus.

Readers of this journal may quibble at the ambiguous roles presidents play in Taft's narrative. They make diplomatic appointments, of course, and they are the ones who must be convinced to carry out international liberal policies. Yet most presidents remain pragmatic, and none appears to buy completely into the international liberal movement. On more than occasion, our protagonists push their ideals too hard and wind up getting dumped by the President (particularly Bullitt by Franklin Roosevelt, Bowles by Kennedy). The president-diplomat relationship is complex, and deserves explication.

Taft is also less clear in defining the challenges to international liberalism, isolationism and ultraliberalism. Other terms, like "isolationist liberalism" and "reactionary unilateralism," keep drifting into the story without being connected to the original classification. Traditional understandings of isolationism are stretched to include the Republican right wing of the 1950s, the unilateral forays of the Reagan years, and 1980s peace movements, which are based "on a solipsistic assumption that the United States and its dependencies embrace the entire world" (p. 272). Some of these may have evolved out of pre-World War II isolationism, and they may share opposition to the coupling of international activism with anti-Communism advocated by the international liberals, but to lump them all under the same rubric is confusing. Likewise, ultraliberals — a term seemingly designed to offend (p. viii) — seem to differ from the Wilsonians only in their greater zeal and lesser pragmatism. The distinctions are subtle, to be sure, and deserve clearer delineation, especially since Chester Bowles, Sumner Welles, and others seem to straddle both camps.

Some of these confusions come home to roost in describing the post-Vietnam period. The solution is not clear, even for Taft. The U.S., having naively extended

202 | PRESIDENTIAL STUDIES QUARTERLY

the reach of its idealism into the Third World in the 1950s (following the example of Chester Bowles), got its wings singed in Vietnam. In the ensuing confusion of purpose, the U.S. compromised its long-standing anti-Communist policy thrust. "[I]t seemed that no U.S. client anywhere in the world could rely on Washington's backing unless it was democratic" (p. 274). The author faults divided government, Carter's "imperialism of sensitivity", Reagan's unilateralism (though less at fault than a meddling Congress), public ignorance, interest groups, and Soviet manipulation of American and European opinion. These interpretations are arguable, particularly the last; the notion that opponents of Reagan's dramatic military buildup of his Central American policies were Soviet dupes is hard to swallow.

International liberalism may have risen from the ashes in 1991. It is worth noting that of the rationales offered for the Persian Gulf War—jobs, oil, and stopping aggression—only the last resonated among the American public. But despite the capture of Manuel Noriega, the defeat of Iraq, and the failed coup in Libya, translating American ideals into foreign policy remains an open question.

BRUCE NESMITH

Assistant Professor of Political Science
Coe College

Book Note

CARNEGIE COUNCIL ON ETHICS AND INTERNATIONAL AFFAIRS, *Ethical Traditions and World Change*, Vol. 5, Ethics and International Affairs Series (New York: Carnegie Council on Ethics and International Affairs, 1991), paperbound, $10.00 (ISSN 0892-6794).

Students of the Presidency may be interested in an essay by Kenneth Thompson, professor of government and foreign affairs at the University of Virginia and director of the White Burkett Miller Center of Public Affairs. In an essay entitled "The Decline of International Studies," Professor Thompson criticizes "the spectacular irrelevance of most education in international affairs to present and future international crises." Professor Thompson is critical of what he finds to be a permissive policy of the Bush Administration toward Iraq prior to the August 2, 1990, invasion of Kuwait. He states, in part: "Not only Saddam but some of his predecessors had told western observers, including the present writer, that if Egypt, Iran, or Syria should falter, Iraq would prove itself the hardline militaristic state in the region. Reservists assigned to the Pentagon for temporary duty in the spring of 1990 shared with friends reports of Iraqi troops massing on the borders of Kuwait. The handwriting was on the wall. . . . It is as though Bush administration officials, like Rip Van Winkle, had slept through the late 1940s and 1950s when the reconstituted political and strategic language was used to describe the Soviet threat . . ." (p. 243).

Other contributors to this collection are Terry Nardin, Cho-yun Hsu, Alberto R. Coll, John E. Becker (writing on "the vision thing"), Chris Brown, James H. Billington, Charles W. Kegley, Jr., Greg Russell, Robert L. Phillips, David A. Crocker, Stephen Haggard, Thomas G. Weiss and Larry Minear, and Jerrold D. Green.

The major thrust of this volume is broader than the Presidency alone, but it discusses relevant global issues.

WILLIAM C. SPRAGENS

Spragens Research/Analysis
Herndon, Virginia
Professor Emeritus of Political Science
Bowling Green State University

Guest Editorial
Term Limits—and Beyond

ROBERT SEELE
Trustee
James Monroe Memorial Foundation

Interest in the term limit issue is rising all over this country and, despite occasional setbacks, all indications point to significant advances for this laudable idea both at the state and at the federal levels. As we approach the year 2000 and enter a new century—the 21st Century!—the following worthy ideas are submitted in the hope and with the expectation they will strengthen our governmental processes and be enacted into law before the presidential election of the year 2000. While the year 2000 is significant in and of itself, it has the undoubted advantage of eliminating all—or nearly all—of the present personalities in current leadership positions at all government levels. The debates then can turn wholly on the merits of these issues.

I   *Term Limits.* House of Representatives 12 years and Senate 12 years or 18 years.

II   *Extend House of Representatives term* from present two years to four years, thus eliminating the constant need to "run" for reelection during each term. The many reasons for four year terms are obvious. When term extension is phased in over two elections, the laudable and important presidential midterm election which is, in fact, a referendum on the presidency will be preserved, i.e. one half the House will be up for election at each two year cycle.

III   *Limit all legislative sessions* to six months and no longer. Such limits are entirely consistent with the intentions and actions of our founding fathers. While they were long unwritten, limits on sessions were the normal procedure most often in past years.

IV   *Limit severely all legislative staffs.* The unprincipled, unplanned, helter skelter growth in this area has ballooned way out of hand and is not only exceedingly costly, but also, counterproductive and it is an embarrassment bordering on a national scandal.

V   *Change voting day from Tuesday to Sunday* as is done throughout Europe and all over Latin and South America. At present no more than 50.1% of the electorate votes and the trendline is downward. Such low voter participation is, in actual fact, a national disgrace. Better governance will come over time when more of the electorate votes.

Letters to the Editor

13 October 1990

Dear Mr. Hoxie:

I was very pleased to receive your letter of September 24th informing me that my article had been accepted for publication in your journal. I would also like to thank you for your prompt reply. Many journals tie up articles for months, leaving authors in the limbo between acceptance at one place or sending it off to another. Your consideration is much appreciated.

Last, I was under the impression that I was a member of the Center. If I am mistaken, I will certainly be glad to apply at this time. I have found your journal to be very useful and interesting. More important, I believe that it fills a gap which has existed in the world of scholarly journals.

Again, thank you for your interest in my work.

Sincerely,
MARY C. BRENNAN
Assistant Professor of History
Southwest Texas State University
San Marcos, Texas 78666-4616

April 5, 1991

To Whom It May Concern:

I hope the following suggestions for changes to the presidential election process are useful. Though I realize that some of these ideas could be difficult to implement, I feel strongly that what I'm suggesting would significantly improve the present situation. I hope you agree.

Here's what I suggest:

— All candidates for President should be required to inform the electorate of the names and relevant backgrounds of their choices for the major cabinet positions (e.g., state, defense, justice, interior, education) at least one month before election day, and repeatedly thereafter up to election day.

— Aspiring presidential and vice presidential candidates should be required to have had a specific college-level education in political science as well as in U.S. and world history and geography, and to have had some measure of experience in dealing with domestic and international issues. I assume that a constitutional amendment would be needed to bring this about, but since a relevant educational background and experience is required for military officers and high-level civilian managers, then why not for the CEO of the country?

— A constitutional amendment should be passed to eliminate the largely ceremonial office of Vice President. Since the vice presidency isn't an elective office in the true sense of the word, I suggest that after that office is eliminated the Secretary of State should then be first in line to become President in the event of death or incapacitation of the sitting President. The highest-ranking Senator from the President's political party (or if there is no such person, then the Senate Majority Leader) could be President of the U.S. Senate.

— If a constitutional amendment to eliminate the office of Vice President is simply not feasible, then each potential nominee for President should be required to publicize the name and relevant background of his or her Vice Presidential nominee at least one week before his or her party's nominating convention begins. The requirement for such an advance announcement would be consistent with the pre-convention exposure that aspiring presidential nominees get. Moreover I believe this requirement could help prevent nominations of inexperienced or unqualified persons.

— Debates and speeches by presidential candidates should be required to concentrate on the party platform and on other relevant major issues. As it now stands, the details of party platforms have become virtually invisible to the electorate. No doubt this would be difficult to enforce. To provide an incentive for adherence to this requirement, perhaps moderators of debates could be paid on the basis of how well they enforce this requirement, and perhaps presidential candidates could have the amount of their campaign funds depend on how well they meet this requirement.

— Neither the results of polls nor predictions of the outcome of a presidential election should be allowed to be published or otherwise disseminated to the general public. To do so should be a serious offense with a stiff penalty for offenders. In my opinion, enforcement of this suggestion would encourage voters to make up their minds on the basis of written and spoken analyses rather than simply joining the perceived "band-wagon." To those who would object on constitutional grounds, perhaps a sufficient counter-argument would be that conflicting ideals necessarily leads to exceptions to the concept of a totally free press: e.g., restrictions on what can be published about court proceedings while a trial is in progress, and on what can be published about matters affecting national security.

— Every political advertisement for a presidential candidate should be required to contain a signed statement by the candidate (in large letters, easy to identify) saying that he or she agrees with the entire content of the ad.

— Political advertisements, brochures, etc., for presidential candidates should not be permitted during the final week before election day. As it now stands, that final week of high-pitched persuasive efforts demeans what should be a sober process and a thoughtful moment in the country's history.

As can be seen, it's clear to me that the presidential election process needs significant improvements. If my ideas aren't likely to improve that process, then I hope the people in your organization will at least be stimulated by them to develop their own ideas to attain that objective. Whichever ideas prevail, I hope your organization will work to have them become laws.

> Sincerely,
> MICHAEL KUDLICK
> 39 Atalaya Terrace
> San Francisco, CA 94117

September 10, 1991

Dear Mr. Hoxie:
Thank you for the invitation to attend the Leadership Conference on November 1–3, 1991. A prior engagement makes it impossible for me to attend. I have been impressed with the good work of the Center. Keep it up.

> Sincerely,
> CHARLES F. HERMANN
> *Director*
> Mershon Center
> The Ohio State University
> 199 West 10th Avenue
> Columbus, OH 43201-2399

October 21, 1991

Letter to Editor:
Will our Leader have the fibre of Reform:
Reasonably, can any national Leader form the courage to lend his strength and support for Reform, to address the cries of disparagement by the ordinary People.
Or has the reliance on a System, bounded any human elected to the highest award a Democracy can offer, to the very political controls that have seized from public domain their duty of responsibility, the meaningful attention of serving open full government.
Reflection shows an indifferent attitude toward the civil freedom and little faith in the representatives taking unilateral steps to satisfy the centers of partisan pressure, called control, from the larger portion of constituents.
"The Constitution belongs to the People." Its strongest delivery will be from

a broader action, not the emphasis of political scheming. Changes in modification or adaption are the deserved duty of the widest representation of Citizens.

"Constitutional actions must always be a refreshing of the Country's unity and purpose." A declaration to respond to voters wishes in agreement to promoting a Balanced Budget Amendment, a Limited Terms Amendment, are a sophistry to the People, without a foundation to preserve original "fundamental Rights accorde to U.S. Citizens."

Constructive amendments must pass all tests in studied free discourse, in manifest tests of support through four debates. Millions of voters must set the stage, Delegates, free of Party, must study and debate, the Convention must be in overwhelming approval, the at large Public then must accept by a demanding plurality.

God bless all our Country, meaningfully.
PHILIP C. KENYON
111-4 Shawomet Ave.
Somerset, MA 02726

October 27, 1991

Dear Editor,

I am still not convinced that separate Presidential libraries are the *best* manner in which to keep certain documents. They are indeed expensive and not always located in places of easy access. Perhaps Bob Moos' original thought on the libraries being "equivalents of pyramids" still has some validity. We may have not truly answered, "Who do they serve?"

As to the presidential documents themselves, I would ask Don W. Wilson if he sees any "blandness" to the newer documents. In other words, has there been a mind-set by recent presidents to have their papers as simplistic and drab as possible since they *know* these papers will be "public property?" I know that I would be reluctant to put my true feelings to paper if I knew thousands of persons could/would see them. The microscopic scrutiny we put the President under may inhibit the individual in ways we cannot understand or appreciate, and the documents could suffer because of this process. Just being the most conspicuous person on the Earth is quite enough for any person, but then to have your papers, correspondences and other documents at easy access may pose dilemmas never envisioned by the Presidential Records Act of 1978. I would ponder how truly reflective the public papers of any president are to the individual and his (her someday) Presidency.

Cordially,
ROBERT D. HATFIELD
8728 Huron
Taylor, MI 48180

November 12, 1991

Dear Dr. Hoxie:

Concerning Deputy Assistant Secretary David L. Mack's essay, "The Middle East After the Persian Gulf Conflict," I would first like to send my congratulations to you Dr. Hoxie and the Center for a bit of history that I was not aware of, but I am now and I as well as millions of Americans owe you and the Center our utmost gratitude — I am speaking of the Center's involvement in "nudging" Israel and Egypt toward what appears to be a lasting peace between one another in the Middle East today.

However, I must take exception to Secretary Mack's view that negotiations between the parties in the area should be based on United Nations Resolutions 242 and 338 — that is "peace for land."

It is most unfortunate to watch the largest and most respected democracy in the world denigrate and pressure the only democracy in the Middle East — Israel, the only country in the world that has voted right down the line with the United States on every important vote taken in the UN, including this country's darkest days during the Vietnam War.

The United States Government constantly insinuates that Israel stands in the way of peace. But if one looks clearly at the dispute in the Middle East between Arab and Israeli; between Moslem and Jew, one will walk away with the opposite view.

The PLO, quite clearly believes fervently that the obtaining of the West Bank and Gaza is merely the first step to the dismantling of the State of Israel. The PLO has gone on to add that once Israel is no more, then the new Palestinian State will become democratic. Let me expose the truthfulness of this declaration and expose it for what it truly is — a compete fabrication!

The purported commitment to a future democracy in Palestine was set forth in a resolution of the Eighth Palestine National Assembly adopted 20 years ago. The carefully ambiguous resolution declares in pertinent part that "the future State of Palestine will be a democratic state in which all enjoy the same rights and obligations."

The ambiguity of the resolution lies in the meaning of the word, "all."

The PLO would have the United States believe that the word, "all" encompasses all Palestinians and Israelis. But according to the constitution (Palestine National Covenant) of the PLO and the Koran, which statements must be conceded to more authoritative than the above resolution, very few Israelis would be given rights whatsoever in the so-called Democratic State of Palestine.

The position taken by the PLO toward the Jews is more conclusively enunciated in a document called the Palestine National Covenant. In its original (1964) version it read that the Jewish people of Palestinian origin (which would be interpreted as those living in the country before 1948) would be recognized as Palestinians and permitted to stay in the new democratic state.

The Covenant was revised in 1968 and again in 1971 to read that "only those Jews who have been living in Palestine permanently before the beginning of what the PLO and Yasser Arafat call the Zionist invasion, i.e., 1917, would be considered Palestinians; the rest would be considered aliens and expelled."

How many Jews lived in Palestine before 1948? Answer, about 500,000 or less. How many Jews lived in Palestine in 1917? Answer, around 80,000.

Since there are close to four million Jews in Israel today, it follows that the PLO plans to expel 98 percent of the Jewish population if Israel is dismantled, and that will happen if the West Bank and the Gaza go back to Arab control.

Of course, the Palestinian desire to reduce the number of Jews is understandable. The Jewish majority stands in the way of the true PLO goal—an Arab-Islamic Palestine.

The Koran also contradicts the PLO's purported commitment to democracy. Under its doctrine, Jews will only be allowed to exist as a minority in an Arab State much like the (few that are left) Christians in Lebanon. For Islam recognizes neither independence nor equality for Jews or Christians.

The Jews like all the "People of the Book" have to be fought until they submit to the supremacy of Islam (Koran IX, 29).

I realize this seems hard, but one only has to see Iran to know the truthfulness of these statements.

> MICHAEL BUSSIO
> 720 Coleman Avenue
> Suite N
> Menlo Park, CA 94025
> Former Editor/Publisher *World Affairs Newsletter*

November 15, 1991

Dear Gordon:

If the rest of your conference at the Marriott Hotel was as interesting and charged as the dinner my wife and I attended on Friday night, I know that the weekend in Richmond was a grand success. All of us want to also congratulate and compliment you on the way you organized a host committee here in Richmond. I was, frankly, rather surprised to see the depth of that committee and their interest in attending some of the Center's sessions.

We also appreciate your group having selected Richmond as the site for this year's meeting. Certainly, any meeting devoted to the study of the Bill of Rights would have to consider having its site in Virginia. It was my understanding that your group's trip to Montpelier was also a resounding success.

Rebecca and I enjoyed having an opportunity to meet and chat with you. We hope that we will have a chance to be with you again in the future.

> *Sincerely yours,*
> THOMAS N. ALLEN
> *Chairman*
> East Coast Oil Corporation
> 1420 East Commerce Road
> Richmond, Virginia 23224-7598

November 15, 1991

Dear Dr. Hoxie:

I want to express my warmest appreciation to you and the Center for the wonderful experience I so much enjoyed at this year's Annual Leadership Conference. I am unable to tell you how much I have learned and benefitted from my association with you and all the members of the Center.

Every phase and aspect of this year's Leadership Conference was, from my perspective, a great success. The issue panel topics and participants, the distinguished speakers, and the special events were all educational and stimulating. Although I certainly could never appreciate the effort and dedication necessary to coordinate such a project, please allow me to thank and congratulate both you and the entire Center staff. Everyone concerned offered advice and assistance throughout the Conference, making my experience one I could never forget.

Between now and the 1992 Student Symposium, I will concentrate on promoting the Center and its wonderful attributes here on the University of Wyoming campus. Although our University is now suffering budget reductions, I hope to convince those officials concerned that sending a student reprsentative to the Symposium generates rewards for all. I will surely be attending, and I trust the University will again this year agree to sponsor another student participant. I have also made arrangements with the Arts and Sciences College Coordinator to assist in attracting applicants for the Gitelson Essay Awards.

This year's Fellows are a wonderful group, and I plan to remain in close contact with these fine friends whose companionship I will always cherish. To be considered a part of the Center is an honor and thrill for me, and I want to serve its cause as much as it has benefitted me.

Thank you again, Dr. Hoxie, for all you have done for me.

Sincerely,
NICK EVANS
1991–92 Center Fellow
University of Wyoming

November 22, 1991

Dear Gordon:

Enclosed is the brochure on the PBS Adult Learning Program based on the plenary sessions at the Eisenhower Symposium last year. Many PBS affiliates will be showing the program. If you check with your local affiliate they will tell you if they are going to run it. The show is also being used by colleges and universities around the country that work with PBS.

We also have a book coming out, entitled *The Eisenhower Legacy*, which is due for publication in the next month or so. As soon as that is available, we will send you a copy.

Please keep in touch. With all good wishes for a Happy Thanksgiving.

Best wishes,
SHIRLEY ANNE WARSHAW
Director
Eisenhower Symposium
Gettysburg College
Gettysburg, Pennsylvania 17325-1486

News Notes

A. 23rd Annual Student Symposium

The twenty-third Annual Student Symposium of the Center for the Study of the Presidency will convene at the Hyatt Regency Washington on Capitol Hill the weekend of March 20–22, 1992. It will have as its theme "Selecting the President, the Vice President, and the Congress." In this quadrennial year in which we select the President and Vice President, members of the House of Representatives and one-third of the members of the Senate, the leadership of both the executive and legislative branches of our national government have been invited to address the symposium and respond to commentaries and questions. All Center members who are college or university students are invited to participate. All other Center members are invited to be special guest observers.

The President has been invited to deliver the keynote address. Other invited speakers include Director Robert Gates of the Central Intelligence Agency; Chairman Colin Powell of the Joint Chiefs of Staff; the new White House Chief of Staff, Samuel K. Skinner; Speaker of the House Foley; and, from the Center's Board of Trustees, James R. Jones, Chairman and CEO, The American Stock Exchange. Jones was the youngest White House Chief of Staff, serving with President Johnson. Subsequently he served in the Congress, 1973–87 (D) Oklahoma and was Chairman of the Budget Committee in the House.

This year the 16 issue panels include the presidential primaries, campaign financing, the media and the pollsters, roles of the Vice President, presidential debates, and selecting presidents and prime ministers. The concluding Sunday panel features media leaders.

One of the most exciting Symposium events is the Gitelson Essay Awards for the undergraduate college and university students. The winners will be announced at the Saturday evening dinner session. The essay topic is the same as the symposium theme.

American Airlines is the official conference carrier. Their substantially reduced fares may be secured by calling 1-800-433-1790 and asking for STAR FILE #14324G.

When President Eisenhower inspired this Annual Symposium, he emphasized it should be for "students old and young." For further information regarding both the essay program and the symposium please write:

Symposium Coordinators
Maria Rossi or Maura Zottner
Center for the Study of the Presidency
208 East 75th Street
New York, NY 10021
OR CALL
(212) 249-1200

B. Center to be Honored by Newcomen Society

The Newcomen Society of the United States, a non-profit corporation which makes annual citations for excellence both to American business corporations and to educational institutions, has selected the Center for the Study of the Presidency to be honored in 1992. This will be at a dinner at the Union League Club in New York City on Thursday, April 23, 1992.

James Fritz, President of the Society, will make the award presentation. Responding for the Center's Board will be David Eisenhower, whose grandfather inspired the Center's founding, and Gordon Hoxie, the Center's Chairman and President. The Society is named for Thomas Newcomen, the English engineer, who in 1712 invented the first practical steam engine.

The Society, which has honored leading American corporations, selected the Center for its 1992 award in recognition of its educational and research roles related to the American political system.

For further information regarding the dinner write:

Maria Rossi or Maura Zottner
Newcomen Dinner Coordinators
Center for the Study of the Presidency
208 East 75th Street
New York, NY 10021
OR CALL
(212) 249-1200